AFRICAN ETHNOGRAPHIC STUDIES OF THE 20TH CENTURY

Volume 46

THE PREMISE OF INEQUALITY IN RUANDA

THE PREMISE OF INEQUALITY IN RUANDA

A Study of Political Relations in a Central African Kingdom

JACQUES J. MAQUET

LONDON AND NEW YORK

First published in 1961 by Oxford University Press for the International African Institute.

This edition first published in 2018
by Routledge
2 Park Square, Milton Park, Abingdon, Oxon OX14 4RN

and by Routledge
711 Third Avenue, New York, NY 10017

Routledge is an imprint of the Taylor & Francis Group, an informa business

© 1961 International African Institute

All rights reserved. No part of this book may be reprinted or reproduced or utilised in any form or by any electronic, mechanical, or other means, now known or hereafter invented, including photocopying and recording, or in any information storage or retrieval system, without permission in writing from the publishers.

Trademark notice: Product or corporate names may be trademarks or registered trademarks, and are used only for identification and explanation without intent to infringe.

British Library Cataloguing in Publication Data
A catalogue record for this book is available from the British Library

ISBN: 978-0-8153-8713-8 (Set)
ISBN: 978-0-429-48813-9 (Set) (ebk)
ISBN: 978-1-138-59574-3 (Volume 46) (hbk)
ISBN: 978-0-429-48816-0 (Volume 46) (ebk)

Publisher's Note
The publisher has gone to great lengths to ensure the quality of this reprint but points out that some imperfections in the original copies may be apparent.

Disclaimer
The publisher has made every effort to trace copyright holders and would welcome correspondence from those they have been unable to trace.

Tutsi lord and Hutu client

THE PREMISE OF
INEQUALITY IN RUANDA

A STUDY OF POLITICAL RELATIONS IN
A CENTRAL AFRICAN KINGDOM

JACQUES J. MAQUET

Published for the
INTERNATIONAL AFRICAN INSTITUTE
by the
OXFORD UNIVERSITY PRESS
LONDON   IBADAN   ACCRA
1961

Oxford University Press, Amen House, London E.C.4

GLASGOW NEW YORK TORONTO MELBOURNE WELLINGTON
BOMBAY CALCUTTA MADRAS KARACHI KUALA LUMPUR
CAPE TOWN IBADAN NAIROBI ACCRA

© International African Institute, 1961

PRINTED IN GREAT BRITAIN

CONTENTS

INTRODUCTION	1
I. THE COUNTRY AND ITS PEOPLE	7
1. Physical environment	7
2. Human occupation	10
3. Food	14
4. Clothing and shelter	19
5. Health	22
II. THE SYSTEM OF KINSHIP AND AFFINITY	29
1. Descent groups	29
(a) *Inzu, ubwoko, umulyango*	30
(b) Organization and activities of the *inzu*	35
(c) Social roles within the *inzu*	39
(d) Organization and activities of the *umulyango* and the *ubwoko*	45
2. The descent group of Ego's mother	47
3. Ego's cross-line relatives	50
4. Ego's affines	52
(a) The spouses of Ego's kin	52
(b) The kin of Ego's wife	54
5. Some comments on kinship principles in Ruanda	57
(a) Analytical table of kinship terms	57
(b) Concluding remarks	61
III. MARRIAGE AND THE FAMILY	64
1. Marriage	64
(a) The choice of the spouse	64
(b) The bride-wealth	69
(c) The wedding ceremonies	71
(d) Polygynous unions	72
(e) Divorce	73
(f) Celibacy	74
2. The Family	75
(a) Sexual relations	76
(b) Economic co-operation	80
(c) Procreational function	81
(d) Socialization	85
(e) Ritual function	87
IV. ECONOMIC PRODUCTION	89
1. Land tenure	89
2. Rights over cattle	91
3. Inheritance rules	92
4. Labour	94

vi THE PREMISE OF INEQUALITY IN RUANDA

V. POLITICAL ORGANIZATION	96
1. Definitions	96
(a) Intragroup political organization	96
(b) Power	99
(c) Social power	99
(d) Intergroup political relations	100
2. Description of the administrative structure	101
(a) Districts, hills, and neighbourhoods	101
(b) Taxes	102
3. Analysis of the administrative structure	103
(a) Fiscal function	104
(b) Maintenance of the central rulers in power	106
(c) Social cohesion	107
4. Description of the military structure	109
(a) Recruitment	109
(b) The warriors' section	110
(c) The herdsmen's section	111
(d) Tribute due by the army	113
(e) Advantages for the members	114
5. Analysis of the military structure	115
(a) Warlike function	115
(b) Socialization	117
(c) Army and lineage	119
(d) Redistribution of wealth	120
(e) Protection	122
6. The central government	124
(a) The king	124
(b) The queen-mother	126
(c) The *biru*	126
(d) The council of the high chiefs	128
VI. THE CLIENTAGE STRUCTURE	129
1. Description of the *buhake* institution	129
(a) The client's rights	129
(b) The client's obligations	130
(c) End of the *buhake* relation	131
2. Analysis of the clientage structure	133
(a) Notion of feudality	133
(b) Caste structure	135
(c) Protection by identification	136
(d) Social cohesion	138
(e) Maintenance of caste privileges	139
(f) Feudal and political structures	142
VII. THE PROBLEM OF TUTSI DOMINATION	143
1. Frame and background of the domination system	143
2. The sociological problem of domination	147
(a) Caste society and social cohesion	148
(b) Exploitation and protection of Hutu	152
(c) Delegation and centralization of political power	155
3. The function of the political organization in Ruanda	157

CONTENTS   vii

VIII. THE PREMISE OF INEQUALITY   160

1. Definitions   160
2. The ruler's and subject's social roles   161
3. Formulation of the inequality premise   163
4. The theorems   165
    Theorem One   165
    Theorem Two   166
    Theorem Three   166
    Theorem Four   167
    Theorem Five   168
    Theorem Six   168
    Theorem Seven   169
    Theorem Eight   169
5. Origin of the inequality premise   170

APPENDICES   173

1. Translation from Ruanda of the questionnaire on political organization   173
2. Computation of answers given to the questionnaire by a sample of 300 Tutsi   177
3. Bibliography   186

INDEX   195

ILLUSTRATIONS

Tutsi lord and Hutu client		*frontispiece*
1. The Virunga volcanoes		*facing page* 22
2. Intore warrior dancing		23
3. The late king, Charles Mutara Rudahigwa		118
4. The queen-mother, Radegonde Nyiramavugo		119
5. The dynastic drums, with enemies' trophies		134
6. A Hutu diviner		135

MAPS AND DIAGRAMS

1. Physical map of Ruanda		6
2. Kinship diagram A		30
3. Kinship diagram B		31
4. Kinship diagram C		33
5. Map of the districts of ancient Ruanda		*facing page* 102
6. Diagram of the administrative, military, and feudal structures of Ruanda		140

INTRODUCTION

THE greater part of this work is directly concerned with the description and analysis of the political organization of Ruanda. The first chapters, however, are devoted to other aspects of the social system: kinship and affinity, marriage and family. As the whole system of social relations in Ruanda constituted a closely knit fabric, it was thought that an understanding of the political institutions necessitates also some treatment of the other structures of human relations. Moreover, a brief account of the physical environment, the quest for food, shelter, and health, and some demographic data have been included because these elements, if external to the pattern of political relations, set the limits within which the Ruanda system of domination grew.

This study refers to the period immediately preceding the time when Ruanda was submitted to the influence of Western culture through its European agents. That is to say, in the continuously moving historical stream, we have chosen to study the particular configuration of the Ruanda political organization at the moment when it had been moulded by the action of many forces, but not by the full impact of European contacts. For reasons mentioned later, the 'zero point' of direct European influence on Ruanda society is not difficult to assess. It is in the first decade of this century. Ruanda social structure did not undergo any significant modification due to European influence until roughly 1910. This date is fortunately not very distant, and around 1950 it was still possible to interview many people who had been young when the old régime was still a working concern. As far as we know, there had been also no direct and continuous contact between Arabs and Ruanda prior to that time.

To remind the reader that we are describing structures and institutions which no longer exist, at least in their entirety, my account is given in the past tense even when it refers to features which are still functioning today. The expressions 'today', 'now', 'at the present time', &c., refer to the period 1950–1 during which basic research was carried out in Ruanda.

As a social anthropologist of the *Institut pour la Recherche Scientifique en Afrique Centrale*, I carried out field work in Ruanda

2 THE PREMISE OF INEQUALITY IN RUANDA

for two years, from December 1949 to November 1951. During that period information was secured by continuous observation and by informal interviews with Africans and Europeans. Some administrative officers and missionaries, keenly interested in the society and culture of the Ruanda, have contributed much information and stimulating opinions.

In addition to this work, three systematic inquiries on specific subjects have been completed: political organization, kinship and family structures, and cosmological and ethical systems. Each of these inquiries was prepared by a preliminary survey on the subject, on the basis of which schedules of topics and specific questions were framed.

The preliminary survey of political organization enabled me to collect a considerable amount of information on that subject. Consequently, a later inquiry could aim primarily at checking and making more precise what was already known. To achieve this purpose a hundred-question schedule was devised. It was the object of each question that it should fulfil as adequately as possible the following conditions: to be neutral (formulated in such a way as not to suggest that the investigator preferred one answer rather than another), significant (likely to clarify obscure or controversial issues), concrete (such as 'Were there more or less people in group A than in group B?') rather than abstract (such as 'Give a definition of the administrative organization'), and simple (to be answered by 'yes', 'no', or one word). This last requirement was particularly important as it made possible a summing up of the answers. A translation of this questionnaire is given as Appendix One.

The choice of informants was made according to the following procedure. About a dozen persons, Africans and Europeans, who had been living for many years in Ruanda and had been in close contact with many members of the African community, were asked to give a list of Ruanda (Hutu, Tutsi, and Twa) who, in their opinion, would be familiar with the pre-European political structure, particularly from direct experience. The importance of listing people living in all the different regions of the country was stressed. By collating the various lists I finally obtained a set of about 350 names of men scattered everywhere in the country.

In order to interview them, I had to move between seventy-four different places which were about evenly distributed through the

INTRODUCTION

whole area of Ruanda. This took several months. With the help of two assistants, Messrs. G. Sebyeza and M. Sekanyambo, to whom I had given some training in interviewing and recording data, 326 informants were eventually interviewed. The aim of the inquiry was explained to them in small groups, but each interview was privately held to prevent informants from influencing each other's answers. In order to make sure that answers could be accurately recorded, the questionnaire had been printed and the answers of each informant were written on a separate copy.

As might have been expected, the more competent persons on political organization were Tutsi and in fact more than ninety per cent. of our informants were Tutsi. Since the number of Hutu and Twa was too small to be of any significance (there was, in fact, only one Twa!) their interviews were not taken into account in the computation of the results. A few more interviews were discarded on other grounds (such as suspicion about the sincerity or the mental ability of the informant). In the end the number of interviews used in the summing up was reduced to 300.

To count up the answers, some questions had to be modified. For instance, the question, 'Give the name of your patrilineage head', was replaced by, 'Do they know the name of their patrilineage head?' The computation of answers for the whole of Ruanda is given as Appendix Two.

Obviously, this class of 300 informants does not constitute a random sample representative of the total Ruanda population: the informants are practically all Tutsi and have been chosen according to certain criteria. This does not invalidate our procedure, however, as our aim was not to assess the opinions and knowledge of the whole of the Ruanda population on their past political organization, but to discover as accurately as possible what that organization was. This is why we attempted to interview only the most informed persons on the subject and to take into account the divergence of their views.

On kinship, family, and related subjects, the preliminary survey did not give as much information as the preliminary political survey revealed. Consequently, another procedure had to be adopted. A very comprehensive schedule of topics to be brought into the interview was elaborated. There were 542 items distributed under sixty-two headings to be covered with each

4 THE PREMISE OF INEQUALITY IN RUANDA

informant. Sixteen Hutu and twenty Tutsi informants were interviewed. Two junior administrative officers, Messrs. E. Finoulst and G. De Clercq, who were taking a six-month course of training in anthropology, participated in the different stages of this inquiry, as did Mr. S. Naigisiki, who acted as assistant and interpreter.

The inquiry into the cosmological and ethical systems was carried out on similar lines. A schedule of thirty-five headings, under each of which several points were listed, was used in several collective and individual interviews.

This research from 1949 to 1951 forms the main basis for my *Système des relations sociales dans le Ruanda ancien*, published in 1954. But I have spent two other research periods in Ruanda (December 1952–December 1955 and September 1956–September 1957) on more specific topics. What was observed in these later periods, however, bearing on the topic of the earlier study, has been taken into account in the present volume.

Secondarily, the present study of Ruanda is based on literary sources published both before and after 1954. These are fully listed in the Bibliography.

*   *   *

All my field work in Ruanda was sponsored by the *Institut pour la Recherche Scientifique en Afrique Centrale* (I.R.S.A.C.) for which I am deeply grateful. At the same time I assumed the functions of Head of the Scientific Research Centre of I.R.S.A.C. in Astrida. I wish to extend my thanks particularly to Professor L. van den Berghe, Director of I.R.S.A.C. The late Professor F. Olbrechts, when he was Chairman of the *Commission des Sciences de l'Homme* of I.R.S.A.C., also greatly encouraged my research.

For guidance in planning the research project on Ruanda and for supervision of all its later stages, I gratefully acknowledge my indebtedness to Professor Daryll Forde.

I should also like to thank Miss Barbara Pym, of the International African Institute, London, who very kindly corrected the first typescript, and Dr. R. J. Apthorpe, of the Rhodes-Livingstone Institute for Social Research, Lusaka, for his patient and invaluable help in preparing this edition of my book.

*   *   *

INTRODUCTION

I have given Ruanda words in the orthography now customary in Ruanda-Urundi. Articles and prefixes have been omitted wherever possible, as for instance in the words *hutu, tutsi, twa, ruanda, garagu*. The prefix has been kept in words widely used and which, if reduced to their radicals, might not be easily recognized. This is the case with the words *mwami* and *buhake*, whose roots are *-aami* and *-hake*.

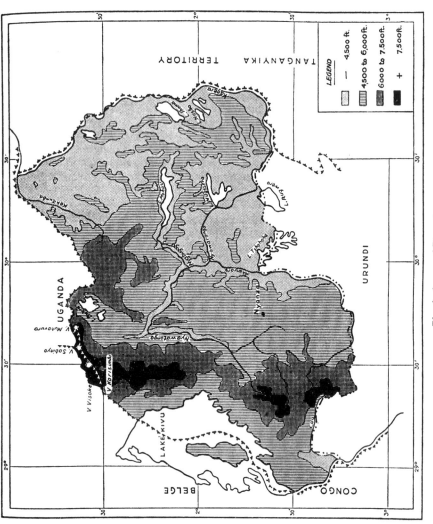
Physical map of Ruanda.

CHAPTER I

THE COUNTRY AND ITS PEOPLE

I. PHYSICAL ENVIRONMENT

THE Kingdom of Ruanda lies within latitudes 1° 20' to 2° 50' south and longitudes 28° 50' to 30° 55' east. Physically it is a part of the elongated highland zone extending at varying elevations from the Red Sea to Lake Nyasa. This East African highland zone is characterized by large blocks of upland and the giant cracks of the rift valley system.

Ruanda is situated on the western border of the central region of this zone. It is a high plateau in which numerous rivers cut deep valleys separating a multitude of hills. The main feature of Ruanda orography is the chain of mountains with an elevation from 2,250 to 3,000 metres (6,750 to 9,000 feet) which separates the Congo and Nile drainage basins. This has a north-south trend approximately fifteen to twenty-five miles east of Lake Kivu (elevation: 1,460 metres or 4,380 feet) and forms, with the northern part of the Ruzizi river, the western boundary of Ruanda. From this mountainous chain to the east, elevations fall gradually to the Kagera River Valley, the eastern limit of Ruanda. The greater part of the Kagera here consists of swamps which may be as much as sixteen miles broad. The elevation of the region along the Kagera is from 1,300 to 1,500 metres (3,900 to 4,500 feet).

The northern boundaries of the country are not as clearly defined by physical factors, except in the west by the Virunga volcanic massif including eight peaks, the highest of which, Karisimbi, reaches 4,507 metres (14,873 feet). The Akanyaru and Lua rivers—which form part of the southern border of the kingdom, separating it from its Burundi neighbour—cannot be considered as natural frontiers, as they are not difficult to cross.[1] Ruanda's relief, together with its central situation in Africa

[1] The present-day political boundaries of Ruanda do not include the whole territory which was politically and culturally part of the kingdom in the past. There are Ruanda populations in the north, in the Kivu Province of the Belgian Congo (between the actual border and Rutshuru), and in the Kigezi District of Uganda (along the actual border).

B

8 THE PREMISE OF INEQUALITY IN RUANDA

(about 1,000 miles from the two nearest sea-ports, Mombasa and Dar-es-Salaam), probably accounts for the country's long isolation from Arab and European contacts, in spite of its easily accessible frontiers in the north and south. Although slaves were occasionally sold to the African middlemen in touch with Arab traders operating in the neighbourhood of Ruanda, it seems that the traders themselves never penetrated the country. At all events Ruanda was never a regular place of supply. The first European reported to have been in the country was Count G. A. von Götzen, a German officer leading a scientific and military expedition across Africa from the Indian to the Atlantic Ocean. He stayed in Ruanda only for a few weeks, in 1894.

The interior highlands, which have been compared to the massif of Abyssinia and to the mountains of Bohemia, or even to Switzerland and Tibet, are not very large. Their longest north-south extent in a straight line is about 100 miles, the extent from west to east being about 140 miles. The area of present-day Ruanda is 26,338 square kilometres (10,166 square miles). In 1907 Professor Jan Czekanowski, a member of the Duke of Mecklenburg's expedition to Central Africa, estimated it to cover about 28,900 square kilometres.[2]

The climatic effects of equatorial latitude are mitigated by the elevation. In the Congo-Nile mountain chain the temperature may drop to freezing point, but the greater part of Ruanda enjoys a temperate climate. The average is about 20° C. (68° F.), and the maximal variations (which are greater between day and night than between the seasons) rarely exceed 10° C. (18° F.) above or under the average. In the eastern lower part the temperature is, of course, higher.

Similar distinctions must be made for rainfall in the high mountains of the west, the highlands of the middle country, and the Kagera lower region of the east. In the first region rainfall averages 1,250 mm. a year (50 inches), in the second it is between 1,250 and 1,000 mm. (50 and 40 inches) and in the third less than 1,000 mm. (40 inches).[3] These figures alone do not have very much bearing on soil fertility, as the significance of rainfall depends on other factors, such as volume and intensity of precipitations, declivity of ground, type of vegetation, and characteristics of the soil.

[2] Czekanowski, 1917, p. 114.   [3] Ministère des Colonies, 1951b, p. 65.

THE COUNTRY AND ITS PEOPLE 9

There is as much as a one-month range of variations in the dates of the rainy and dry seasons each year. The precipitations are very irregular. Sometimes for a few weeks there is heavy rainfall lasting ten or twelve hours followed by a few dry days, at other times there is a 2- or 3-hour shower every day. Besides this fundamental irregularity there is no uniformity throughout the country. Owing to the very uneven relief, neighbouring regions or even neighbouring groups of hills and valleys, may have quite dissimilar climates.

Although it is believed that the country was covered with forest in the remote past, now only three per cent. of the surface of Ruanda is woodland; even if savannah with trees is taken into account the figure is not brought up to more than 6·5 per cent.[4] At the beginning of the century the figures were almost certainly not higher, and very likely lower. Indeed, the policy of the Administration has been to attempt to protect by regulation the forests which were left and to promote the replanting of trees. The present-day typical Ruanda landscape, eucalyptus-covered hills and roads bordered by three or four lines of trees, is new. Fifty years ago the country had an even more denuded appearance than it has today.

The result of the scarcity of trees in a country of steep hills has been erosion. Torrential rainfall has washed off the more fertile top soil. The deterioration of the ground has been a long process which has not yet been reversed. The north-western part of Ruanda provides an exception to the general poverty. Here the soil is of volcanic origin, formed from recent lava, and rich. The land at the bottom of valleys everywhere is, of course, notably better than on the slopes.

A good top-soil is important not only for cultivation: allowing a slow infiltration of water, it helps to form subterranean watersheds situated not too deeply underground. A decrease in this top-soil has had the effect that some of these practically superficial water reserves which feed sources have drained away. I have been told more than once by old people that in such or such a place there was a water source when they were young. When digging a well now one has to go very deep.

These phenomena, erosion, impoverishment of soil, and drying up of sub-soil, are not to be attributed only to the action of the purely natural factors mentioned (the heavy rainfalls and the

[4] Ministère des Colonies, 1951b, p. 331.

10 THE PREMISE OF INEQUALITY IN RUANDA

orography of the country). They are due to the conjunction of these physical circumstances with the particular way in which the human occupation of the land has taken place.

2. HUMAN OCCUPATION

Several hypotheses have been advanced in attempts to reconstruct the history of the human occupations of Ruanda. We are not concerned with them here. Let us summarize only those features which are of significance for our purpose and which have a high degree of probability.

The present population of Ruanda is clearly composed of three groups: Twa, Hutu, and Tutsi. These groups are very unequal numerically. In the middle of 1956, according to a Government demographic survey, the Twa constituted 0·67 per cent. of the total Ruanda population, the Hutu 82·74 per cent., and the Tutsi 16·59 per cent.[5] Differences that are immediately noticeable between these groups concern their activities, their social statuses, and their physical types. The Twa are hunters, potters and iron-workers. Twa hunters are not numerous, as game is rare in most parts of Ruanda owing to the scarcity of forest. Some of them make a living as singers, dancers, and buffoons. The Hutu are agriculturists and the Tutsi pastoralists. The statuses of the three groups are hierarchically ranked. The Tutsi group constitutes an aristocracy, the Hutu are commoners, and the Twa are said, half jokingly, by most of the other Ruanda, to be more akin to monkeys than to human beings. A definite physical appearance is considered typical of each group. According to the socially accepted descriptions of the three stereotypes the typical Twa is short, pygmoid rather than pigmy, with a head low in the crown, face and nose flat, cheek-bones prominent, forehead bulging, eyes narrow and slightly oblique. Hutu characteristics are woolly hair, flat broad nose, thick lips often everted, and middle stature. Tutsi are very slender and tall. They often have a straight nose and a light brown skin colour. The objective measurements of Professor Jean Hiernaux do not entirely coincide with these stereotypes.[6]

[5] These figures have been kindly communicated by Mr. J. Revelard who was at that time in charge of the Ruanda-Urundi Demographic Surveys (Endemoru).

[6] Hiernaux, 1956b, pp. 34-53. Cf. Czekanowski, 1917, pp. 122-34. See the interesting photographs in Czekanowski, 1911, plates 1-61 and in Hiernaux, 1956b, plates VI-VII.

THE COUNTRY AND ITS PEOPLE

The Twa are thought to have been the first inhabitants of Ruanda. This may be inferred from the general reconstruction of the vast human migrations that are supposed to have taken place in Africa in the remote past, and according to which Pygmies and Pygmoids would appear to be the most ancient inhabitants of that part of Africa. Whatever the validity of this hypothesis, the Twa, being hunters and collectors of fruits, seeds, and roots, did not greatly modify the natural vegetal cover of the country.

It was left to the Hutu hoe-cultivators to begin the transformation of the country. The time of their arrival, either after or contemporary with that of the Twa, is immaterial in this connexion. The important fact is that the Hutu had to begin the clearing of grasses, shrubs, and bushes and eventually the felling of forests to make their fields. The extent to which this process of deforestation had been carried out before the arrival of the Tutsi is difficult to assess. It is unlikely, however, that the Hutu were so numerous as to have to cultivate such considerable tracts of the country as to disrupt its natural equilibrium. It is very likely that the increase of population and the cattle-pressure following the Tutsi arrival has been a determining factor in this processs.

The Tutsi immigration into the country is an historical fact attested by the traditions of Ruanda and of neighbouring peoples. Their occupation of Ruanda is an episode of the great southbound pastoral migration which resulted in the formation of the different societies which Baumann terms *Circle of the Lakes*,[7] Schapera, the *Lacustrine Bantu*,[8] and Meinhard, the *Interlacustrine Province*.[9] Pastoral peoples who according to Seligman's classification were 'half Hamites' (probably of eastern Hamitic origin),[10] for an unknown reason migrated with their large herds of long-horned cattle into an area delimited in the west by the Central African rift valley from Lake Tanganyika to Lake Albert, in the north and east by Lakes Kyoga and Victoria, and in the south by a line running westwards from Muanza Bay (Lake Victoria) to the Malagarasi River. Incorporating the Bantu agriculturists previously settled in that area, they constituted a number of political units (such as Nyoro, Toro, Nkole, Ganda, Sogo, Mpororo,

---

[7] Baumann and Westermann, 1948, pp. 215-23.   [8] Schapera, 1929, p. 83.

[9] Meinhard, 1947a and b. See also Roscoe, 1924.

[10] Cf. Seligman, 1930, p. 97, pp. 157 ff.

12 THE PREMISE OF INEQUALITY IN RUANDA

Ruanda, Burundi, Ha, Karagwe). It is not known where these pastoralists came from.

Because of cultural and physical similarities the Galla or Somali country of Southern Abyssinia has been advanced as their possible place of origin. As the invaders have completely adopted the Bantu language of the agriculturists, the lack of linguistic clues so important in such questions is a great setback to any historical reconstruction. It should be noted in this connexion that the use of the linguistic term 'Hamites' to denote Tutsi, who do not speak a Hamitic language at all, is unfortunate and misleading. Dr. Meinhard's suggestion of using a term not burdened with linguistic connotations such as 'Ethiopians' or 'Ethiopoids' should be considered.[11] The population movement which brought the invaders to Ruanda is probably at least four centuries old. The present ruler is traditionally the fortieth king of Ruanda. We know the names of thirty-nine predecessors, but it is possible that the list is incomplete. On the other hand it seems that the first nineteen are legendary figures. Taking account of this and assuming that a reign lasts about twenty years, we go back to the sixteenth century.[12]

As the Tutsi migration seems to have been gradual and peaceful, an infiltration rather than a conquest, it is probable that at the beginning their cattle grazed on the unoccupied grasslands. But the population increased as more Tutsi kept on entering the country and more land had to be tilled to feed them. Cattle were also increasing and the Hutu had to move from the most fertile soil, in the bottom of valleys, because during the dry season these places were the only ones where cattle could find fresh grass. This process must have been in operation for a few centuries to produce the situation as we know it now.

Statistics are not available for the 1900–10 period, with which this study is concerned, but we may from the present figures (with some modifications) get a fairly good idea of the situation at the beginning of this century. The population was estimated on 31 December 1949, to be 1,870,410 souls: in 1956, 2,374,136, which

[11] Cf. Meinhard, 1947a, p. 3.
[12] According to Meyer, 1913, the pastoral invasion took place in two ways. The first, at the beginning of this millenium reached the north-east of the Province; the second, in the fifteenth and sixteenth centuries brought them farther southward. According to Kagame and Delmas, the first Hamitic populations invaded the country in the eleventh and twelfth centuries. (Gouvernement du Ruanda-Urundi), (1956), p. 9.

THE COUNTRY AND ITS PEOPLE 13

gives a density of 235·8 per square mile or 91·9 per square kilo-metre.[13] This density is among the highest in Africa, south of the Sahara.[14] What may we infer from these figures as regards the population at the beginning of this century? According to the available statistics for the last fifteen years, when the circumstances are favourable the yearly increase of Ruanda population may reach three per cent. This increased ratio could hardly have been main-tained over the whole of the last fifty years, mainly because the 'favourable circumstances' refer to medical amenities, new hygienic practices and the reduction of famine. Such conditions were by no means prevalent when the Europeans occupied the country in 1899.[15] Even since 1935, however, events have not always been favourable, as for three years (1941–2–3) there was a decrease of population due to a severe scarcity of food. Con-sequently it seems safe to assume that during the decades preceding the European occupation, the population was already very dense. According to Captain Bethe, it numbered about 2,000,000 in 1899.[16] In 1907, Czekanowski estimated the Ruanda population at approximately 1,710,000.[17]

According to a detailed survey made by the Department of Agriculture, there are about 60,000 to 70,000 families (out of a total of about 380,000 families) more than can be adequately fed by the country.[18] There is also an excess of cattle. In 1950 there

[13] There is a census for the male and able-bodied adults who are taxpayers. To obtain the total number of the population (females, old people, and children) the number of taxpayers in each administrative district is multiplied by a certain coefficient which is determined in each case by a sample-census of a few hills.

[14] For comparative purposes, there are a few density figures for some African territories according to present political boundaries: Uganda: 52·8 per square mile; Tanganyika: 20·7; Belgian Congo: 12·9; Nigeria: 92·0; Sierra Leone: 66·5. All these figures, taken from Hailey, 1957, p. 143, refer to the years 1948-52.

[15] Captain Bethe, a German officer, obtained from the king in 1899 Ruanda's acceptance of the Imperial Government's protection. There was no treaty, only an oral agreement which was followed by a permanent occupation by the German authorities. The first Christian mission was established in 1900, at Isavi, by the White Fathers. Belgian troops took possession of Ruanda during the First World War in 1916. The Belgian occupation of Ruanda-Urundi was confirmed by the Orts-Milner Agreement in 1919. In 1924, Belgium agreed to administer Ruanda-Urundi under the supervision of the Permanent Mandates Commission of the League of Nations. After the Second World War, Ruanda-Urundi became a United Nations Organization Trusteeship Territory admin-istered by Belgium. Cf. Jentgen, 1947, pp. 9-11, 83-9

[16] Quoted by Czekanowski, 1917, p. 109 n.   [17] See Czekanowski, 1917, p. 114.

[18] This study is based on an estimate of the optimum cultivated area needed by a family, the quality of the soil being taken into account. A similar method has been used in the case of cattle. Cf. Ministère des Colonies, 1951b, pp. 343-7.

14 THE PREMISE OF INEQUALITY IN RUANDA

were about 450,000 head of cattle for which cattle tax was paid, but in fact they are considerably more numerous. It is estimated that out of these 450,000 there is a surplus of 200,000. Again, although veterinary assistance has lessened the incidence of many cattle diseases, it is highly probable that there has been an excessive cattle population for a very long time.

This overpopulation by both men and cattle, which is increasingly rapidly transforming the country into a desert, is the most pressing problem for those who are in charge of the country at the present time. But—and this is why I have stressed it so much—the type of human occupation which is responsible for it had prevailed for several hundred years at the time chosen for this study. The Ruanda thus have long had to adapt themselves to an ecological situation allowing them a very narrow security margin in the fulfilment of the primary condition for survival, food.

3. FOOD

It is mainly by agriculture and cattle-rearing that the people managed to get from the land as much food as their implements and their abilities allowed.

Hunting played very little part in their quest for food. Only the Twa, for whom hunting was a traditional occupation, ate game, which is another reason why they were despised by the Hutu and Tutsi. Hunting was significant in two connexions only. In the first place it was a means of providing the Tutsi with a supply of skins and ivory. Skins were used at the court for clothing and ornament, and war dancers wore loin-cloths made of leopard or civet skins and head-dresses decorated with the long white hair of colobus monkeys. In the second place the Tutsi regarded hunting as a sport. They liked to show their adroitness with spears and javelins, bows and arrows. But the meat of the quarry was left to Twa who had tracked the game, and to dogs.

Fishing has never been very much practised, though lakes in Ruanda are numerous, Kivu on the western border, Mohasi, Bulera, Mugesera, &c. Before the introduction of tilapia (a fish well adapted to these waters and excellent to eat) into these lakes in 1936, the kind of fish to be found there was neither very abundant, nor edible. In any case, the eating of fish, even when very good according to European standards, was regarded as disgusting. Even now it is very difficult to persuade people to eat

THE COUNTRY AND ITS PEOPLE

tilapia. Fishermen sell it mainly to foreigners: Congolese, Europeans, etc., but they themselves eat it very rarely.

Agriculture was the principal Hutu occupation. The Tutsi considered this kind of manual work below their dignity and the Twa preferred other tasks. Cultivators used the hoe (*isuka*) and a kind of bill-hook (*umuhoro*) as their main agricultural implements.[19] The main cultivated plants were beans and peas, sorghum, eleusine, sweet potatoes, cassava, maize. Besides these basic foodstuffs, there was also a garden cultivation of other plants used to complement the main dishes or to make them more tasty. These were pumpkins and other varieties of gourds, groundnuts, yams, tomatoes, shallots, and red peppers. Around the huts there were groves of bananas, which were widely used as food as well as in banana-beer.

The yearly calendar of agricultural activities was as follows.

Long rainy season

October. There were usually a few rainy days in September. In October the rains began and were not expected to be very abundant. Soil was prepared for the sowing period which began later in the month. Beans, peas, maize, pumpkins, eleusine, and groundnuts were sown or planted. Banana trees were pricked out.

November. Sowing went on. Because of the rains it was possible to plant sweet potatoes and cassava even on hill-tops. Bean fields were weeded.

December. New plots to be used later on were filled. At the end of the month harvesting began.

Short dry season

January. Peas and beans were harvested. Sorghum, maize, and eleusine were planted, and, in the valleys, potatoes and cassava. Beans were thrashed.

February. Late planting time for sorghum. Sweet potatoes and cassava were planted at the bottom of valleys. Eleusine fields were weeded.

Short rainy season

March. Beans were sown, and sweet potatoes and cassava planted on hill-tops. Sorghum was weeded. Second weeding of eleusine.

[19] See Czekanowski, 1917, pp. 136, 140.

16   THE PREMISE OF INEQUALITY IN RUANDA

April. Tillage of fallow-land in preparation for potato planting next month. Planting of yams, gourds.

May and first half of June. Second tillage of sorghum fields. Beans were weeded. Potatoes were planted. Banana groves were cleared of grass. Cassava planted on hill-tops was gathered.

Long dry season

June, second part. Sweet potatoes and cassava planted in the bottom of valleys. Granaries were stocked.

July. Harvesting of beans, sorghum, maize.

August. Tillage of soil.

September. Tillage went on. At the end of the month there could be an early sowing of beans.[20]

In agricultural tasks, there was no specialization by sex. Men and women worked together in the fields. Although to a large extent the Hutu culture was permeated by the Tutsi scale of values, they did not share the noblemen's disdain for agricultural work. Their ideal type of successful man was that of a rich and hard-working peasant. They were proud of such a reputation when they achieved it, although they recognized that the status of a powerful Tutsi was much higher. But it belonged to another order practically closed to them. In a hierarchical society, certain ideal types may embody values that are for a lower stratum at the same time supreme but not sought after.

Cattle were never reared for their meat in Ruanda. The Tutsi and Hutu appreciated meat very much, but cattle were not usually slaughtered just to be eaten, except occasionally as when a barren cow was getting old. But the contribution of cattle to the diet was great: milk and butter were the food *par excellence* for Tutsi noblemen. The Hutu also liked dairy products very much, but a good supply of them required a larger number of cows than a Hutu would normally possess. Only cows feeding calves were milked. During the dry season their production was very low. In recent years, the average milk production was only from 1 to 1·5 litres a day (from about $1\frac{3}{4}$ pints to $2\frac{1}{4}$ pints) including that taken by the calf. Hides were formerly used for clothing purposes.

As may be expected in a society dominated by pastoralists, livestock was a major focus of interest in Ruanda culture. Its importance in the political structure—which will be considered

[20] See Schumacher, 1942 and Everaerts, 1947, pp. 61-69.

THE COUNTRY AND ITS PEOPLE 17

later on—adds still further to its interest. There was a very elaborate series of prescriptions and taboos concerning the care of cattle, and a very full terminology which took into account the differences in colour of skin, in shape and length of horns, and in origin of possession or ownership, &c.[21] According to experts, Ruanda empirical knowledge of cattle-rearing was quite good.

In this field there was a very strict division of labour by sex. Cattle could be cared for only by men. This restriction was based on magical beliefs regarding impurity, as females before puberty and after menopause were permitted to take care of the livestock. The strictest prohibitions were on women in their menstruating periods. Hutu were not excluded from cattle rearing, and in fact most of the menial tasks were performed by Hutu servants or clients.

The Tutsi were not nomadic pastoralists. Cattle moved according to the seasons from valleys to hills, but usually in the same area. It might happen, however, that when the drought was particularly severe herds had to be led to another area which might be some distance away. But this did not imply any change of residence for the owners of the cattle which were accompanied only by shepherds.

When in October grass began to grow again, the cows were lean and starving. As they recovered strength on new grass, their milk came back. In November rains were sufficient to allow grazing on the hills. Flies were myriad in December. Then the short dry season began. In January, however, there was still too much water in the valleys for cattle to pasture there, and they stayed in kraals, near huts. In February and March they went out again on to the hills. With the rains flies came again. Milk output increased. In April pastures reserved for the dry season were closed. At the beginning of the dry season (end of May, beginning of June) milk diminished as the grass dried up, and grazing was confined to the valleys. July was not a bad month because cows could pasture on the harvested fields. Flies disappeared in the dry season. August and September were the two worst months for cattle.[22]

Sheep and goats were also kept for their skin and their milk. The Hutu ate goat-flesh but mutton was ritually forbidden. Even today it arouses a very marked repugnance and only the shameless Twa will eat it.

[21] Cf. Vanhove, 1941, pp. 46-59.   [22] Schumacher, 1942.

18   THE PREMISE OF INEQUALITY IN RUANDA

Fermented beverages were popular in Ruanda. There were three varieties: those with a sorghum base, those with a banana base, and hydromel. As these drinks were made in each household, their alcoholic content varied greatly. According to the experts, however, their nutritive value was generally considerable. The Tutsi did not drink sorghum-beer (*amarwa*) which they thought was fit only for children and Hutu. It is not as strong as banana-beer (*urwagwa*) and hydromel (*ubwuki*), which may contain 11.5° of alcohol.[23] Hydromel results from the fermentation of a must which is an aqueous solution of honey.

The Tutsi diet was based mainly on dairy products and was more liquid than solid. When still lying on his bed a Tutsi began his day with a pot of curdled milk (about $1\frac{1}{2}$ pints). At noon, before his siesta, he again took about the same amount. Around six p.m. when talking with his friends and clients, he drank, and offered, hydromel or banana-beer. At about half past eight or nine p.m. everybody left his hut and he took his evening meal with his wife (or one of his wives), his young children of both sexes and his daughters even after puberty. A usual menu was sweet bananas (or beans) cooked in water, cut in small pieces which were eaten with hot salted butter, and some sort of 'bread' made with a sorghum flour paste and, of course, milk was drunk. On the rare occasions when they had meat it was boiled, cut in small pieces, and eaten with hot salted butter. After that, when the women had left, the evening was spent with friends and clients, in long, subtle, and witty conversations, while beer and hydromel were served again.

The Hutu ate more food, but it was less refined. They consumed much less milk and butter, if any. They took two main meals a day, one in the beginning of the afternoon and one in the evening. They made a kind of porridge with beans, peas, or maize. Sweet potatoes, regarded as too common to eat by the Tutsi, were consumed in large quantities by the Hutu. A present day evaluation is about seven pounds a day per adult. In the morning, while working in the fields, they ate one or two snacks made of the remains of the preceding evening meal. They drank mainly banana and sorghum beer.

The Twa apparently enjoyed eating much meat and drinking much beer when and where they could get it. Their diet was very

[23] Ministère des Colonies, 1941b, pp. 52 f.

THE COUNTRY AND ITS PEOPLE 19

irregular, dependent on circumstances—a good hunt or a generous reward for dancing and singing.

The Tutsi had a strictly controlled attitude towards solid food. They behaved as if the need for nourishment was, if not shameful, at least beneath their dignity. The taking of a meal was something to be done privately. Friends were offered beer or milk, but they were not asked to share a whole meal. When travelling the Tutsi were not supposed to eat solid food and if the journey did not exceed two or even three days, they very often actually did not eat. It is said that a true Tutsi subsists only on milk and beer and some old men take pride in boasting of it. This attitude towards solid food might be explained as an attempt on the part of the conquering pastoralists to stress their independence of the foodstuffs produced by and characteristic of commoners and on a deeper level as an affirmation of what we might term a fundamental difference between themselves and Hutu. The Tutsi, according to their legends, came from another world. They were human beings like the Hutu, but not in quite the same way. This interpretation of the Tutsi attitude to food is supported by their emphasis on greediness in the Hutu character, and gluttony in the Twa. In most of the tales in which Hutu appeared, they were conspicuous by their overeating. For the Twa this feature was still more stressed. Another fact significant in this respect was the very strong prohibition on Hutu servants attending the meals of their Tutsi masters to reveal what they ate. This prohibition was magically sanctioned.

4. CLOTHING AND SHELTER

In the highlands, especially during the rainy season and at night, adequate covering against cold and damp is needed. Boys and girls, however, go completely naked as long as they are *abana* (children), that is up to the age of eight or nine for girls and ten or eleven for boys. As children usually do not go very far from the compounds, they may find some protection against cold either inside the hut or by picking up a skin or blanket. But the great number of diseases of the respiratory organs among children is a sign of their inadequate protection against bad weather.

The traditional Twa garment was a sheep skin. The Hutu wore bark-cloth as a sort of skirt from the waist down to the knees.

20 THE PREMISE OF INEQUALITY IN RUANDA

On top of this men might add a goat skin and women a piece of cow-hide in which they eventually carried their babies on their backs. Before the Europeans came, important Tutsi had already for some time replaced the traditional cow-hide of the pastoralists or the bark-cloth borrowed from the agricultural group with large cotton cloths, white or light coloured, elegantly draped. The Tutsi wore two, one as a kind of long, narrow skirt, and the other flowing and tied on the shoulders. Both men and women wore them in this way. These goods were imported by African traders coming from the east where they bought them from Arab merchants. Up to their marriage Tutsi girls wore only a very short loin-cloth made of cow-hide.

Tutsi men had their hair cut in such a way as to leave a few tufts shaped according to a traditional and extremely elegant pattern (*amasunzu*). Unmarried girls, Hutu as well as Tutsi, had their hair cut the same way. The heads of Hutu men and Hutu and Tutsi women were shaved. Necklaces and bracelets in white, blue, and red beadwork were favourite ornaments. There were no artificial bodily deformations such as flattening of the head, chipping of teeth or circumcision. Everybody went barefooted.

The dwelling unit was a compound (*rugo*) consisting of at least three huts, each almost always situated in a circular enclosure intersecting and communicating with the other enclosures of the compound. Huts were of the beehive type usual among the interlacustrine peoples, made of reed and grass. There was a 'bed-sitting' hut (*kambere*), another, where pots, baskets, &c. were kept (*kigonii*), and a kitchen (*kagondo*). Hutu boys and girls under the age of puberty slept in the kitchen if there was no special hut for them. In addition there were granaries, and the small hut devoted to the ancestral spirits, &c. The circular fences were ficus hedges, much higher than a man. This pattern of combined circular fences made possible an almost unlimited extension of the compound without its losing its compactness. Indeed, compounds of rich Tutsi constituted a kind of intricate labyrinth in which it was easy to lose one's way. Whatever the number of enclosures, there was only one narrow communication with the outside world. The open enclosed area might be very large and was used as a kraal in which cattle spent the night during certain periods of the year at least. There was no difference of pattern between Hutu

THE COUNTRY AND ITS PEOPLE 21

and Tutsi compounds. Only the size and number of huts and enclosures were different.[24]

These compounds, usually surrounded and more or less hidden by banana groves, were scattered throughout the country. They were on the top or on the slopes of hills, never in the valleys which were flooded every year at the end of the rainy season. They were usually rather isolated but even when they were not far from each other (and they were never so near together as to have two adjacent hedges) they did not constitute villages in the sense of concentrated clusters of dwellings situated near the centre of the territory worked by the inhabitants. There was, however, some grouping on a predominantly local basis of people who were all personally acquainted with each other. They could be described, following Murdock's terminology, as *neighbourhoods*.[25] These neighbourhoods were made up of a certain number of compounds (from twenty to sixty) situated on a hill (*umusozi*) or a part of a hill (*umurenge*). The people living there had a few common activities: mutual aid in the building of huts and in the performance of certain agricultural tasks, and recreational gatherings (such as dancing, jumping competitions, arrow shooting, &c.). They showed a certain *esprit de corps* in taking the side of one of their members in a dispute against a member of another similar community. The word used to designate the members of such groups expressed this idea of neighbourhood. They were called *abazimya muriro*, 'those who put out the fire', people very often needed. One important person in the group such as a lineage-head, was appointed as neighbourhood-head (*umukoresha*) by the traditional administrative authority to take charge of the collection of dues and tribute-labour of a hill or, more frequently, of a group of hills (*umutware w'umosozi*). He acted as an intermediary between his neighbours and the hill chief. The group could refuse the appointment of a certain person and another would be chosen. These neighbourhoods had no communal place for meeting, exchanging goods, or worshipping.

The same pattern of local grouping was to be found throughout

---

[24] Cf. Czekanowski, 117, p. 200 ff; Pauwels, 1953; Vincent, 1954, pp. 12-15.

[25] Murdock, 1949, p. 80. The definition of village given in Royal Anthropological Institute, 1951, p. 64. ('a territorially separate collection of homesteads, which is regarded as a distinct unit and of such a size that its inhabitants can all be personally acquainted') cannot be applied to the Ruanda type of local community.

22   THE PREMISE OF INEQUALITY IN RUANDA

Ruanda. The exception was the place where the royal court happened to be established. At the end of the nineteenth century the most permanent site was Nyanza, which was and still is regarded as the capital. One or two thousand people lived there, but Nyanza was not a village or a town. It was rather the great homestead of the king surrounded by the small temporary dwellings occupied by the different chiefs when they came to the court to pay a more or less long and obligatory visit to their sovereign. The king had other residences throughout the country where he stayed regularly.

Markets do not appear to have been numerous in Ruanda before the European occupation. Goods were exchanged mainly through other channels; the tribute of subject, dues of clients, gifts from the lords, &c. At all events the few markets where goods from abroad, such as rock-salt coming from the Lake Edward region, were exchanged, did not become centres of villages as in many other parts of Africa.

5. HEALTH

The general health of a people is as significant a part of the background of their culture and social institutions as are physical environment or demography. We can only conjecture about the situation before Europeans came, but there is some evidence.

The health of a group of people depends partly on their diet. The present day diet is lacking in animal proteins, vegetable fats (containing vitamins A, D, and E), and green vegetables.[26] We have no reason to believe that there was a higher consumption of meat fifty years ago, or that there were oleaginous plants growing which have disappeared and that the habit of eating green vegetables has been lost. According to nutritionists, these shortcomings cannot be compensated by a consumption, however abundant, of carbohydrates, a high percentage of which is to be found in maize, sorghum, peas, and beans. Also, if a fairly adequate consumption of the latter foodstuffs is possible now (in the sense that the total annual yield for the country is sufficient for the total number of people), it is not to be assumed that the total production was as high fifty years ago as it is now. On the contrary, the figures we have indicate that fifty years ago, the production of maize, sorghum, peas, and beans was much lower than today.

[26] Ministère des Colonies, 1951b, p. 56; Close, 1955.

PLATE 1

The Virunga volcanoes

PLATE 2

Intore warrior dancing

THE COUNTRY AND ITS PEOPLE 23

It should also be pointed out that the supply of the staple foods was usually short at the end of the dry season and that starvation periods, in which many people died, were occurring several times in a life-time. For instance in a thirty-year period (1900–30) among the events used as references to assess the age of people, three famines are remembered: in 1908, 1918, and 1924.

The above considerations take into account only the total production of available food in the country. But it is obvious that in a society composed of several groups very unequal in power, access to food was not the same for everybody. It seems that we may safely infer that the normal diet of many Hutu was barely adequate to sustain people who had to spend a considerable amount of physical effort in agricultural tasks.

In the preparation of meals, two facts relevant to health should be mentioned. Firstly, the methods of cooking very often resulted in a diminution of the nutritive value of food. For instance, beans cooked in water lose from one-sixth to one-fifth of their carbohydrates.[27] Secondly, the standards of cleanliness in food preparation were very high among the Tutsi, though more for magical than for hygienic reasons. This applies particularly to milk. To avoid flies and dust, receptacles containing milk were always closed with basketwork conic covers adorned with elongated geometric patterns. It is believed that if milk comes into contact with anything impure, the cow would be harmed. The contaminating substances were not always connected with the Western idea of dirtiness. For instance water was considered dangerous to milk. Consequently the wooden vessels in which milk was kept were not washed out with water but with cows' urine.

The equatorial situation of Ruanda, combined with the rather cold climate due to its elevation, resulted in the spreading of diseases characteristic of tropical as well as of temperate regions. Yaws, typhoid fever, tuberculosis, recurring fevers, and a large variety of intestinal diseases are quite common in Ruanda today.[28] They are not new diseases resulting from new conditions introduced by the European occupation, such as malaria, which was unknown in Ruanda except in the narrow strip adjacent to the Ruzizi River until roads were built permitting a very rapid transportation of people, or some venereal diseases which spread

[27] Ministère des Colonies, 1951b, p. 49-51.
[28] Cf. Lestrade, 1955; Vincent, 1953, pp. 16-18.

c

24   THE PREMISE OF INEQUALITY IN RUANDA

from the great commercial centres where there is an important transient foreign population of Africans from the Congo, Arabs, Indians, and Europeans. They are not new in so far as the factors favouring their spread have been in existence for a very long time. I have already mentioned the inadequate clothing of children. Bark-cloth and hides which were not washed, grass and reed huts and enclosures where cattle were living near the dwellings, which were never built in the valleys, were effective deterrents to corporal cleanliness. The Tutsi took hot baths and washed and rubbed themselves with perfumed butter, but the Hutu, particularly the women, did not seem to wash completely very often, if ever.[29]

Defences against these diseases were, as one may expect, very inferior compared with those which Western medical science can now provide. When somebody was ill and the usual remedies known to every old person did not work, he had to have recourse to a herbal expert. I have been told by a missionary who had studied the question for several years that knowledge of these medicinal plants was very often extremely penetrating and that cures, especially in dysentery and other intestinal diseases, were quite often successful. These remedies were collected or administered in a magical context. When that course of action did not produce the expected results, the diviner (*mupfumu*) had to be consulted. He was an interpreter of the will of God (Imana), which he could read in the patterns made by knuckle-bones, in the viscera of chickens, rams, and bulls, or even by a certain intuition without the help of any apparatus. Some diviners used a medium, usually a female possessed by Biheko, an important spirit of the dead, or were possessed themselves. The diviner was asked to identify the malevolent agent sending the illness, which could be either a *muzimu* (spirit of a dead person) or a *murozi* (sorcerer). If the spirit was identified, the diviner could tell what would appease him, and could offer some counter-magic to deal with a sorcerer.[30]

These resorts to the non-material world probably had the useful function of making bearable a situation in which nothing could otherwise be done to alter the course of the illness. It is doubtful, however, if this method had any other effect on the patient's health.

[29] Cf. Czekanowski, 1917, pp. 118-21.   [30] See photographs in Maquet, 1957.

THE COUNTRY AND ITS PEOPLE

The conditions favouring contamination by different diseases and the very limited defences against them permit us to assume that illness and mortality through these diseases must have been very high and a constant threat to everybody.

These brief notes on health conditions in Ruanda would be incomplete without a mention of mental health. We are not attempting here an assessment of the neuroses and psychoses which can be found in Ruanda or to the number of people affected by them and who, in the Western world, would be considered in need of psychiatric treatment. There is not sufficient information on these matters at present. But we would like to consider very briefly conditions which are likely to result in psychological tensions.

We have already mentioned the circumstances which make life objectively hard (a barely sufficient diet, starvation periods, and diseases). In addition it was often dangerous. When informants were asked what sort of reputation they particularly wished to avoid, they did not usually answer by listing the opposites of those particular qualities which they would like to have attributed to them, but by pointing to some definite reputation in which danger might be inherent. Above all, a Tutsi feared to be regarded as an enemy of the king. It was no doubt partly because he felt a genuine respect for the king, but mainly because to be thought of as an enemy of the king was extremely dangerous. It could mean dispossession of everything, the severance of all social relations, exile, or even death. He also feared to be considered a traitor to his chief. This was a less dangerous reputation, although it entailed sanctions: if a client had been disloyal to his lord the latter might take back from him all the cattle he had previously given him and eventually all his cattle. The Hutu said that they feared an accusation of witchcraft, for such an accusation could certainly mean immediate death. There was little that could be done actively to avoid such a danger except to be a good neighbour, to be envied by nobody, to have no enemies, and especially to have a powerful protector. The Hutu were also afraid of acquiring any reputation which could result in their losing the protection of the lord to whom they owed allegiance and consequently leaving them exposed and defenceless against the arbitrary actions of the powerful.[31]

[31] Cf. Maquet, 1954a, or Maquet, 1958.

26   THE PREMISE OF INEQUALITY IN RUANDA

Twa, as people living an active and dangerous life, and regarded as almost sub-human, had little to fear except being deprived of food by their master's whim.

All these dangers were real enough and no behaviour could ensure complete immunity. But most people appear to have felt that with some skill and right conduct they were avoidable and consequently did not constitute oppressive threats. Frustrations entailed by starvation and Tutsi requirements were regarded in pre-European days as part of an immutable natural and social order. Ruanda men and women were not inclined to speculate on the impossible, and any order of things other than that they knew belonged definitely for them to the sphere of the impossible. We shall see later on that a deep belief in the fundamental inequality of men had pervaded the ethos of the whole society, and had helped a great deal in the acceptance of frustrating conditions. Consequently these have not led to the usual feeling of aggressiveness or resentment.

Let us now turn to the invisible world as the Ruanda conceived it.[32] Although it was dominated by Imana, a god essentially powerful and good, it was a disquietening world. Indeed the spirits of the dead (*bazimu*), whatever their temper when they were in this world, were thought of as bad. The direct ascendants of the father's and mother's lines were usually protective if their living descendants had observed the proper filial behaviour, if they had not neglected prohibitions and avoidances, and if they had not forgotten offerings. But all other *bazimu* belonging to the same patrilineage were always harmful. *Bazimu* of other lineages were less dangerous unless there were feuds between the particular kin groups concerned. Among the spirits of the dead, a small clique, called the *imandwa*, was particularly powerful and might be helpful to those who had been initiated into the sect of Ryangombe, their chief.[33] Apart from these exceptions, ghosts were essentially malevolent towards living people. At best they did not harm. Of the two categories of men who had special relations with the invisible world, diviners and sorcerers, the latter were definitely considered to be criminals who either used poison (or other deadly substances as for instance when they mixed in food a powder made from the lungs of a person who had died from tuberculosis), or magical

---

[32] Maquet, 1958, pp. 526-30; Pauwels, 1958.
[33] See photographs in Maquet, 1957.

THE COUNTRY AND ITS PEOPLE 27

means (sending a *muzimu* to strangle somebody, acting through lightning or an animal, or using spells).[34]

What was the impact of this frightening world on the everyday life of Ruanda people? It seems that it was not ever-present in their daily lives. The Ruanda considered that most of the events in the human sphere as well as in the material world may be understood without reference to the action of the supernatural world. Some antecedent events or acts were considered as natural causes of the consequent ones. To get a cold at the beginning of the dry or rainy season was considered due to the change of weather. It was known that yaws could be got by contagion. Even death was very often interpreted without any magical explanation. It was expected for instance that people would die because of old age. When beans were sown on poor soil, a bad crop would not mean that the field had been bewitched. Thus when recurrences had been observed or when 'causes' had been discovered in the sphere of physical or human phenomena, events happening according to these recurrences or following their causes were considered as intelligible without any reference to the supernatural world. But when events appeared inexplicable in terms of these natural antecedents or causes, or were attended by some peculiar circumstances, intervention of spirits or sorcerers were suspected and a diviner was consulted. If somebody had tuberculosis and no one among his ascendants or the people with whom he lived had suffered from that disease, it was thought that the cause was a sorcerer. If somebody died from an illness usually considered 'natural', but his death occurred a few days after a theft of which he was the supposed culprit, he was said to have been magically striken at the request of the robbed person.

Even as regards his own death, the individual Ruanda seems to have taken a rather 'secular' view. All our informants agree that to die meant almost exclusively simply to quit life. They believed that they would become *bazimu*, but this left them rather indifferent. To abandon children, cows, fields, and friends was sad for people. But it was accepted without dramatization, as one of those facts which were in the normal order of things.

To sum up, freedom from want, frustrations, and objective fears was far from being achieved in Ruanda. Moreover, supernatural

[34] Cf. Czekanowski, 1917, pp. 302 f.; Arnoux, 1912-13; Pauwels, 1949b; Bourgeois, 1956.

agents instead of being comforting were always potential enemies. There appear to have been certain defences, however. Firstly, there was a belief in the immutability of natural and social order; consequently this order and its frustrations were accepted as a matter of course. Secondly, there was always a means, whatever its efficacy, of coping with dangers and consequently people were able to hope that they would not be defenceless against them. We may thus conclude that social and natural conditions in Ruanda did not seem to prevent the bulk of people from enjoying the amount of psychological security necessary to go on living without tensions and anxieties such as disturb mental balance.

CHAPTER II

THE SYSTEM OF KINSHIP AND AFFINITY [1]

1. DESCENT GROUPS

AMONG the Ruanda people, Tutsi as well as Hutu, the social principle of descent was agnatic. When any informant is asked who are his ascendants, he always answers by giving the names of his father, his paternal grandfather, his paternal great grandfather up to some male ancestor beyond whom he is unable to go. He does not mention his mother nor any of her ascendants.

Questions on the actual groupings founded on this principle and their functions elicit less unanimous and clear answers. The reason is that kinship groups have undoubtedly undergone a slow process of change in several respects during the Tutsi occupation of the country. What we know of its history [2] is quite sufficient to convince us that there has been a progressive territorial expansion under one dynasty of rulers together with an intensification of the

[1] In order to make clear the connotations of the main concepts used in this chapter, here are a few definitions:

Ego's *kin* are his socially recognized relatives to whom he is connected through parent-child and-or sibling links. *Consanguineal* and *cognatic* relatives are used as synonyms for kin.

Ego's *affines* are his socially recognized relatives to whom he is connected through a marriage link. This link may be the first traced from Ego (the affines are then Ego's spouse's kin) or the kinship link may be the first one traced (the affines are then Ego's kin's spouse).

Ego's *patrilineal* or *agnatic* relatives are those of his kin who descend by male links from the same male ancestor as Ego.

Ego's *matrilineal* or *uterine* relatives are those of his kin who descend by female links from the same ancestress as Ego.

Ego's *cross-line* relatives are those of his kin who are neither patrilineally nor matrilineally related to him.

Ego's *paternal* or *patrilateral* relatives are those of his kin to whom he is connected through his father.

Ego's *maternal* or *matrilateral* relatives are those of his kin to whom he is connected through his mother.

To sum up:

	are *kin* (or consanguineal relatives or cognates) who can be distinguished as	1. patrilineal (or agnatic) 2. matrilineal (or uterine) 3. cross-line
Relatives	or as	1. paternal (or patrilateral) 2. maternal (or matrilateral)
	and *affines* who can be distinguished as	1. kin of Ego's spouse 2. spouses of Ego's kin.

[2] See for instances, Pagès, 1933.

degrees of control exerted by that central authority on the territory. These processes have necessarily had an impact on the autonomy and social significance of Hutu and Tutsi kinship groups, on their connexion with a particular tract of land, and on their functions. We shall not be concerned here with any reconstruction of these processes but only with them as they existed in the immediate pre-European days. It should be borne in mind, however, that this was the period of an evolution. This explains the sometimes confused picture given by some informants.

(a) *Inzu, ubwoko, umulyango*

Hutu and Tutsi recognized a patrilineal kin group (*inzu*)[3] which included all who could actually trace their agnatic relationship through usually no more than four or five ascendent genealogical links to an ancestor recognized as the original ancestor of the group.

Members of the inzu of a male Ego were: Br, Si, Fa, FaSi, FaBr, FaBrSo, FaBrDa, FaFa, FaFaBr, FaFaSi, FaFaBrSo, FaFaBrDa, FaFaBrSoSo, FaFaBrSoDa.[4]

Ego's sororal nephews and nieces (SiSo, SiDa) and his paternal cross-cousins (FaSiSo and FaSiDa) did not belong to his *inzu*. However they participated in some of its activities if they lived with their maternal uncle (Ego), which happened when the bride-wealth for their mother (Ego's Si) had not been entirely paid.

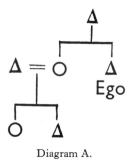

Diagram A.

Other generations above Ego's (that of FaFaFa, &c.) or under his (that of SoSoSo, &c.), were not necessarily included in Ego's

[3] *Inzu* means also hut.
[4] I follow the symbolization system used by Murdock, 1949.

THE SYSTEM OF KINSHIP AND AFFINITY 31

inzu. Their inclusion depended on the situation of Ego's generation with regard to the ancestor recognized as the originator of the group. Suppose a new inzu had begun with F (Diagram B), in the sense that F's descendants referred to themselves as 'people of F' rather than as 'people of A' (as F referred to himself). In that case, Ego would not consider E (FaFaFaFa) as of his inzu although he knew that he was the father of his great-grandfather.

Or suppose that D was considered as the origin of the inzu. In that case Ego's son, J, was separated from D by five links. It was quite possible that if, for instance, G had had many children and had been a man of standing and repute, J and K (and all G's descendants in their generations) would some day refer to themselves as 'people of G'. As long as Ego was living, however, J would consider himself as a member of the same inzu as his father and Ego would not think of his son as belonging to another inzu. One informant, Kayijuka, told us that one of his great-grandchildren will probably take the initiative in forming the new inzu of 'people of Kayijuka'.[5]

Although the inzu was a transitory group about six generations deep, it must be understood that the formation of a new inzu was not rigidly determined and did not automatically happen at the birth of the first child in the seventh generation. The operative factors were mainly the fast growing number of inzu members after a few generations (in genealogies collected, the sixth

Δ A
|
Δ B
|
Δ C
|
Δ D
|
Δ E
|
Δ F
|
Δ G
|
Δ H
|
Δ Ego
|
Δ J
|
Δ K

Diagram B.

[5] This was no boast as Kayijuka is now a very important political personality in Ruanda. It may be of interest to mention that Kayijuka was at the court, as a young nobleman, when the first Europeans entered the country. At that time there was a considerable amount of suspicion on both sides. A missionary asked him to point out the queen-mother among the women who were present at the Court. This was prohibited as it was feared that the White Fathers could harm her by magic. Kayijuka did it, however, and for that reason, when the visitors had gone, he was blinded with a red hot iron. But as on the following day he addressed somebody by name after having recognized the voice, it was believed that the operation had not been a success and it was performed a second time. Kayijuka is now a loyal courtier of the king.

32 THE PREMISE OF INEQUALITY IN RUANDA

generation alone seems to comprise about 100 persons), the existence of a man prominent (by wealth, political functions, &c.) among the ascendants closer than the fifth, or a change of residence. The first two factors were usually realized in the span of six generations. If they were not, and if the inzu remained a small group of, say, a dozen people, these and their descendants went on referring to themselves as 'people of' an ancestor of the seventh, eighth, or ninth generation. One informant told us that his own inzu, already six generations deep, was not yet numerous enough to be split into new ones though it probably would be after two more generations. The fact that the ancestor of a new inzu was chosen, and was not simply the son of the ancestor of the former inzu, shows that there was a definite emphasis on the personal prominence of the ancestor.

Among the Tutsi, it seems that inzu tended to grow rather large before segmenting. In their intrigues for power, it was an advantage to be connected by agnatic links to many and important people. Consequently, before initiating the formation of a new inzu, the Tutsi were very cautious: they did not want to diminish their social power by severing their connexions with the members of their present inzu. Besides, a change of residence was a less compelling reason for the Tutsi to split the inzu: they were not attached to a particular region to the same extent as the Hutu; when appointed to different offices, they often had to move from one part of the country to another and they frequently travelled to the court.

The formation of a new inzu was not necessarily a segmentation resulting in the concomitant formation of two new units of the same age and importance. It could happen that among the inzu 'people of A', those of the sixth generation who were the descendants of B preferred to think of themselves as 'people of B' because B was a famous warrior and they were numerous enough to constitute an inzu of their own. This did not compel those of the sixth generation who were descendants of C and D to do the same. They would go on considering themselves 'people of A'. After a couple more generations, when the number of the descendants of F had increased, they would refer to themselves as 'people of F' who was a rich owner of cows, and the descendants of G as 'people of G' because he had been an important province chief, whereas the descendants of C would some day take the name of 'people of E' if they moved into another region.

THE SYSTEM OF KINSHIP AND AFFINITY

The *ubwoko* was the largest kin group of the patrilineal type. Its members recognized a traditional bond of common descent in the paternal line, but were definitely unable to trace their

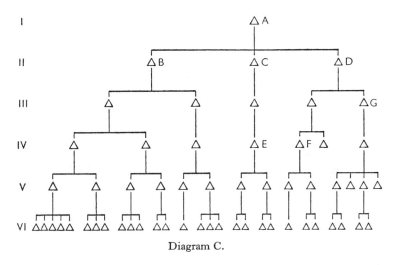

Diagram C.

relationship to the ancestor who was, perhaps, mythical. Two members of the same ubwoko have an idea of a certain kinship tie between them, but nothing more. Ubwoko were geographically dispersed.

There were thirteen such groupings in Ruanda: Abanyiginya (the royal ubwoko), Abega (the ubwoko from which the queens usually came), Abatsoba, Abacyaba, Abasinga, Abatira, Abakono, Abaniakarama, Abazigaba, Abagesera, Ababanda, Abaha, Abashambo. This number was consistent for a very long time. Ubwoko were permanent groups.[6]

Larger in membership than inzu and smaller than ubwoko, a third kinship group called *umulyango* existed in Ruanda. What it was is not quite clear in the mind of most of our informants. This is due, I think, to the fact that umulyango varied considerably in their degree of organization, corporateness, and functions. But also there was some uncertainty in terminology: the same group, say the Abahindiro, has been referred to by our informants sometimes as inzu, and sometimes as umulyango.

[6] See Czekanowski, 1917, pp. 41-45 and 235 f.

34 THE PREMISE OF INEQUALITY IN RUANDA

Umulyango appears to have been the group of living people who would have belonged to the same inzu if that primitive inzu had not split into new ones. This explains the fluidity of the use of the term. For instance the word 'Abareganshuro' (people of Mureganshuro) has meant first 'the members of the inzu of Mureganshuro'; then, after the splitting of that inzu, 'the members of the umulyango of Mureganshuro'. When an inzu divided into different new ones, the ancestor of the former one became the ancestor of the umulyango. Thus the umulyango link existed between members of different inzu having the same origin.

As may be expected, the strength of these links was quite different at the time of the splitting and a few generations afterwards. This accounts for the fact that in some cases the umulyango appears almost as a corporate group very similar to an inzu, and in other cases as a purely nominal group.

The span of life of an umulyango seems less defined than that of an inzu. It is doubtful, however, whether it was longer. Suppose inzu A splits into B and C and becomes umulyango A. Six generations later inzu B splits into inzu D and E and becomes umulyango B. At that time it is very likely that the primitive ancestor being twelve generations past will not be clearly remembered and that, except for some extraordinary reason, he will be superseded by the ancestor of umulyango B.

Descent groups in Ruanda were thus of two different types A permanent group, the ubwoko which fulfilled the definition of patriclan (if exogamy be excluded from that definition) and two temporary groups, inzu and umulyango, the second being rather the surviving shadow of the first. The latter were both patrilineages. As they were not segments in the same sense as among, e.g. the Nuer, it would be misleading to differentiate them according to the terminology of Evans-Pritchard.[7] We would suggest calling inzu a primary and umulyango a secondary patrilineage in order to convey the idea that the umulyango originated from the inzu and that the inzu's functions were more important for the individual and society at large than those of the umulyango.[8]

---

[7] Evans-Pritchard, 1940, pp. 192-4.

[8] Members of the inzu were called *bavandimwe* (which primarily means sibling), agnatic relatives, *benewacu* and relatives, affines included, *abacu*.

THE SYSTEM OF KINSHIP AND AFFINITY 35

(b) Organization and activities of the inzu

The primary patrilineage had a head who was usually called *umutware w'inzu* (chief of the inzu). Sometimes he was designated *umutware w'umulyango* (chief of the umulyango) even when his group was clearly an inzu. Among the Hutu, particularly in the north (Bugoyi, Mulera, Ndorwa), he was often called *umukungu*.

The man who first formed a new inzu did not necessarily become its head: he could choose its chief from among his uncles, brothers, cousins, or sons. Then the lineage head chose his successor. He was usually the eldest son but he could be any son or a nephew. If the person chosen seemed unacceptable to the Ruanda administrative authority, a meeting of the inzu was held and the political chief asked them to choose another inzu head. If the objections came from the group itself, they could resort to the umulyango head—if the umulyango concerned was still a strong group—or to the administrative authority, or in the case of an Hutu inzu which depended on only one lord for its cattle (*shebuja*), to him.

In addition to presiding over the collective activities of his lineage, the head had some power of his own. He was a judge in disputes between the members of his inzu; he also had the right to punish a member of his inzu who had wronged another, except in the case of murder, when the political authority was responsible for the punishment. Anyway, those who were dissatisfied with the decisions of the lineage head could always appeal to the political chief. Sometimes the lineage head legislated for the members of the inzu. A Hutu informant told us that his grandfather, who was the inzu head, had prohibited cross-cousin marriage in his inzu. The lineage head also detailed members for military service and assigned individual contributions to the tax required by the authorities. Officially and towards individual outsiders, he acted as the representative of the inzu. When a girl of his inzu ran away from her husband, he tried to settle the dispute with the head of the husband's inzu. He was responsible for the inzu's tax contribution and for handing over to the political authority any member of the lineage who had committed a crime against an outsider.

The significance of the inzu as a collective body was apparent in ritual, marriage, mutual aid, and blood-feud. In the ritual

36   THE PREMISE OF INEQUALITY IN RUANDA

sphere, there was the initiation of a member of the inzu into the Ryangombe sect. Ryangombe was supposed to have been during his life the chief of a small band of friends and clients. He was accidentally killed by a buffalo during a hunting party. Unwilling to leave Ryangombe, his friends threw themselves on the buffalo's horns. Imana gave them a special place, the Karisimbi, a former volcano, where they were believed to enjoy a notably more agreeable life than the other spirits. In order to have the privilege of joining them there and of enjoying their protection while living, Ruanda had to be initiated into Ryangombe's sect (to be initiated: *kubandwa*). This sect was not a permanent organization, in the sense that churches are. It was only for an initiation ceremony that people who were members of the candidate's inzu as well as members of the sect, came together. An initiator and the different people who were going to impersonate the imandwa (Ryangombe's friends) were chosen from the inzu concerned. The initiation ceremony took place in a hut, secretly (in the sense that non-initiates were not admitted, but not in the sense that affiliation to the sect was kept secret). It was an occasion for the gathering of the inzu as the great majority of its members, men and women, particularly among the Hutu, were initiated.

A second collective ritual was celebrated yearly in the inzu to honour the ancestor of the lineage (*guterekera*: to make an offering to a *muzimu*—a spirit). Presents were offered in the little hut dedicated to the ancestor's spirit in the lineage head's compound. They consisted of what the deceased person liked most in life (milk, hydromel, beans, &c.). This celebration lasted six days and six nights and took place after the sorghum harvesting, in July. There was a kind of ritual meal at the inzu head's compound in which every descendant of the ancestor participated (a cow, a goat, or beans were eaten according to the means of the people). This custom was more widespread among the Hutu than among the Tutsi, where, also, more restraint in eating, drinking, and feasting was observed.

Another collective activity of the inzu was the meeting of councils in which all the important members of the inzu sat. Sometimes all the adults joined, but it was certain that the opinions of only the old, wealthy, and politically powerful men would prevail. The questions discussed concerned proposals of

THE SYSTEM OF KINSHIP AND AFFINITY 37

marriage coming from another inzu or to be made to another inzu, and whether the council thought that a connexion with such or such lineage was to be accepted, sought, or avoided. A certain number of disputes that the lineage head could not or would not settle alone were submitted to the council. When somebody had lost his cattle and was ruined, the council could determine and apportion a collective contribution to help him out of his difficulties. Finally, blood-feuds were discussed. When a member of the group had been killed by a member of another all the kinsmen of the victim attempted to retaliate by taking of the life of a kinsman of the offender. Compensation was not usual. I was told, however, by the Hutu of Bugoyi that there the murderer's group could prevent the taking of vengeance by handing over a beautiful girl. Political authority kept the feuds under strict control. Permission to retaliate had to be obtained from the king and when it was granted and vengeance had been achieved, the feud was at an end. No further vengeance could be taken. Sometimes the king made representatives of the two lineages share a meal.

As the preceding paragraphs suggest, there was no clear-cut division between the powers of the head and of the council. It was a question of the particular traditions in each inzu and of the individual characters of the persons concerned. Usually, however, the inzu was an oligarchy rather than a monarchy. The head could not rule in opposition to the men of standing in his lineage; they had the means to put pressure on him and then there was the possibility of recourse to the political chiefs, always glad to interfere in a domain which was not completely under their control.

The obligations and rights of the individual members of a primary patrilineage were many. There was first a prohibition on sexual intercourse within the group, which applied to relations whether in or out of wedlock. It was feared that the mating of descendants from the same inzu ancestor would produce sickly and malformed children. A few informants add that exogamy was necessary to promote connexions between descent-groups, these connexions being thought of as beneficial in a vague way. The Ruanda did not distinguish incestuous relations from prohibited relations because of consanguinity. For them all the latter were incestuous. But they recognized order in the degrees of gravity in

38 THE PREMISE OF INEQUALITY IN RUANDA

incestuous relationships. The most serious in the inzu would be between Ego and Da or Ego and FaSi. These were said never to occur. Incest was viewed with horror as a beastly thing, a view reflected in one of the words used to describe it, *ubuhene*. The root of this word is *ihene* (goat) because, as an informant put it, only he-goats pair with their mothers and sisters. A breach of this rule was the concern of everybody in the group as it was likely to bring about calamities affecting them all.

Another duty of a member of a primary lineage *vis-à-vis* any of his kinsmen was that of rendering assistance when he was in difficulties (as for instance when a father was unable to help his son to pay bride-wealth or when the cows of a herdsman had been killed by an illness). This obligation was particularly binding when the misfortune was no fault of the victim, but even if it was, aid was often given. As has been mentioned, the lineage-head or the council usually determined the amount to be contributed by everybody. But mutual help was also an individual duty.

A kinsman could enlist the help of the wise and experienced men of his inzu when he had to go to the tribunal. He was accompanied by them, and was helped not only by their advice but also and sometimes mainly by the mere fact of their moral support. The chief who was judging could see the power of the group behind the plaintiff or the defendant.

Inzu solidarity operated both actively and passively in blood-feuds. All adult kinsmen of the victim were obliged to take up arms and carry out vengeance. Kinsmen of the murderer had to defend themselves and all adult males of his inzu had to accept the risk of being killed because of their kinsman's crime.

When a member of the inzu died, all others met in the deceased's hut and watched by the corpse for eight days. After this the corpse was not buried but thrown away in some isolated place, such as the top of a rocky hill, which could be used by the people of any inzu living nearby. Mourning lasted two months for a man and one month for a woman. During that period there was a prohibition on intercourse for people very closely connected with the deceased (his son, his wife, his son's wife, his father). At the end of the mourning period all the inzu gathered together again. There was a beer-feast and obligatory intercourse for all the inzu members with their own spouses. When there was no spouse, as

THE SYSTEM OF KINSHIP AND AFFINITY 39

for instance with a widow, intercourse took place with a brother or a parallel cousin of the deceased husband.

Among the Hutu when the inzu as such possessed fields (*ingobii* or *ubukonde*), as happened particularly in the northern area (Bugoyi, Mulera, Ndorwa), the individual member had a right to a plot (*isambo*). He could not sell such a plot, but could let it (at a rent of about one hoe for two years). If the ancestor has received cows from a lord (*shebuja*), these cows, or rather their offspring, were the property of the inzu which happened to have some pasture land. Among the Tutsi there were usually no land rights vested in the inzu. Tutsi as well as Hutu inzu had no sacred place other than the ancestor's shrine in the *rugo* (enclosure) of the lineage-head and the small huts in the enclosure of each descendant.

From this one may infer that the lineage group at the end of the nineteenth century was not a group with a territorial basis. It is very likely that a territorial lineage group was common among the Hutu and had persisted in the north where Hutu were predominant and where Tutsi occupation had always been scanty and superficial (there were very few Tutsi settlers in that region, apart from administrative chiefs).[9] On the other hand all the activities of the inzu just described implied a rather close co-residence (which is, of course, different from the concept of a territorial basis). These frequent gatherings, blood-feuds, and the rendering of help in difficult circumstances would hardly have been possible if the members of the group had been living in scattered places several days' journey apart. This explains also the crucial importance of the change of residence in the formation of a new inzu. When a branch of an inzu had to leave and settle elsewhere, it was bound to become a new inzu because the former relations with the members of the inzu who did not move could not have been maintained, at least among the Hutu and ordinary Tutsi. This was less important for Tutsi chiefs who were in any case moving about and travelling frequently.

(c) Social roles within the inzu

Following the authors of *Toward a General Theory of Action*, social role is understood here as the totality of reciprocal

[9] For an account of the specific structure of the kinship system in the north of Ruanda, the present-day districts (*territorires*) of Kisenyi, Ruhengeri and part of Biumba, see Hertefelt, 1959.

D

40 THE PREMISE OF INEQUALITY IN RUANDA

interactions of Ego and Alter once an organized system of interaction between themselves has become stabilized. 'Alter expects Ego to behave in given situational conditions in certain relatively specific ways, or at least within relatively specific limits.'[10]

Members of an inzu were supposed to have more confidence in each other and to be readier to help and sympathize with each other than with outsiders. Within the inzu itself, each member was expected to assume a certain role which defined, within narrow limits, expected behaviour towards other lineage members. Before these intra-inzu roles are described, a list of kinship terms used within the inzu to address or designate members, will be given. Some characteristics of these behaviour patterns are reflected in the terminology, as, for instance, the predominance within the lineage of the horizontal or generation principle of grouping over the vertical grouping by branches of the lineage.

Data will be presented first and implications analysed at a later stage. Our point of reference will be the conventional Ego. All the terms and their symbolizations are to be understood as relating to Ego who is a male (Tutsi, Hutu, or Twa). The same terms are used by a male as by a female, except where otherwise indicated: f.s. (female speaking) and m.s. (male speaking).

Role	Term of address	Term of reference
I. The generation of Ego's father		
Fa	Data	Data
FaBr	Data	Datawacu (father-our)
FaSi	Mama	Masenge (mother through father)
FaFaBrSo	Data	Datawacu
FaFaBrDa	Mama	Masenge
FaFaFaBrSoSo	Data	Datawacu
FaFaFaBrSoDa	Mama	Masenge
II. The generation of Ego's grandfather		
FaFa	Sogokuru (kuru = great)	Sogokuru
FaFaBr	Sogokuru	Sogokuru
FaFaSi	Nyogokuru	Nyogokuru
FaFaFaBrSo	Sogokuru	Sogokuru
FaFaFaBrDa	Nyogokuru	Nyogokuru
III. The generation of Ego's great-grandfather		
FaFaFa	Sogokuru	Sogokuruza
FaFaFaBr	Sogokuru	Sogokuruza
FaFaFaSi	Nyogokuru	Nyogokuruza

[10] Parsons and Shils, 1951, p. 19.

THE SYSTEM OF KINSHIP AND AFFINITY

Role	Term of address	Term of reference
IV. The other generations above		
Ancestor		Igisokuru
V. Ego's generation		
Br, ½ pat Br	Muvandinwe (from same womb)	Mwenedata (child of father)
YoBr, ½ YoBr (pat)	Muvandimwe	Murumunawanjye (murumu = little)
ElBr, ½ pat ElBr	Muvandimwe	Mukutuwahjye (mukuru = great)
Br (f.s.)	Muvandimwe	Musazawanjye (wanjye = my)
Si, ½ pat Si	Muvandimwe	Mwenedata
YoSi, ½ pat YoSi	Muvandimwe	Murumunawanjye
ElSi, ½ pat ElSi	Muvandimwe	Mukurumwanjye (Mukuru = great)
Si (m.s.)		Mushikiwanjye
FaBrSo	Muvandimwe	Mwenedatawacu (child of our Fa)
FaBrSo (f.s.)		Musazawacu
FaBrDa	Muvandimwe	Mwenedatawacu
FaBrDa (m.s.)		Mushikiwacu
FaFaBrSoSo	Muvandimwe	Mwenedatawacu
FaFaBrSoDa	Muvandimwe	Mwenedatawacu
FaFaFaBrSoSoSo	Muvandimwe	Mwenedatawacu
FaFaFaBrSoSoDa	Muvandimwe	Mwenedatawacu
VI. The generation of Ego's son		
So	Mwana (child)	Muhunguwanjye (boy–my)
Da	Mwana (child)	Mukobwawanjye (girl–my)
BrSo (m.s.)	Mwana (child)	Muhunguwacu (boy–our)
BrSo (f.s.)	Mwana (child)	Musengenezawanjye
BrDa (m.s.)	Mwana (child)	Mukobwawacu (girl–our)
BrDa (f.s.)	Mwana (child)	Musengenezawanjye
FaBrSoSo (m.s.)	Mwana (child)	Muhunguwacu
FaBrSoSo (f.s.)	Mwana (child)	Muzengenezawacu
FaBrSoDa (m.s.)	Mwana (child)	Mukobwawacu
FaBrSoDa (f.s.)	Mwana (child)	Musengenezawacu
FaFaBrSoSoSo (m.s.)	Mwana (child)	Muhunguwacu
FaFaBrSoSoSo (f.s.)	Mwana (child)	Muzengenezawacu
FaFaBrSoSoDa (m.s.)	Mwana (child)	Mukobwawacu
FaFaBrSoSoDa (f.s.)	Mwana (child)	Muzengenezawacu
VII. The generation of Ego's grandchildren		
SoSo	Mwana	Muzukuruwanjye
SoDa	Mwana	Muzukuruwanjye
BrSoSo	Mwana	Muzukuruwacu
BrSoDa	Mwana	Muzukuruwacu
FaBrSoSoSo	Mwana	Muzukuruwacu
FaBrSoSoDa	Mwana	Muzukuruwacu

42   THE PREMISE OF INEQUALITY IN RUANDA

Role	Term of address	Term of reference
VIII. The generation of Ego's great grandchildren		
SoSoSo	Mwana	Muzukuruza
SoSoDa	Mwana	Muzukuruza
IX. The other generations under		
Descendant		Ubuvivi[11]

Let us now turn to the description of the most important of these roles.

During all his father's lifetime, Ego remained subject to his authority, though before puberty the young son was allowed to show some familiarity in his relations with his father. Even at that early age, however, the interests and comfort of his father predominated, and it seems that the weakness of a child was not considered a reason for giving. him relatively more food and other comforts than his father. When he reached puberty and was initiated into the Ryangombe sect, he was treated more severely and had to behave as an obedient servant of his father. He could not go to sleep before his father, or get up after him in the morning, without permission. He had to stay near the gate of the fence, to close it at night and open it in the morning, instead of sitting near the fire. This was especially true among the Hutu who did not have servants. There the son had to tend the cattle (goats, sheep, and eventually cows) with the help of his sisters. His training in different men's activities was given to him by his father. Among the Tutsi, where such training included dancing, composition of poetry, and the use of weapons, different specialists were required. The training was given at the court of a chief or of the king. But even when separated from his father for a long time, the young Tutsi was expected to manifest the same attitude of obedience.

When his son was getting married, the father, Hutu as well as Tutsi, had to help him to pay the bride-wealth. Marriage did not change the son's attitude towards his father, who still had the right to inflict severe punishments if disobeyed. He could curse him, which amounted to complete ostracism and being obliged to flee to a region where he was not known and consequently where it was extremely difficult for him to make a living. The father could carry out less severe but more humiliating punishments, such as beating his son with a stick or preventing him from sleeping with his wife for some time by monopolizing her; (it should be noted that

[11] Compare with Vanhove, 1941, pp. 11-16.

THE SYSTEM OF KINSHIP AND AFFINITY 43

the absence of a taboo on sex-relations between father-in-law and daughter-in-law may have induced some severe fathers to punish their sons in this way). As long as their fathers lived, sons were never emancipated.[12]

The father had a slightly different attitude towards his daughter, though she certainly had to obey and respect him. Like the boys the girls went to sleep later than their parents and got up earlier. They participated in a large measure in the domestic chores, among the Hutu. They were more closely associated with their mother, the father did not have the task of punishing them, and they were never beaten by him after puberty. They were said usually to have great influence on their father and could get what they wanted from him. When they married the father received the bride-wealth, but he had to supply some of the counter-gifts. Marriage did not cut the links between the girl and her inzu which remained her inzu. But her close connexion with her husband's inzu sometimes divided her loyalties, though I was told that this was rare and anyway not a part of her expected behaviour. *Amahitamo yaje, umwana ni uwa se* (when a choice has to be made, one is the child of one's father).

Ego regarded his paternal uncle very much as another father. He referred to him as 'our father'. Like the father, the father's brother had the right to punish. This is why a man who had committed some offence did not dare to take refuge with his paternal uncle. Their relations were, however, more cordial and less tense: the paternal uncle was the usual intermediary between Ego and Fa when the former wanted to obtain something from the latter. Ego, for instance, told his FaBr first when he wished to marry. There was no significant difference of behaviour towards the father's brothers, unless the relative ages of Ego and his FaBr were exceptional. If the nephew and his uncle were about the same age, there was a more familiar relationship between them. If FaBr was about as old as Fa, the attitude was more polite and respectful.

The paternal aunt (FaSi) had perhaps a still more prominent position. As she had received no part of her father's heritage, she felt free to ask from her father or from her brothers whatever she wanted for her nephews (Ego's children). Moreover, as her nephews could marry her daughers without any very urgent

[12] Cf. Vincent, 1954, pp. 106-14.

44   THE PREMISE OF INEQUALITY IN RUANDA

obligation to pay the bride-wealth, she could exert further pressure on her brothers by not agreeing to the marriage; finally, she had the power to curse her nephews and nieces. All this accounted for the importance of her role in the inzu. Nieces and nephews very often turned to her and she was often said to love them more than her own children. This difference between FaBr's and FaSi's attitudes toward Ego is perhaps reflected in the terminology. FaBr referred to his nephew by the word *muhunguwacu* (our-boy) and to his niece by *mukobwawacu* (our-girl), whereas the FaSi referred to both of them by *musengeneza-wanjye* (my niece/nephew). This last word contains the possessive 'my' used in kinship terminology usually for only the primary relatives, whereas the term of reference used by the FaBr includes the form 'our' usually used for secondary or more distant relatives.

Between Ego and the members of the generations alternate to his own, there were symmetrical relations of great familiarity and joking, with a preponderant sexual theme. The grandfather called his granddaughters his little wives and his grandsons his love rivals. The reason given for this familiarity is that it helped to cheer up the old people and to train the young ones in socially enjoyable talk. Grandfathers also participated in the socialization of the grandchildren by transmitting proverbs, legends, tales of past history, and mythological conceptions in which a great deal of the Ruanda view of the world was embodied.

As regards siblings, Ego was expected to have a respectful attitude towards his eldest brother, *uwamboneye izuba* (the first who saw the sun) even if the latter happened not to inherit the paternal authority over his brothers. In these cases he was honoured more than his brother who wielded the paternal authority. The eldest brother's advice was always asked by his siblings. Other brothers were expected to assume what we would call fraternal attitudes. But as brothers competed for their father's favour and had to share his heritage, there was under this appearance of cordiality a very deep rivalry and mutual distrust. It should be noted that all that is said of siblings applied both to half paternal siblings and to full siblings. In a descent group founded on agnatic principles the distinction of full and half paternal siblings is largely irrelevant.

Sisters were also expected to respect and obey their oldest brother. After they had reached puberty, however, he could not enforce obedience. The oldest sister's role was somewhat similar

THE SYSTEM OF KINSHIP AND AFFINITY 45

to the oldest brother's as regards her younger sisters. But the importance of seniority was less stressed among sisters than among brothers. There was often rivalry between married sisters as there was no taboo on intercourse between a woman and her sister's husband.

Sisters and brothers were playmates during their childhood. After puberty their relations were restricted, but certainly not to the point of avoidance. As girls did not inherit from the father, as they were the prospective paternal aunts of the future children of their brothers, the relations between siblings of opposite sexes did not manifest the same covert strain as that between brothers.

Parallel paternal male cousins of Ego were assimilated to his brothers, but as there was no inheritance rivalry, and as Ego was not required to manifest a particular respect for his eldest cousin, Ego's actual relation with his parallel cousins was in fact more fraternal than with his brothers. Ego considered the daughters of his paternal uncle as sisters with whom there was a marriage prohibition. There was consequently a certain reserve between them which, however, did not prevent them from exchanging obscene jokes at a celebration or a gathering, but any sexual acts were severely tabooed.

(d) Organization and activities of the umulyango and the ubwoko

The two other descent groups may be described much more briefly. The secondary patrilineage when it had just divided from the primary group continued to share in the previous functions of the formerly united inzu. There were still gatherings of the descendants of the umulyango's ancestor, mutual aid, judgements in disputes, and participation in the blood-feuds. But gradually these activities were confined more and more within the new inzu and after an intermediate period, the umulyango generally disappeared as a corporate group.[13] Obviously if the splitting was due to a change of residence or a dispute, the functions of the former inzu were very quickly assumed by the new one and relations with other branches of the former inzu (which then constituted an umulyango) were not very close.

Did the umulyango as such have any special characteristics or activities? All our informants agree on the rule of exogamy.

---

[13] For a definition of a corporate group see Radcliffe-Brown and Forde, 1950, p. 41.

46 THE PREMISE OF INEQUALITY IN RUANDA

When the umulyango had a head (chosen in a similar way to the inzu head), he is said to have had the power to give orders to the heads of the component inzu and to draw up general rules for all the umulyango members. I was told, for instance, that the chief of a certain umulyango had ruled that the members should not marry girls of the ubwoko of the Abacyaba. This prohibition about 150 years old is still observed. When the secondary lineage had a head, he fulfilled very much the same function as an 'appeal court' for all decisions taken within the inzu. Such an umulyango organization existed among Hutu and Tutsi, but seems to have been more common in the important Tutsi lineages.

The patriclan (ubwoko) had no head and no collective activities. It was usually agamous, although there may have been an exogamy rule in one particular clan. An animal species was associated with each clan. Its members were not allowed to kill any of them and were even obliged to protect them. The animal was not thought of as a reincarnation of the ancestor's spirit but probably only as a living symbol of the clan.[14]

Unlike the inzu and the umulyango, any ubwoko could have both Tutsi and Hutu among its members. There was no purely Hutu or purely Tutsi patriclan. When asked if this meant that Tutsi and Hutu of the same clan descended from the same ancestor, Tutsi answered that it did not. They explain it by the relationships which have linked Hutu to Tutsi as clients or servants. After some time the Hutu were identified with the group of their master. Such identification was particularly easy since Tutsi frequently emigrated from one region of Ruanda to another with their Hutu clients and servants. Some Hutu told me that as Gatutsi, Gahutu, and Gatwa (mythical figures who, as their names indicate, were supposed to be ancestors of the three groups) were brothers, it is not impossible that Tutsi and Hutu of one clan could have had the same ancestor. At all events clansmen who were of different socio-'racial' groups did not exhibit any solidarity at all and behaved towards each other as complete strangers.

As has been said, Ego's wife belonged to her own patrilineage for ever. This is why the social role of Ego's wife has not been mentioned in this section. But as she took part in many of the

---

[14] Some examples of the totemic animals of patriclans are: Abazigaba, the leopard (*ingwe*), Abasinga, the hawk (*sakabaka*), Abega, the frog (*igikeli*), Abagesera, the wagtail (*nyamanza*), Abacyaba, the hyena (*impyisi*).

THE SYSTEM OF KINSHIP AND AFFINITY 47

activities of her husband's inzu and was not bound by all the obligations common to the members of her own inzu, a few words should be added about her behaviour in this connexion.

She participated in the cult of Ego's (=her husband's) ancestor and of her own ancestor, but she was not allowed to build a shrine in honour of her ancestor in Ego's enclosure. She gave the ritual gifts at the birth of a child in her own inzu as well as in Ego's inzu, and did the same at marriage ceremonies. In times of mourning, Ego's inzu was predominant: his wife had to practise sexual abstention for two or three months when Ego's parents died. For her own parents she was not bound by any such observances. She received protection from her husband's group, but from her own only when she had disputes with Ego's lineage

2. THE DESCENT GROUP OF EGO'S MOTHER

A man (or a woman) was not a member of his mother's patri-lineage, which is why in the preceding section only his agnates were considered. But the picture of Ego's position in kinship relations would be incomplete if it were limited to that. Ego's mother's agnates were not complete strangers to him. In everyday life, he met them often and his culture provided him with roles to assume in these circumstances. In some cases Ego's behaviour to 'maternal' kin was very similar to that which he was expected to observe towards the agnatic counterpart of that kin.

Role	Term of address	Term of reference
I. The generation of Ego's mother		
Mo	Mama	Mama
MoBr	Data	Marume
MoSi	Mama	Mamawacu
MoFaBrSo	Data	Marume
MoFaBrDa	Mama	Mamawacu
MoFaFaBrSoSo	Data	Marume
MoFaFaBrSoDa	Mama	Mamawacu
II. The generation of Ego's maternal grandfather		
MoFa	Sogokuru	Sogokuru
MoFaBr	Sogokuru	Sogokuru
MoFaSi	Nyogokuru	Nyogokuru
III. The generation of Ego's maternal great-grandfather		
MoFaFa	Sogokuru	Sogokuruza
MoFaFaBr	Sogokuru	Sogokuruza
MoFaFaSi	Nyogokuru	Nyogokuruza

48 THE PREMISE OF INEQUALITY IN RUANDA

Role	Term of address	Term of reference
IV. Ego's generation		
MoBrSo	Name, nickname or Muvandimwe	Mubyarawanjye (one with with whom to beget-mine)
MoBrDa	Name, nickname or Muvandimwe	Mubyarawanjye
MoFaBrSoSo	Name, nickname or Mwana	Mubyarawacu (one with whom to beget-our)
MoFaBrSoDa	Name, nickname or Mwana	Mubyarawacu
MoFaFaBrSoSoSo	Mwana	Mubyarawacu
MoFaFaBrSoSoDa	Mwana	Mubyarawacu[15]

Ego's mother, who was the link between Ego and her descent group, was not a figure of authority to the same extent as Ego's father. Her children had to behave respectfully and obediently towards her, but as she was a wife of their father, they saw that she, like they themselves, had to submit to an authority in the home. Moreover, Ruanda placed a very high value on their children and they were more important for the father than his wife. Consequently the children knew that from their father's point of view their mother did not enjoy a status superior to their own. Consequently the mother-son and mother-daughter relations were usually free and affectionate. Very often the mother, when widowed and old, came and lived with one of her children, whereas the old widower frequently lived alone.

The relationship between Ego and his maternal uncle was one of extreme restraint. It was not avoidance: they spoke to each other and Ego came and called on him from time to time. These attitudes were not completely symmetrical: the uncle seemed to consider his nephews only as nuisances. For him they brought ill-luck and they were treated accordingly: they were not allowed to look into his granaries or to milk his cows, and they ate with the servants, The uncle seemed to do all he could to induce them to keep away. But they visited him because there they met his children with whom they were traditionally permitted to have very familiar relationships. The maternal uncle was afraid that Ego would have intercourse with his daughter and that her betrothal to somebody else would thereby be broken. He was also afraid that if Ego married her he would not easily obtain bride-wealth from his brother-in-law. All these reasons were understandable enough.

[15] We do not mention here the maternal half-siblings because they do not belong to their mother's descent group. They are referred to as *Mwenemama* (child of mother).

THE SYSTEM OF KINSHIP AND AFFINITY 49

Why did they not operate in the case of FaSi? As mother of Ego's paternal cross-cousins, with whom Ego could enjoy the same familiarities, she could have reacted in the same way. We have seen that, on the contrary, she was extremely cordial to her nephews. The only reason seems to be that her nephews belonged to her own lineage, whereas her daughters did not. Consequently she was less interested in bride-wealths, &c. Her husband (FaSiHu) probably reacted in the same way as MoBr.

The relations of Ego with his maternal aunt (MoSi) were supposed to be similar to his relations with his mother, but in fact great trust and affection did not often exist between them because of the usually tense relations of the aunt with Ego's mother, her sister. If, for instance, Ego's aunt's husband (MoSiHu) neglected his wife and preferred his sister-in-law (Ego's Mo), with whom intercourse was not taboo, the relations between the two sisters became tense. The incest taboo applied to the relations between Ego and MoSi (as an extension of the incest prohibition between Ego and his Mo) and also MoSiDa (although she did not belong to Mo's inzu). In the latter case, the reason was that for Ego, his maternal parallel cousins were assimilated to his paternal parallel cousins. He had consequently to consider her as his sister. In the next generation this incest taboo still existed (between So and MoSiDaDa, i.e. between any male and his FaMoSiDaDa). The incest between Ego's male descendants and his MoSi's female descendants through females lasted, I was told, as long as the original sibling relation (between Mo and MoSi) was remembered.

Between Ego and his maternal grandfather, the relations were very similar to those between him and his paternal grandfather. As we may expect, the fact that his maternal grandmother did not belong to the maternal patrilineage did not prevent her from being considered as a grandmother and not only as MoFaWi.

As has just been indicated, Ego could enjoy with his female maternal cross-cousins great familiarity expressed in practical jokes, pleasant talk, and erotic games. But as long as the girls were unmarried anything more than caressing and petting (erotic kissing seems to have been unknown among Ruanda) was prohibited. It was only after the female cross-cousins' marriages that sexual intercourse with them was tolerated. This behaviour was extended to wives of male cross-cousins (MoBrSoWi).

50   THE PREMISE OF INEQUALITY IN RUANDA

3. EGO'S CROSS-LINE RELATIVES

The cross-line relatives of Ego are people who are socially recognized as related to him although they do not belong either to his parents' descent groups or to the category of his relatives by affinity.

In Ruanda, the category of cross-line relatives was limited to Ego's paternal cross-cousins, his maternal parallel cousins, their descendants, his sororal nephews and nieces, and their descendants.

Paternal cross-cousins did not belong to Ego's father's patrilineage since they were members of their own father's (FaSiHu of Ego) lineage. It could be said that they were agnates of FaSiHu who was himself an affine of Ego. It seems, however, that the link between Ego and his paternal cross-cousins was their mother (FaSi) and not their father (FaSiHu). This is why I do not include Ego's paternal cross-cousins among Ego's affines.

Maternal cross-cousins were not Ego's cross-line relatives because they were related to Ego as agnates of Ego's mother. On the contrary maternal parallel cousins of Ego were cross-line relatives of Ego's mother: her sororal nephews and nieces. Ego was not related to them through his MoSiHu but through his MoSi as the term of reference used by Ego indicates: child-of-my-maternal-aunt (*mwenemamawacu*). This is why I regard them as Ego's cross-line relatives.

Ego was related to his sororal nephews and nieces through his sister in spite of the fact that her children belonged to her husband's agnatic group.

Role	Term of address	Term of reference
FaSiSo	Name, nickname or Muvandimwe	Mubyarawanjye
FaSiDa	Muvandimwe	Mubyarawanjye
MoSiSo	Muvandimwe	Mwenemamawacu
MoSiDa	Muvandimwe	Mwenemamawacu
SiSo	Mwana	Mwishywawanjye
SiDa	Mwana	Mwishywawanjye

Familiarity, jesting, erotic games without actual intercourse before marriage, were the relations of paternal cross-cousins (as well as maternal cross-cousins) of the opposite sex. The difference was that paternal cross-cousins had to assist each other and often fought together in blood-feuds although, as they did not belong to the same inzu, they could not be killed in retaliation.

THE SYSTEM OF KINSHIP AND AFFINITY 51

This privileged sexual partnership is not to be understood as an unrestricted freedom irrespective of circumstances. From the point of view of a married woman sex relations with these relatives were privileged in the sense that her husband could not divorce her or dismiss her on these grounds as he could do if the lover was not a relative of that category. For the lover himself, it did not make much difference as the woman was always regarded as being responsible for adultery ('she should have refused'); the husband usually had no claim against him although the lover might have to endure some punishment such as being beaten if caught in the act. We may say, however, that intercourse with a woman relative was privileged for a man in the sense that his wife was supposed not to resent it. In any case these relations were kept secret as far as possible, and it was regarded as seriously lacking in respect to indulge in them when the spouse was not away. When the spouse was absent, travelling for a long time, they were considered normal.

This tolerance concerned only married women. Before marriage girls were supposed to remain virgin. When an unmarried girl became pregnant, she was either killed with the infant or sent away, usually to an island on Lake Kivu where she was left to die, unless rescued and taken by a man of a very much despised tribe, the Shi, living on the western shore of the lake (the present Belgian Congo side). Of course, such a drastic course of action was not always followed, but this was the traditional rule. When the unmarried girl was impregnated by a cousin, these dreadful consequences could be more easily avoided if the parents wanted to exert pressure on the lover to make him marry the girl. But this is the only sense in which it may be said that sexual intercourse for an unmarried girl with a relative was privileged.

On the contrary, maternal parallel cousins of Ego had to be treated with restraint. Although not members of his patrilineage, as were his paternal parallel cousins, his attitude towards them and particularly towards the girls was supposed to be very similar. The incest taboo existed between Ego's descendents and his parallel cousins' descendents until such time as the fact that the two mothers were sisters had been forgotten.

Towards his sororal nieces and nephews, Ego's role was similar to his avuncular role *vis-à-vis* his brother's children. He could not marry or have intercourse with his sororal nieces. His behaviour

52 THE PREMISE OF INEQUALITY IN RUANDA

was expected to be protective, but he had no authority over his sister's children unless bride-wealth had not been paid for her.

4. EGO'S AFFINES

Following *Notes and Queries*, I shall distinguish two classes among the relatives by marriage. First, those in which the affinal link is the first traced from Ego, i.e. kin of the spouse; secondly, those in which the kinship link is the first one traced, i.e. persons who have married kinsmen and kinswomen.[16]

I shall begin with the second class: spouses of members of Ego's patrilineage, of Ego's mother's patrilineage and their own agnatic relatives. Not all of these spouses were considered by Ruanda to be significantly related to Ego. They say, for instance, that the wife of the maternal uncle (MoBrWi) is just a stranger, whereas there was a particular code of behaviour laid down towards the wife of the paternal uncle (FaBrWi). Among affines I include, besides these spouses of Ego's consanguineal relatives, the consanguineal relatives of these spouses, such as DaHuFa, SoWiFa, &c.

(a) *The Spouses of Ego's Kin*

This is the nomenclature of the second class of Ego's affines.

Role	Term of address	Term of reference
I. The generation of Ego's father		
FaWi	Mama	Mukadata (wife of Fa)
FaBrWi	Mama	Mukadatawacu (wife of FaBr)
FaSiHu	Name	Mugabo wa masenge (husband of FaSi)
MoSiHu	Name	Mugabo wa mamawacu (husband of MoSi)
II. The generation of Ego's grandfather		
FaFaWi	Nyogokuru	Nyogokuru
MoFaWi	Nyogokuru	Nyogokuru
III. Ego's generation		
BrWi (m.s.)	Name, nickname or Muvandimwe	Mugore wacu (wife-our)
BrWi (f.s.)	Name, nickname or Muvandimwe	Muramukazi wanjye
SiHu (f.s.)	Name, nickname or Muvandimwe	Mugabowacu (husband-our)
SiHu (m.s.)	Name, nickname or Muvandimwe	Muramu wanjye

[16] Royal Anthropological Institute, 1951, p. 87.

THE SYSTEM OF KINSHIP AND AFFINITY 53

Role	Term of address	Term of reference
FaBrDaHu (f.s.)	Name, nickname or Muvandimwe	Mugabo wacu
FaBrSoWi (m.s.)	Name, nickname or Muvandimwe	Mugore wacu
FaSiSoWi (m.s.)	Name, nickname or Muvandimwe	Mugore wacu
FaSiDaHu (f.s.)	Name, nickname or Muvandimwe	Mugabo wacu
MoSiSoWi (m.s.)	Name, nickname or Muvandimwe	Mugore wacu
MoSiDaHu (f.s.)	Name, nickname or Muvandimwe	Mugabo wacu
MoBrDaHu (f.s.)	Name, Nickname or Muvandimwe	Mugabo wacu
MoBrSoWi (m.s.)	Name, nickname or Muvandimwe	Mugore wacu
FaFaBrSoSoWi (m.s.) &c.	Name, nickname or Muvandimwe	Mugore wacu
DaHuFa, DaHuMo, SoWiFa, SoWiMo		Muwana wanjye

IV. The generation of Ego's son.

SoWi	Mwana	Mukazanawanjye (female-mine-through-marriage)
DaHu	Mwana	Mukwewanjye (... male ...)
BrSoWi	Mwana	Mukazanawacu (... our)
SiSoWi	Mwana	Mukazanawacu (... our)
BrDaHu	Mwana	Mukwewacu (... our)
SiDaHu	Mwana	Mukwewacu (... our)
FaBrSoSoWi	Mwana	Mukazanawacu
FaBrSoDaHu &c.	Mwana	Mukwewacu

V. The generation of Ego's grandchildren

SoSoWi	Mwana	Mukazanawacu
SoDaHu	Mwana	Mukwewacu
DaDaHu	Mwana	Mukwewacu
DaSoWi	Mwana	Mukazanawacu
BrSoSoWi	Mwana	Mukazanawacu
SiSoSoWi &c.	Mwana	Mukazanawacu

Grandparents by affinity were regarded in the same way as grandparents by consanguinity. Relations with them were symmetrically playful and familiar.

The two uncles by affinity (FaSiHu and MoSiHu) were treated with respect because they were older than their nephews and with sympathy in so far as their wives got along well with them. If they did not, the nephews tended to side with their aunts. The ideal behaviour, however, was to act towards the aunts' husband with rather more confidence than towards mere outsiders.

54   THE PREMISE OF INEQUALITY IN RUANDA

The paternal uncle's wife (FaBrWi) was more deeply connected with Ego's inzu. She bore children who were Ego's parallel cousins; there was no incest taboo between her and Ego's father and if her husband died, she might become a wife of Ego's father. For all these reasons, respectful and almost filial behaviour towards her was expected from Ego.

For the affinal relatives of Ego's generation, the rule was quite simple. There was no incest taboo; there was on the contrary a privileged sexual partnership (as described earlier in connexion with the paternal cross-cousins) between a male Ego on the one hand and on the other the wives of his brothers, parallel cousins, and cross-cousins. And the same *mutatis mutandis* when Ego is female.

Between Ego and his daughter-in-law (SoWi) there was no incest prohibition, although there was between a female Ego and her son-in-law (her DaHu). This was rationalized by saying that the SoWi is for Ego a little spouse and not a daughter, whereas for the son-in-law, his wife's mother is his mother. As may be imagined the role of SoWi, 'daughter' and rival of her HuMo, was not an easy one as regards Ego and Ego's wife. Her ambivalent situation was reflected in her traditionally expected behaviour. She had to behave respectfully, obediently, and affectionately, as a daughter, towards her parents-in-law, and at the same time she was expected to assume almost an avoidance attitude: she was not allowed to pronounce their names nor even words which sounded similar.

Ego's daughter's husband was expected to conform to the same verbal taboos as regards his father-in-law (Ego) and his mother-in-law (Ego's wife). He was not allowed to eat at his parents-in-law's until his wife had had a child. Even then he never spoke if not invited to. After a certain period of time, however, when the marriage was stable and had produced a few children, relations eventually became freer, though they remained always rather reserved.

All other affines of generations following that of Ego were designated by the same term, even if they were not connected through his patrilineal descendents, DaDaHu for instance.

(b) The kin of Ego's wife

Let us now consider the other class of affines, that in which the affinal link is first traced from Ego. These are the consanguineal

THE SYSTEM OF KINSHIP AND AFFINITY   55

relatives of Ego's spouse among whom we have included the patrilineal kin of the spouse's mother. More exactly, in this total class of potential affines, the Ruanda chose a few of them who they considered as relatives of Ego because for one reason or another they had a certain role to play in his social or cultural life. The others had been neglected. It has been necessary in this case to distinguish between a male and a female Ego.

Role	Term of address	Term of reference
I. The first generation above Ego: Male speaking		
WiFa	Sogokuru	Databukwe (father through marriage)
WiMo	Nyogokuru	Mabukwe
WiFaBr	Sogokuru	Databukwe
WiFaSi	Nyogokuru	Mabukwe
WiMoBr	Sogokuru	Databukwe
WiFaFaBrSoSo &c.	Sogokuru	Databukwe
Female speaking		
HuFa	Sogokuru	Databukwe
HuMo	Nyogokuru	Mabukwe
HuFaBr	Sogokuru	Databukwe
HuFaSi	Nyogokuru	Mabukwe
HuMoBr	Sogokuru	Databukwe
HuFaFaBrSoSo	Sogokuru	Databukwe
II. The second generation above Ego: Male speaking		
WiFaFa	Sogokuru	Sogokuru
WiFaFaBr	Sogokuru	Sogokuru
WiFaMo	Nyogokuru	Nyogokuru
WiMoFa &c.	Sogokuru	Sogokuru
Female speaking		
HuFaFa	Sogokuru	Sogokuru
HuFaFaBr	Sogokuru	Sogokuru
HuMoFa	Sogokuru	Sogokuru
HuFaMo &c.	Nyogokuru	Nyogokuru
III. Ego's generation: Male speaking		
WiSi	Name	Muramukaziwanjye
WiFaBrDa	Name	Muramukaziwanjye
WiMoSiDa	Name	Muramukaziwanjye
WiSiHu	Name	Musanzirewanjye
WiFaBrDaHu	Name	Musanzirewacu
WiMoSiDaHu	Name	Musanzirewacu
WiBr	Name	Muramuwanjye
WiBrWi	Name	Muramuwanjye

56 THE PREMISE OF INEQUALITY IN RUANDA

Role	Term of address	Term of reference
WiFaBrSo	Name	Muramuwacu
WiMoSiSo	Name	Muramuwacu
WiFaSiSo	Name	Muramuwacu
WiFaSiDa	Name	Muramuwacu
WiMoBrSo	Name	Muramuwacu
WiMoBrDa	Name	Muramuwacu
Female speaking		
HuBr	Name	Mugabowacu
HuSi	Name	Muramukaziwanjye
HuFaBrSo	Name	Mugabowacu
HuMoSiSo	Name	Mugabowacu
HuFaSiSo	Name	Mugabowacu
HuFaSiDa	Name	Mukebawanjye (my rival)
HuMoBrSo	Name	Mugabowacu
HuMoBrDa	Name	Mukebawanjye
HuMoSiDa	Name	Muramukaziwanjye
HuFaBrDa	Name	Muramukaziwanjye
HuWi	Name	Mukebawanjye
HuBrWi	Name	Mukebawacu (our rival)
HuFaBrSoWi	Name	Mukebawacu (our rival)
HuMoSiSoWi	Name	Mukebawacu (our rival)

As has just been mentioned in connexion with the SoWi and the DaHu roles, Ego and his wife were expected to behave respectfully, with restraint as well as with affection towards their parents-in-law. This was reflected in the terminology. WiFa, WiMo, HuFa, HuMo were addressed by the term used for the grandparents. We know that Ego's conduct towards his grandparents was extremely familiar. He had to use the same term for in-laws and was not allowed to pronounce their name. As the preceding nomenclature indicates, the use of the same term of address was extended to all in-laws of the generation above Ego's one. There was again no distinction between the grandparents and great-grandparents who were patrilineal ascendents of the spouse and those who were only in the maternal line.

Ego's conduct towards his wife's relatives of the same generation depended mainly on the privileged sex partnership. The determination of those who could be partners was conditioned by the simple principle which assimilates a person to his siblings and parallel cousins. According to this, Ego could have sex relations with those who were assimilated to his wife: her sisters and her parallel cousins. The same applied to a female Ego: her privileged partners are thus her husband's brothers and parallel cousins.

We have indicated what was meant by a sexual privileged

THE SYSTEM OF KINSHIP AND AFFINITY 57

partnership among cross-cousins and that this was only one aspect of wider behaviour patterns of familiarity and joking. The relations between Ego and certain of his affines should be understood in the same sense.

These relations were reciprocal in the sense that the husband of Ego's partner was also the privileged partner of Ego's wife, as the two husbands had the same relationships of affinity with each other's wives. This reciprocity seemed essential to the working of the system, which otherwise would have been probably too frustrating. The case of the wife of Ego's wife's brother (WiBrWi) confirms this interpretation. Although she was quite unrelated to Ego, there was a kind of 'incest' taboo concerning any relation with her. There was a strict avoidance (Ego was not allowed to stay alone with his WiBrWi) and such a relation was considered to bring ill-luck not only to the partners but to the lineages concerned. The reason for that prohibition, I was told, was that the husband of WiBrWi, being the brother of Ego's wife, was prevented by the incest-taboo from having any reciprocal relations with her. It appears, however, that the common resentment of Ego and his WiBrWi against their common in-laws may have been such that these sanctions were not a sufficient deterrent.

These different patterns of behaviour were expressed in terminology. Ego referred by the same term to his wife's female parallel cousins and by another to her cross-cousins and male parallel cousins. There was also a special term to designate those who are husbands of privileged partners. A female Ego used terms in which similar distinctions appeared.

5. SOME COMMENTS ON KINSHIP PRINCIPLES IN RUANDA

(a) Analytical table of kinship terms

The attention I have given and have still to give to kinship terminology rests on the assumption that the use of kinship terms indicates what aspects, among the many that could be stressed in a kinship system, have been actually emphasized in a particular society. Terminology indicates first the principles according to which, among the almost unlimited mass of possible relationships some have been given a name and are thus considered as social roles. Secondly, terminology shows the lines of cleavage according to which the totality of relationships have been separated in different classes.

58 THE PREMISE OF INEQUALITY IN RUANDA

To investigate systematically the social significance of kinship terminology, some procedure should be adopted whereby every term is analysed from a set of relevant viewpoints. In order to do this we are setting them in the following table. The table recapitulates the sixty-one kinship terms mentioned in the preceding sections and for each of them gives eleven characteristics. In this choice I have followed closely the chapter 'Analysis of Kinship' in Murdock's *Social Structure*.[17]

			1.	2.	3.	4.	5.	6.	7.	8.	9.	10.	11.
[18]Sogo-kuru	a	dr	–	+	+	+	–	+	o	–	–	c
[18]Sogo-kuru	r	dr	+	+	+	+	–	+	–	–	–	c
Nyogo-kuru	a	dr	–	+	+	+	–	+	o	–	–	c
Nyogo-kuru	r	dr	+	+	+	+	–	+	–	–	–	c
Sogo-kuru-za	r	dr	+	+	–	+	–	+	–	–	–	c
Nyogo-kuru-za	r	dr	–	+	–	+	–	+	–	–	–	c
Isogo-kuru	r	dr	+	+	–	–	–	+	o	–	–	d
Data	a	e	+	+	–	+	o	+	–	–	o	c
Data	r	e	+	+	–	–	o	+	–	–	o	d
Mama	a	e	+	+	+	+	o	+	–	–	o	c
Mama	r	e	+	+	–	–	o	+	–	–	o	d
Data-wacu	r	dr	+	+	–	–	+	+	–	–	–	c
Ma-senge	r	ds	+	+	–	–	+	+	–	–	–	c
Mama-wacu	r	dr	+	+	–	–	+	+	–	–	–	c
Ma-rume	r	dr	+	+	–	–	+	+	–	–	–	c
Maku-data-wacu	r	dr	+	+	–	–	+	+	–	–	–	d
Mu-gabo-wa-ma-senge	r	ds	+	+	–	–	+	+	–	–	–	c
Mu-gabo-wa-mama-wacu	r	ds	+	+	–	–	+	+	–	–	–	c
Data-bukwe	r	dr	+	+	–	+	–	+	–	–	–	c
Ma-bukwe	r	dr	+	+	–	+	–	+	–	–	–	c
Mu-vandimwe	a	dr	+	–	+	+	–	–	–	–	–	c
Mw-ene-data	r	ds	+	–	–	–	+	–	–	–	–	c
Mu-rumuna-wanjye	r	dr	+	–	–	–	+	+	+	–	–	d
Mu-saza-wanjye	r	dr	+	+	–	–	+	+	–	+	–	d
Mu-kuru-wanjye	r	dr	+	–	–	–	+	+	+	–	–	d
Mu-shiki-wanjye	r	ds	+	+	–	–	+	+	–	+	–	d
Mw-ene-datu-wacu	r	dr	+	–	–	–	+	–	–	–	–	c
Mu-shiki-wacu	r	dr	+	+	–	–	+	+	–	+	–	d
Mu-byara-wanjye	r	dr	+	–	–	–	–	–	–	–	–	c
Mu-byara-wacu	r	dr	+	–	–	–	+	–	–	–	–	c
Mu-gore-wanjye	r	dr	+	+	–	–	o	+	–	+	o	d
Mu-gore-wacu	r	dr	+	+	–	–	–	+	–	+	–	c
Mu-ramu-kazi-wanjye	r	dr	+	+	–	–	–	+	–	–	–	c
Mu-gabo-wanjye	r	dr	+	+	–	–	o	+	–	+	o	d
Mu-gabo-wacu	r	dr	+	+	–	–	–	+	–	+	–	c
Mu-ramu-wanjye	r	dr	+	+	–	–	–	+	–	–	–	d
Mu-saza-wacu	r	dr	+	+	–	–	+	+	–	+	–	d
M-wena-wacu	r	dr	+	–	–	–	+	+	–	–	–	c
Ba-mwana-wanjye	r	dr	+	–	–	–	–	–	–	–	–	c
Mu-ramu-wacu	r	dr	+	–	–	–	+	+	–	–	–	c
Mu-sanzire-wanjye	r	dr	+	+	–	–	+	–	–	+	–	d

[17] Murdock, 1949, pp. 91-112. Quotations in the following paragraphs come from p. 98.

[18] *a* means address; *r* reference.

THE SYSTEM OF KINSHIP AND AFFINITY 59

		1.	2.	3.	4.	5.	6.	7.	8.	9.	10.	11.
Mu-sanzire-wacu	r	dr	+	+	−	−	+	−	−	+	−	c
Mu-keba-wanjye	r	dr	+	+	−	−	+	+	−	+	−	d
Mu-keba-wacu	r	dr	+	+	−	+	+	−	−	+	−	c
Mw-ana	a	e	−	−	+	+	−	+	o	−	−	c
Mu-hungu-wanjye	r	dr	+	+	−	−	o	+	−	−	o	d
Mu-kobwa-wanjye	r	dr	+	+	−	−	o	+	−	−	o	d
Mu-kobwa-wacu	r	dr	+	+	−	+	+	+	−	+	−	c
Mu-hungu-wacu	r	dr	+	+	−	+	+	+	−	+	−	c
Mu-sengeneza-wanjye	r	dr	+	−	−	−	+	+	−	+	−	c
Mu-sengeneza-wacu	r	dr	+	−	−	+	+	+	−	+	−	c
Mu-kazana-wanjye	r	dr	+	+	−	−	+	+	−	−	−	d
Mu-kwe-wanjye	r	dr	+	+	−	−	+	+	−	−	−	d
Mu-kazana-wacu	r	dr	−	+	−	−	−	+	o	−	−	c
Mu-kwe-wacu	r	dr	−	+	−	−	−	+	o	−	−	c
Mw-uzukuru-wanjye	r	dr	+	−	−	−	+	+	−	−	−	c
Mw-uzukuru-wacu	r	dr	+	−	−	−	+	+	−	−	−	c
Mw-uzukuru-za	r	dr	+	−	−	−	+	+	−	−	−	c
Ubuvivi	r	e	−	−	−	−	+	+	o	−	−	c
Mw-ene-mama	r	ds	+	−	−	−	+	−	−	−	−	c
Mu-ka-data	r	ds	+	+	−	−	+	−	−	−	−	d

1. Linguistic structure.
2. Denotes generation.
3. Denotes sex.
4. Denotes affinity and consanguinity.
5. Denotes lineality and collaterality.
6. Denotes bifurcation.
7. Denotes polarity.
8. Denotes age in generation.
9. Denotes speaker's sex.
10. Denotes decendence of link.
11. Range of application.

In the first vertical line the linguistic structure of the term is given. An elementary term (symbolized by 'e' in the table) is 'an irreducible word which cannot be analysed into component lexical elements with kinship meanings', a derivative term (symbolized by 'dr') is 'compounded from an elementary term and some other lexical element which does not have primarily a kinship meaning' and a descriptive term (symbolized by 'ds') 'combines two or more elementary terms to denote a specific relative'.

In the second line a cross (+) indicates that the term is never applied to two individuals to different generations. The dash (−) points out that it can be so used.

The third characteristic is the sex of the person designated by the term. Again (+) indicates that the term is only applicable to males or females and (−) that it may be applied to persons of either sex.

A cross in the fourth line shows that the term may indicate certain individuals among both affinal and consangulneal relatives of Ego; a hyphen denotes that the term can be applied only either to affines or only to consanguineal kinsfolk. In the assessment of this characteristic, the patrilineal descent group of Ego's mother has been considered as a group of consanguineal relatives of Ego.

60 THE PREMISE OF INEQUALITY IN RUANDA

In the following column (—) indicates that the term may be applied only to individuals who belong to the same direct line (people who either descend from one another or have all the same ascendants) or only to persons who are collaterals. For instance if the term A may be applied only to Ego's paternal uncle, Ego's paternal uncle's son, and Ego's paternal uncle's grandson, we say that it denotes only people of the same line. If the term B may be applied to Ego's paternal uncle and to Ego's paternal uncle's cousins, we may say that it denotes only collaterals. A (+) means that the term may be applied to a class of individuals, some of whom are collaterals and some belonging to the same line.

In the sixth line there is a cross for the terms which indicate the sex of the relative who is the link between Ego and the role designated by the term, and there is a hyphen for terms which do not denote the sex of the link. The symbol (o) means that there is no link. When there are several links, only the person directly connected to Ego has been considered. For instance if the same term denotes MoBrSo and MoSiSo but not FaBrSo and FaSiSo, only the direct link to Ego, i.e. Mo has been considered. Consequently in this case the term is bifurcate although it does neglect the sex of the second link: Br or Si.

There is polarity when the two participants in a relationship do not refer to each other by the same term. Consequently a (—) means that the term is used reciprocally by the two participants and a (+) that it is not.

The eighth characteristic concerns distinctions of age within the same generation. A hyphen indicates that the term may be used for the complete range of age variations within one generation; a cross means that it applies only to people of a definite age, absolute or relative, within the generation. The symbol (o) means that a term by definition could not denote age differences within a generation as it applies to different generations.

Next, the speaker's sex is considered. There is a dash for terms which may be used by males and females alike and a cross when they are used only by one of the sexes.

The tenth characteristic, as the sixth, is concerned with the person through whom kinship is traced. A dash indicates that the term applies as well if the link is deceased or living and a cross that it applies only when the connecting person is either alive or dead.

THE SYSTEM OF KINSHIP AND AFFINITY 61

The last column of the table indicates the range of application of the term: is it classificatory or denotative? Although the nine preceding characteristics are criteria of the range of application, I have considered as denotative not only the terms which have these nine characteristics, but those which show only characteristics 2, 3, 4, 5, and 6, i.e. generation, sex, distinction between affinity and consanguinity, lineality and collaterality, bifurcation by sex of connecting relative.

If we sum up the different symbols in the vertical lines, we obtain for the sixty-one terms of the table (fifty-five terms of reference and six of address) the following results:

1. Linguistic structure: 6 elementary terms, 48 derivative, 7 descriptive.
2. 54 denote generation, 7 do not.
3. 43 denote sex of the relative, 18 do not.
4. 54 do not cover both affinal and consanguineal relative together and 7 do.
5. 45 do not denote a class of people including lineal and collateral relatives, 16 do.
6. 34 indicate the sex of the person through whom kinship is traced, 19 do not and in 8 cases the question does not arise as there is no link.
7. 50 terms indicate polarity, 11 do not.
8. 59 do not denote age within generation, 2 do, and in 7 cases they ignore age differences by definition.
9. The speaker's sex is indicated in 16 cases, it is not in 45.
10. There is no case in which it is indicated whether the link is living or dead. Thus, except for the 8 cases in which there is no connecting relative, 53 terms ignore that characteristic.
11. 41 terms are classificatory and 20 are denotative.

(b) Concluding remarks

Let me conclude this chapter with a few remarks on the Ruanda system of kinship and affinity. They are suggested by the previous description of kinship roles or by the table.

Descent is reckoned patrilineally and a lineage is a corporate group of agnates. But Ego does not feel that all others are strangers. He lives, as it were, in a cognatic as well as an agnatic world. For help in important questions, when it is necessary for him to assert his rights to be assisted, he turns to his patrilineal kinsmen, but in

62   THE PREMISE OF INEQUALITY IN RUANDA

everyday life, when he needs only some slight service, some advice and sympathy, he asks for and receives it from his maternal relatives as easily as from his paternal ones. Moreover, in matters very important to him concerning playmates, sex partners, and marriageable girls, the two groups stand equal: taboo and tolerance apply to maternal as well as to agnatic cousins. Kinship terms, even terms of reference, used to denote the grandparents are the same in both lines.

If the descent groups tend, in many respects, to merge in a kind of cognatic structure, the distinction between affinity and consanguinity is more clearly maintained. Affines are often identified with their spouses who are Ego's kin, and in a situation subordinate to the latter's from the point of view of Ego (as for instance FaSiHu and MoSiHu), or they are considered only in connexion with privileged sexual access. The distinction between affinal and consanguineal relations is emphasized in terminology as only seven terms out of sixty-one denote both affinity and consanguinity relationships. Among the seven, there are five terms of address.

Generation is another focal point of attention in Ruanda kinship relationships. There are broad behaviour patterns expected from people in their relationships simply because they belong to the same or to different generations. Respect should be shown to the members of the generation immediately above, domination and protection are correct behaviour towards people of the generation immediately under Ego, a certain equality tends to prevail between people belonging to the same generation, and there is a great familiarity among those who belong to alternate generations. This is again clearly supported by kinship terminology: fifty-four terms apply only to people of the same generation, whereas only seven fail to denote the generation of the relative. On the other hand, very little attention is paid to age differences within one generation: two terms only denote them, whereas fifty-two do not (in the seven cases left the question does not arise).

In spite of the principle of assimilation of parallel cousins to siblings the distinction in terminology between lineal and collateral relatives is observed more often than would be expected. In forty-five terms, there is no merging and out of the sixteen cases of merging, it should be mentioned that there are six terms of address in which the failure to distinguish is less

THE SYSTEM OF KINSHIP AND AFFINITY 63

significant because terms of address are more likely to be classificatory.

Another important principle of cleavage among relatives is sex. Very rarely, as the preceding brief survey of the different kinship roles shows, is kinship behaviour the same towards relatives of both sexes. Out of our list of sixty-one terms, forty-three denote the sex of the relative. Further analysis indicates that what is important is sex in connexion with privileged relations. Terminologically, male parallel cousins of Ego's wife are lumped together with her cross-cousins, whereas her female parallel cousins are designated by another word. This is a case in which the principle of sexual privileged partnership has been more operative than other principles such as descent, &c. The eighteen terms ignoring sex denote relatives with whom Ego could not have sexual relations, either because they would be incestuous or because the difference of age would be too great. It could be argued that sex is not such an important principle in kinship as there are only sixteen terms which denote the speaker's sex and forty-five which do not. I do not think that this objection is a valid one, however, because when terms are not written by an anthropologist but are spoken—as they are meant to be when they are used in everyday life—it is clear to anybody whether the speaker is a man or a woman.

To sum up, the Ruanda kinship system seems to have evolved according to principles stressing the importance of generation and the predominance of an almost cognatic system over affinity, keeping a very clear distinction between lineal and collateral relatives and emphasizing sex especially when connected with privileged sexual access.

CHAPTER III

MARRIAGE AND THE FAMILY

I. MARRIAGE

THE family, the social group characterized by common residence, economic co-operation, and reproduction[1] had in Ruanda a conjugal basis[2] that we shall consider in this section.

Married life will not be dealt with here but only the ways and conditions of the establishment of that 'union between a man and a woman such that children born to the woman are then recogized legitimate offspring of both partners'.[3]

(a) *The choice of a spouse*

In a primary marriage (the first that an individual contracts) there were few positive socially recognized criteria of choice and none of them indicated one or a few individuals as preferential partners. Among close kin cross-cousins were possible spouses, but it was generally an unfortunate circumstance that obliged a man to marry his cross-cousin. It was usually either because he was not able to pay bride-wealth immediately, or because his cross-cousin had become pregnant by him. We should add that there was no restricted or generalized exchange among the Ruanda in Lévi-Strauss's sense. On the contrary I was told that because they limited connexions, exchanges were not in favour except in some special circumstances.[4]

In the preceding chapter we have mentioned persons whom Ego was prohibited from marrying because of his relations of kinship or affinity with them. Let me sum up the different categories of these persons.

We may start with that which seems fundamental in the sense

---

[1] Murdock, 1949, p. 1.
[2] Linton, 1936, p. 159.
[3] Royal Anthropological Institute, 1951, p. 110.
[4] Lévi-Strauss, 1949, pp. 189, 322. There is restricted exchange if, when a man of group A gets a woman from group B, it results in a man of group B claiming a woman from group A. Exchange is generalized if when a woman of group A is given to a man of group B, a woman of B must be given to a man of C and a woman of C may be claimed by a man of A.

MARRIAGE AND THE FAMILY 65

that in questions of exogamy, informants mention it first and attempt to relate other categories to it: I refer to the primary patrilineage (inzu). People descending in the paternal line from a common ancestor did not intermarry because they were of the same blood. The same principle was logically extended to the secondary patrilineage (umulyango).

A second extension of the taboo concerned the maternal kinship group and had a double basis. First the idea that it would be unnatural and horrible to conceive a marriage between Ego and his mother and consequently between him and any person assimilated to her (her sisters and female parallel cousins). Second, because of the tendency to recognize the cognatic principle, some matrilateral relatives were tabooed because their paternal counterparts were tabooed. This applied to the maternal parallel cousins.

Only when Ego was a male was there a third extension to his in-laws. The explanation given is that it seemed distasteful that a man could have intercourse with a girl and her mother. Consequently the wife's mother and all the relatives assimilated to the mother were in the prohibited class.

The same taboo included also sororal nieces and grand-nieces of Ego because he had to assume an avuncular attitude towards them, although they belonged to another patrilineage.

A further extension included the spouses of uncles and aunts. The spouse of an aunt was regarded rather as an uncle, and the spouse of an uncle was regarded rather as an aunt.

Ruanda were so eager to form new connexions with unrelated kinship groups that they were very keenly aware of any factor favouring them. Some informants stressed the function of exogamy rules from that point of view. Increase of social communication by marriage does not explain all the particular prohibitions, however, since some of them were concerned with people of a different patrilineage. Taboos on marriage and sex relations (they were co-extensive) had, it appears, in some cases the function of keeping a certain cohesion within the large group of relatives by kinship and affinity by preventing rivalry. Prohibition of relations between Ego and his WiBrWi could not favour social communication, but it certainly made possible harmonious relations between Ego and his WiBr.

Inter-caste marriage was not prohibited between Hutu and

66 THE PREMISE OF INEQUALITY IN RUANDA

Tutsi. Hutu informants say it happened frequently, Tutsi informants claim that such marriages were very rare, but that Tutsi often had Hutu concubines. This discrepancy shows clearly that for a Tutsi to take a Hutu as wife in a primary marriage entailed a loss of prestige. It was resorted to mainly because of poverty. Bride-wealth was lower in these inter-caste unions (not in the sense that the standard bride-wealth among Hutu was much lower than among Tutsi) and a Hutu girl worked harder than a Tutsi. It does not seem on the other hand that the Hutu girl was particularly proud of having a Tutsi husband. But it is not easy to assess the feelings of a girl in that respect, as no informant seems to have cared very much about them. A prosperous Hutu could marry a Tutsi girl, but then the bride-wealth was often greater than for a Tutsi (three cows instead of one). It happened also that a Tutsi cattle-lord (*shebuja*) would grant a daughter to one of his Hutu clients. Here again the feeling of the girl was unknown to informants. Such a match could be eagerly sought by a Hutu social climber, but in general Hutu opinion did not look upon it with favour. In a caste society only a few atypical persons are anxious to get as near as they can to the higher stratum. Hutu and Tutsi informants considered any question suggesting intermarriage with Twa as very insulting.

It was possible to marry a foreign woman, often a war captive who had become a sort of domestic slave. The bride-wealth then had to be paid to her master. Sometimes Ruanda living near the borders married a girl of the neighbouring people (such as Nkole, Rundi) when peaceful relations with that particular people had lasted for some time. There was much reluctance to let a Ruanda girl marry an alien.

Within the borders of Ruanda, local proximity was an important positive factor for Hutu in the choice of a mate. They did not travel very much and as a marriage was primarily a patrilineage affair, they had to know the inzu of the prospective bride or groom and they only knew the groups residing nearby. Tutsi, and particularly those of importance, were less localized than Hutu. They had to go often to the court; they were appointed to administrative charges in one part of the country, then in another one. Consequently inter-regional marriage was favoured as it usefully extended kinship connexions.

What were the qualifications socially considered as the most

MARRIAGE AND THE FAMILY

important for prospective spouses? Among Hutu and Tutsi both patrilineages looked for the right connexion. Has the man's (or girl's) inzu a good reputation? Is it well considered at the king's court? Are they rich? Is it strategic, in present circumstances, to be allied to them? What are the relations between their cattle-lord and ours? Individual qualities considered as socially important were for the prospective wife of a Tutsi that she should be expert at keeping a house very clean, at basket work, and at commanding servants. The Hutu wanted a hard-working wife able to help them in the fields. The Twa appreciated, as we may expect, a skilled potter. The most important qualities of the culturally defined ideal husband was his ability to support economically his wife and their children. That meant for a Tutsi that he should be rich in cattle and clever in political intrigues; for a Hutu that he should be a good labourer and a client appreciated by his lord, and for a Twa that he should be a good craftsman or hunter or a buffoon, liked by his Tutsi protectors. These qualities mentioned by our informants are those which made spouses good partners in the co-operative economic unit of the family. In the mind of Ruanda that aspect of the family was clearly emphasized. Beauty and sex-appeal were also highly appreciated, however, particularly by Tutsi.

The normal marriage age for boys was around twenty-five for Tutsi, seventeen to eighteen for Hutu, and fifteen for Twa. For girls, when 'breasts were fully developed and beginning to fall down' I was told. This gives a rather large range of age. A girl could be married before puberty but she remained with her parents till her first menstruation.

According to informants, virginity was appreciated more than both beauty and ability to co-operate in economic pursuits. This was rationalized in terms of virginity being a guarantee of fertility and of stability in the family. Among the Hutu a small gift was sent to the girl's parents by the husband when the girl was found to be virgin.

The prospective spouse was not chosen by his or her future partner. The boy could express only to his paternal uncle or aunt nothing more than a wish to get married. The father was told of his son's desire and then looked for a suitable girl. When she was found, the inzu council met and the advisability of a connexion with the girl's inzu was discussed. When an agreement was reached on the choice, the boy's father asked for an appointment with the

68   THE PREMISE OF INEQUALITY IN RUANDA

girl's father, allowing a sufficient time for the latter to consult his patrilineage. If the answer was favourable, the meeting took place. Accompanied by a kinsman or a client, the boy's father came to visit the girl's father and offered him a jug of beer. After some preliminary talk, he came to the point and asked for the girl.

These preliminary steps were taken very skilfully. Nobody should ever be directly refused. If the girl's kinsfolk did not want the match, the visit of the boy's father was indefinitely delayed under several pretexts. Nobody should be put in such a position as to lose face. The boy and the girl were never officially consulted during these preparatory stages. If, however, one of them categorically refused the choice made, he was not obliged to marry. But it happened very rarely and the opposition of the individual concerned had to be extremely persistent if it was to succeed.

To marry a certain girl against the consent of one's own and her parents was impossible. But the following procedure could be attempted. The boy hid himself in a place to which he knew the girl would go. When she was coming he spat in her face a certain herb which had been chewed and mixed with milk (*imbazi*). They were then considered married as this was the central rite of any wedding. Often the ordinary wedding ceremonies followed. If, however, the girl's inzu were still opposed to that match, they obliged the girl to whistle and milk a cow. As both these actions were tabooed for a married woman, it was clearly meant that the girl was not married. The boy's father had then to pay a fine to the girl's people as a reparation for the wrong done to the girl's family.[5]

In secondary marriages (any marriage subsequent to the first one) there were not many more cultural criteria determining the choice of the spouse. Sororal polygyny was permitted but rare. In order to obtain new connexions the husband preferred to choose subsequent wives from an inzu other than that of his first wife Another reason given is that to have two or three sisters as wives brought more domestic troubles than wives who were not consanguineal relatives. If, however, his first wife was sterile, the husband was likely to ask for one of her sisters or parallel cousins as a second wife, without paying bride-wealth. But this was not a sororate, for the first wife's sister was not said to give birth to children for her sister: she was regarded as bearing them for

[5] See description of other forms of this type of marriage in Pauwels, 1951, pp. 126-9.

MARRIAGE AND THE FAMILY 69

herself. A widow became the wife of one of her late husband's siblings or agnates designated by the inzu head. Usually an older brother of the husband was chosen. Among the Tutsi this resulted in a levirate: the first husband was still the pater of the children whose genitor was the second husband. Among the Hutu, in similar cases, the genitor was pater. A widower often married a younger sister of his late wife if he was on good terms with his parents-in-law, and if they did not require bride-wealth for the deceased wife's younger sister. This marriage was favoured because it was thought that it was appropriate that the children of the first wife should be brought up by her sister.

(b) The bride-wealth

Bride-wealth had to be paid before the wedding ritual, but payment could sometimes be delayed. In that case more jugs of beer had to be given.

There were some regional variations in the amount of the bride-wealth, but within one region it did not vary very much within each caste. Among Tutsi it was usually one cow plus some jugs of beverage, and one hoe. The bride-wealth proper was the cow, as the beverages were rather contributions to the different celebrations taking place at the wedding. Among Hutu it was one heifer or cow (which could be replaced by about one dozen goats) and a number of jugs of banana-beer. The following table indicates the average bride-wealth paid by Tutsi and Hutu in the central region of Ruanda. Among Twa bride-wealth was composed of a certain number of pots of beverages.

TABLE OF THE STANDARD MARRIAGE GIFTS AND COUNTER-GIFTS IN CENTRAL RUANDA

A. HUTU

Groom's inzu		Bride's inzu
1.	one hoe, one jug of beer after agreement	
Father	————————————————————→	Father
2.	one heifer or twelve to fourteen goats (bride-wealth) from one to three weeks after 1. (gutenbutsa)	
Father	————————————————————→	Father
3.	household equipment on wedding day (ibirongoranywa)	
Groom	←————————————————————	Father
4.	one hoe or one sheep or one goat + jugs of beer at the end of seclusion period	
Groom	←————————————————————	Father

70 THE PREMISE OF INEQUALITY IN RUANDA

TABLE OF THE STANDARD MARRIAGE GIFTS AND COUNTER-GIFTS IN CENTRAL RUANDA—*cont.*

A. HUTU

Groom's inzu		*Bride's inzu*
5.	one hoe or one sheep or one goat (even one heifer) a week after each birth	
Groom	←	Kinsfolk
6.	counter-bride-wealth (stock increase of the bride-wealth) two or three years after marriage	
Father	←	Father

B. TUTSI

1.	one jug of hydromel, one hoe, one *isando* (forked branch of ficas tree)	
Father	⟶	Father
2.	one cow (bride-wealth) (*inkwano*) a few days later	
Father	⟶	Father
3.	one cow (counter-bride-wealth) when the bride leaves her father's homestead	
Father	←	Father
4.	household equipment on wedding day (*indogoranyo*)	
Groom	←	Father
5.	one heifer (*izimano*) on the day following wedding	
Father	⟶	Male abashyitsi
6.	one steer (*izimano*) on the day following wedding	
Father	⟶	Female abashyitsi
7.	jugs of beer, pots of milk, sorghum flour (*imitwa*) at the end of seclusion period	
Groom	←	Father
8.	one cow, jugs of beer, pots of milk at each birth (*ibihembo*)	
Groom	←	Kinsfolk

All our informants agree that bride-wealth was not considered very expensive. Moreover, counter-gifts were about as high. The girl's father had to provide the young couple with household equipment and to give the husband's father a counter-bride-wealth approximately equivalent to the bride-wealth itself. Among Tutsi it was proper to give the counter-gift before the wedding. Hutu gave back another heifer not later than after the third calving of the bride-wealth cow. In addition valuable gifts were given by the wife's kinsfolk after each birth.

MARRIAGE AND THE FAMILY 71

Bride-wealth was definitely not a compensation for the economic loss entailed by the girl's departure from her patrilineage. Her departure was not an impoverishment of her group because it provided it with a new alliance with another descent group; all informants agree on that. Bride-wealth was the socially recognized symbol of the legitimate transfer of fertility from one descent group to another. As long as bride-wealth had not been given, children borne by the woman were considered as belonging to her inzu (they are called *nkuli*). The husband was only their genitor, not their pater.

Bride-wealth received by the girl's father was not to be used only to provide the bride's brother with a wife. There was no direct relation between a man's possibility of getting a wife and his sister's marriage.

(c) The wedding ceremonies

Wedding ceremonies (*ubukwe*) taking place at the groom's father's were very long and complicated. The central rite constituting the wedding was the spitting on the bride's head of chewed herbs mixed with milk, and the placing on her head of a garland made of the leaves of a certain plant (*umuwishywa*). Other rites symbolized the dominance of the patrilineages' interests in the marriage. Both inzu were represented by two groups, the *abashyitsi*, the agnatic relatives of the bride, and *abasangwa*, agnatic relatives of the groom. When the rite was accomplished, *abashyitsi* had to express sorrow by their laments and *abasangwa* to rejoice loudly. Another rite stressed the concern of the kingroups in the intimate relations between the spouses. A younger brother or paternal parallel cousin of the bride had to lie between the new spouses during some part of their first night together (*gucahagati*). The groom had to beg him to leave. I was told that this signified that it was the bride's patrilineage which had to give permission for the first intercourse. Moreover, after the central rite and before the first intercourse, the father and mother of the groom and the father and mother of the bride had to have sexual relations. If the girl's parents (who did not attend the wedding party) were living far away, the young couple sometimes had to wait for a couple of days before having intercourse.[6]

The high value of virginity was also symbolically stressed.

[6] On wedding celebration, see Kagame, 1954, pp. 143-72.

F

72 THE PREMISE OF INEQUALITY IN RUANDA

Firstly, all these ceremonies did not take place when the bride had already been married before or when the girl had been struck by lightning because, as I was told, she was considered to have been raped by the king (thunder being one of the symbols of the king). Secondly, the spreading of the herbs and milk mixture had to be done by surprise and the girl had to cry immediately afterwards. Thirdly, in the first intercourse the girl had to struggle and penetration had to be achieved by force.

For about ten or twelve days the young couple lived semisecluded in a hut in the groom's father's homestead. Then, at the end of that period, there was another ritual celebration (*gutwikurura*) attended by those who were present at the marriage. The central rite of the ceremony was a dance by the new couple in public. After that, the young wife was allowed to cook for her husband for the first time. The latter was given by his father his share of inheritance, and the couple settled in a compound of their own. Residence was occasionally neolocal but usually patrivirilocal (at the HuFa's).

(d) Polygynous unions

Ruanda may be said to be a polygynous society in two senses. Firstly, polygynous unions were culturally preferred. Secondly, probably thirty per cent. of the unions were polygynous.[7] It was no grand scale polygyny. A man rarely had more than four wives. Usually a polygynous Tutsi had two wives, a Hutu three or four, and a Twa two.

Supplementary wives were an economic asset for rich people, as a Tutsi having herds of cattle in different places found it very useful to be able to put a wife in each of his homesteads as manager; but if he had only such cattle as he could care for himself, a second wife was an expense. It was the same for a Hutu: if he had so many plots that he could not cultivate them all by himself and with the help of his wife, a second one was very useful. If not, she was rather expensive.

To have several wives was also to have many children, which were very highly valued by all Ruanda. For Tutsi occupying very high positions, plural union was a means of establishing useful

---

[7] 'Any society in which plural unions, however strongly favoured, actually occur in less than this percentage [set arbitrarily at 20 per cent.] of all marriages, is considered monogamous with respect to the family [. . .]' (Murdock, 1949, p. 28).

MARRIAGE AND THE FAMILY 73

connexions with several inzu. These important chiefs sometimes had more than four wives.

Our informants were aware of these different functions of polygyny, but it did not seem necessary for them to look for reasons why people are polygynous. It appeared obvious to them that everybody wanted to have several wives.

(e) Divorce

Marriage could be ended by divorce (*gutana*). The parents of both spouses and their patrilineage heads usually took part in the various preparatory steps. Nevertheless, divorce was not decided by them, but resulted from the will of the spouses or even from the will of one of them.

Divorce itself was usually preceded by one or several temporary separations (*kwahukana*), although these separations did not necessarily lead to divorce. The wife left her husband and went to her parents', or to her husband's parents', or to her husband's brother's home. She complained that her husband had insulted her, beaten her, neglected her, was lazy, &c. The fathers of both spouses then met, talked to the husband, and tried to persuade him to take his wife back, and her to return to him. Very often it was difficult to convince them because the spouse who initiated the separation merely wanted it to be temporary in order to exert a certain pressure on the other. So married life was resumed.

It is to be noted that whoever felt wronged, it was always the wife who left and that among well-to-do people she was never expelled by her husband. He merely showed her by his behaviour (not spending the night with her, &c.) that she was unwanted, and then she left.

For a divorce the procedure was essentially similar to that of a temporary separation. The wife left when either she or her husband definitely wanted to end the marriage. Of course there was very strong pressure from both kin-groups to keep the marriage going, in order not to break the alliance between the two patrilineages. Consequently, the spouse who wanted divorce had to try to convince both inzu and public opinion at large that he (or she) was in one of the cases socially recognized as providing legitimate grounds for divorce. These grounds were for a wife: repeated ill-treatment by her husband, his failure to support her, and his refusal to cohabit with her. Impotence was not regarded as

74 THE PREMISE OF INEQUALITY IN RUANDA

sufficient grounds, as in that case the wife had the right of co-habitation with one of her husband's agnates. Socially accepted grounds of divorce for a husband were his wife's neglect of domestic duties, or repeated adultery with a non-privileged partner. Sterility was not a reason for divorce as the man could always take another wife.

The divorced woman left with her only belongings—her clothes. Usually the husband gave her new clothes on that occasion. If bride-wealth and counter-gifts had been exchanged, nothing had to be given by either father. If bride-wealth had been paid, but not the counter-gifts, bride-wealth had to be returned except either where children had been born or where there were other marriage links between the two lineages concerned. If bride-wealth had not been paid, children went to live with their mother's kinsfolk unless their father paid the bride-wealth later. If bride-wealth was not returned and there were no children, the children borne by the wife in a following marriage could be claimed by the former husband.

Young children stayed with their divorced mother till they were seven or eight years old. They were then sent to their father's home where they were taken care of by another of his wives. Later on these children could visit their mother whenever they wished.

Divorced women usually married again easily. Their bride-wealth was lower and its payment was delayed till after marriage. But if it was felt that they were responsible for the failure of their previous marriage, then they did not always find another husband.

(f) Celibacy

Voluntary celibacy was unknown in Ruanda. Every man wanted to be married, to have children and a place of his own. Every girl wanted to be a mother. Those who were impotent (*ibiremba*) usually did not marry. Lepers (*ababembe*), the insane (*abasazi*), and people ill with tuberculosis (*abanyagitundu*) were forbidden to marry. Girls who had refused a husband often remained un-married, as few men wanted to take the chance of being refused also. Single people lived with their kinsmen. Sometimes Tutsi bachelors were given a homestead and servants by their fathers.

MARRIAGE AND THE FAMILY

2. THE FAMILY

Two basic types of family were to be found in Ruanda: the nuclear family which was the most widespread, and the polygynous family. The Ruanda polygynous family constituted a type of organization fundamentally different from the nuclear family. It was not just a nuclear family with a few more persons, the secondary wives and their children, but a structure composed of several elements, each of them constituting almost a nuclear family from the sexual, economic, procreational, and educational points of view. On the other hand, the polygynous family was not an aggregate of nuclear families because the uniqueness of the husband gave to the various elements a type of integration different from that merely of a sum of nuclear families.

A nuclear family (*rugo*) was composed of a man, his wife, and their children. It could happen that some additional persons lived with them, such as the widowed mother of one of the spouses or an old female relative (old men usually lived by themselves, with the help of a grandson). There could also be a child, a son, or a daughter of the husband's brother or even of the husband's sister (if the bride-wealth had not been given for his sister), or a child of the wife's brother.

Adopted children were also included in the rugo. These could only be children who had no lineage relatives left. Tutsi children, when adopted by Tutsi, were treated, while they were young, as if they were the adopter's own children; Hutu children if adopted by Tutsi were considered as clients. But adoption did not confer the full status enjoyed by an offspring of the adopter: the ward could marry a descendant of his foster-father. Cases of adoption seem to have been frequent and people appear to have been so eager to adopt that we may suspect that all the advantages were not for the child. The Ruanda highly appreciated all children, and this attitude accounts for the fact that a child was as such always welcomed in a family. Moreover, the man adopting a child expected more material advantages: a girl's marriage brought him the benefit of a new family connexion and boys could be as useful as his sons without having a right to inheritance. Our informants say that most of the boys when grown up fled away, hoping to find some distant relative of their own.

The members of a nuclear family lived in a compound called

76 THE PREMISE OF INEQUALITY IN RUANDA

by the same name, rugo. I have described earlier this complex dwelling place composed of intersecting circular enclosures. In the case of rich people, their clients during their time of service and their servants had huts in the compound.

The compound, surrounded by fields and banana-groves, and not far from pastures, was situated on that part of the paternal homestead given by the father to his son at the latter's wedding. If the father's homestead was not large enough to provide all his sons with areas to live on, the young couple either had to ask the political authority to allocate them a plot, or they had to rent one belonging either to a relative or an unrelated person.

The ideal type of residence of a polygynous family was a compound for each wife surrounded by its own cultivated area. These rugo could be on the same homestead or on several homesteads. The latter arrangement was more frequent with Tutsi than with Hutu. None of these compounds was more important than the others, except occasionally. The husband had no rugo regarded as being more his residence than the others.

Between these two sharply different types of family organization, there were intermediate kinds. If it happened that a Ruanda wanted a second wife, he looked for one even if he could not afford a second compound. She lived then in the same compound as the first wife, in a separate hut. But such an arrangement was regarded as unfortunate, and should be assimilated to that of a nuclear family notwithstanding the plurality of wives.

We will now consider whether and how these types of organization fulfilled the functions that might be expected of any type of family, for some of these functions seem to be fulfilled by all the family structures known, and the others by most of them. The points to be considered are: sexual gratification, economic co-operation, reproduction, socialization, and ritual.

(a) Sexual relations

The Ruanda distinguish the sexual from the procreational function of marriage. Neither the husband, nor apparently the wife, ever feared (except in very unhappy circumstances of poverty) that pregnancy might result from any particular act of intercourse; on the contrary such an event was usually longed for. As some informants said, why have relations with a sterile woman? Sexuality, however, had for them a value in itself.

MARRIAGE AND THE FAMILY

For husband and wife, sex was not only that pleasurable activity in which tensions are released, but it was also linked with feelings of affection and sympathy. Moreover, as some cases of prohibition and obligation make it clear, it was a means of participating in collective feelings and of relating oneself to natural processes and rhythms.

For men, marriage was not the only socially approved means of obtaining sexual gratification. Before marriage young Tutsi were often given Hutu temporary concubines, wives or daughters of their father's clients. Moreover, they, as well as young Hutu, had privileged partners: married cross-cousins, brothers', and parallel cousins' wives. If they had affairs with unrelated women or even related or unrelated girls, the blame and the risk were for the latter more than for themselves. But as these affairs were occasional and had to be kept secret, marriage brought to men stability, continuity, and quietness in their sexual life. Homosexuality was widespread among Tutsi and Hutu young men. For girls, any heterosexual activity before marriage was strictly prohibited and severely sanctioned. After marriage, their sexual needs could be satisfied not only with their husbands but with their privileged partners.

Cohabitation was an obligation for each spouse. Refusal over a certain time—one, two or three weeks according to different informants—was a cause of temporary separation or even of divorce (of course this does not refer to a refusal based on culturally accepted reasons such as illness or menstruation). Frequency of intercourse is said to have been up to three times a day for Tutsi when they were newly married, then once a day for young people, and about once every other day later on. Hutu accounts suggest that the average frequency was not as high in their group (once a day for newly married, every other day for young people, and twice or once a week later on). The difference was attributed to the more leisurely life of Tutsi. 'They were not tired by work in the fields.' Women were said to be more eager than men but I was told by some informants that men thought this 'because they never refused intercourse'. Women, however, had to behave in a restrained way and to leave the initiative to men. It was very improper for a wife to manifest pleasure or to be other than purely passive during love-play and intercourse. Both partners sat or lay on their sides. Coitus with the woman lying on her back

78 THE PREMISE OF INEQUALITY IN RUANDA

under the man was not usually practised. In the polygynous family the husband had to spend two nights with each wife *seriatim* and to have at least one intercourse.

The Ruanda thought that when the sex activity of an individual had begun, he could legitimately expect an opportunity to enjoy intercourse as frequently as was socially thought normal. Some parents were said to be severe towards sexual play among children. When the latter indulged in imitation of adult relations, in masturbation, and other manipulations, they were beaten and flogged. Others were more permissive.[8] Homosexuality was common among young Tutsi when being trained at court, and was almost exclusively ascribed to the lack of heterosexual contacts.

Later in life, sex needs were regarded as requiring satisfaction just as any other natural need. If the husband or wife was not available, it was socially permitted to have another partner (among the privileged ones) even if the absent spouse resented it. The sexual needs of a woman were thought to be more urgent when she was pregnant; intercourse once a week was regarded as a minimum. If her husband was absent, therefore, cohabitation with one of his brothers or parallel cousins was viewed almost with favour. When a husband had been away for a very long time, and if it was not known even if he was still living, though his wife could not obtain a divorce she could cohabit and have children with one of her privileged partners, preferably belonging to her husband's patrilineage. A wife never accompanied her husband on his travels to the court or elsewhere. In such cases the Tutsi took with them a concubine, the daughter of a client for instance.

At the court of the king or of important chiefs, there were a few Tutsi women who were openly servants of the chief or the king (*abaja*). In fact they were courtesans, either the daughters of Tutsi clients of the chief or king, who had been invited by the chief or king to come to the court as servants because of their beauty, or divorced women. They received costly presents and were often well-off, having their own herds of cattle. These presents appear to have been rewards not only for sexual favours but also, and perhaps mainly, for some inside information so useful in that world of intrigue.

The preceding paragraphs should not be understood as implying that the Ruanda emphasized exclusively the physical and

---

[8] Cf. Vincent, 1954, pp. 167-71.

MARRIAGE AND THE FAMILY 79

physiological aspect of sexuality. They do not seem to have thought of sexual relations as the fulfilment of a romantic love between two individuals meant to mate with each other and nobody else. The way spouses were chosen by the two patrilineages prevented any such ideas, for the choosing of spouses rested on the assumption that any boy and any girl of the right age and reasonably attractive could be good partners in marriage and sexuality. But feelings of sympathy and affection developed later as a result of their life together rather than as its basis. According to our informants, love, in the sense of attractiveness based on individual characteristics, was greater in non-marital relations. 'One slept with a certain woman to make her happy because one liked her,' I was told.

Various prohibitions and obligations indicate how sexuality in marriage was related to events concerning the community and the patrilineage. During the mourning period for the husband's father and mother, which lasted one, two or three months according to the region, intercourse was prohibited for both husband and wife. It was also prohibited for one moon after the death of the wife's child, and for two or three moons for the surviving spouse when one of the spouses died. The meaning of this taboo was not only that one had to refrain from enjoying oneself when one should have been in sorrow. It meant also a certain symbolic participation in death or in the diminution of life affecting the patrilineage. This is, I think, what informants have in mind when they say in this connexion that sex is a sacred activity. This interpretation seems to be supported by what happened when a king died. Not only had all Ruanda to be continent for a certain period (some informants said two moons, others one year), but the bulls were separated from cows and rams from sheep. The king (*mwami*) was identified with Ruanda. If he was strong, Ruanda was strong, if he was getting old and weak, he had to commit suicide because he endangered the country's life. In that context, if animals were prevented from mating it was to express symbolically the idea of the death of the community rather than, it seems, to deny them pleasure.

On the other hand, intercourse was obligatory when events fortunate for the patrilineage or the community at large occurred. For instance when a new hut was occupied, when six days had passed after the birth of a child, when the first teeth of the baby

80 THE PREMISE OF INEQUALITY IN RUANDA

were growing, when a child had his hair cut in tufts for the first time, at the initiation into the Ryangombe sect, when a daughter was asked to marry, on the wedding day of a son or a daughter, on the accession of a new king, at sowing time, and at the celebration for July harvesting. All these events were happy and joyful because they were growths or increases in life. Intercourse was also obligatory at the end of the mourning periods when life had to go on and start again after that period of abeyance.

This obligatory intercourse took place between husband and wife. When it was impossible because one of the spouses was absent or dead, one had to rely upon a privileged partner, or, if this was impossible, had to get medicine prepared from certain herbs by a diviner.

There was no prohibition of intercourse between the spouses during the suckling months (the first eighteen to twenty-four).

(b) Economic co-operation

The nuclear family and, to a large extent each wife's compound in polygamous cases, was a self-sufficient unit of economic co-operation. Among rich Tutsi who could afford separate homesteads for their wives, each wife was in fact the superintendent of her own. She had to command her husband's clients, servants, cultivators, and herdsmen. It was no wonder that women who could be entrusted with such responsibilities were respected within their family and in society at large. If the homestead was small, as among ordinary Tutsi, or consisted only of a small cultivated plot, as among most Hutu polygamists, each of these wives had, nevertheless, some economic responsibility, even if it was only that of working by herself in the fields. This important participation of polygynous wives in the management of a small unit of production and consumption, should be studied in relation to the status of women in Ruanda.[9] This status was by no means equal to that of men but it was far from being one of slavery. Tutsi husbands and wives ate together, the wife was consulted by her husband on many problems, and she was treated with much politeness. The Hutu were ruder and more temperamental, but they followed a more or less similar pattern. Under the present administration there are two or three women, widows of Tutsi chiefs, who act as sub-chiefs. The mere fact that it is taken for

[9] See Naigiziki, 1959.

MARRIAGE AND THE FAMILY

granted that a woman may fulfil these functions emphasizes the high status that women have enjoyed in Ruanda society. It is tempting to regard their status as a consequence of the economic responsibilities of the polygynous wives when replacing their husbands.

Besides this form of economic collaboration, wives, in nuclear as well as in polygynous families, had to perform certain economic tasks within the rugo. The activities which belonged exclusively to the wife, though she was sometimes helped by her daughters and certain other females were, for women of any caste: cleaning and brushing the hut and the enclosure, milk churning, and basket-making. In addition to these, Tutsi women made particular objects in basket-work (such as screens used in the hut, very finely woven plates, &c.), butter perfumed with the wood of a certain tree *umubavu* (such butter was used as a cosmetic), and garments in bead work. Hutu women had to cook and to apportion food. In agriculture their particular tasks were to sow and plant, to grind sorghum, and to sift peas. Twa women simply cooked.

The husband's contributions to the economic activities of the compound were, among the Tutsi, cattle-rearing and hunting (for the hides and skins); among the Hutu, hut-building, minding cattle (if they had any), felling the bush, and usually all the agricultural tasks requiring considerable physical strength. Moreover, they prepared bark-cloth and skins and forged iron implements. Among the Twa, husbands hunted and made bows and iron weapons.

The principles underlying this division of economic tasks exclusively performed by males or females were according to informants that men should carry out tasks which either were particularly hard, or required intelligence, had to be performed far from the compound, or were thought 'noble'.

Most other duties could be performed by men or women and were shared between husband and wife according to individual arrangements. Such activities were, for instance, in the case of the Tutsi: watching labourers working in the fields, and supervising them, doing menial tasks such as mending the enclosure, milking the cows or looking after the herds. For the Hutu they were: harvesting, brewing beer, drawing water, cutting and collecting wood, lighting and maintaining fires, making mats and baskets, &c. For the Twa: pot-making and brewing beer.

82 THE PREMISE OF INEQUALITY IN RUANDA

Economic co-operation was not limited to husband and wife. Their children, their relatives living with them, their clients, and servants participated in productive activities. Each compound was supposed to produce the necessary foodstuffs for its inhabitants. In polygynous families the husband sometimes made his wives work together in common fields, but this was not the socially approved pattern.

(c) Procreational function

When a Tutsi informant was asked what the people of his group wished for above all, the answer came immediately: 'Children and cows'. A further question, 'Why?', disclosed that they were not regarded as ultimate values to be sought for themselves but that they were intermediate ones, the means to attain more important fundamental ends—power (*amaboko*) and reputation (*ugukomera*).

To be powerful is to be able to exert significant pressure upon somebody. In Ruanda society that meant, for a Tutsi, to be able to compel somebody to give him tribute in labour or in kind, and to induce assistance in support of his claims. To have many children was almost indispensible for this purpose. Girls, by their marriages, extended family connexions. Boys were sent while very young to the court of the king or of an important chief, and thereby reinforced their father's influence very considerably. He would be able to know from his son what was going on and the king or chief would be constantly reminded of the father by the son's presence, which was considered a great advantage for the father. The boy could also increase the influence of his family by becoming the client of a powerful Tutsi. By this means he obtained protection and cattle for himself and his patrilineage. Finally the matrimonial alliances of his sons could create new links between the father's kin group and his daughters-in-law's lineages. To sum up, from the point of view of power, the significance of children was to provide cattle and connexions. Cattle, as will be explained later on in more detail, had very much the same function as money in our culture: to provide the man who owns it with means to exert pressure on those who do not have enough money of their own and thus need to get some in exchange for services. By connexions is meant here that type of relationship in which one party may require something from another under the covert threat of a sanction.

MARRIAGE AND THE FAMILY 83

Independent of their being instruments of power, children enhanced the reputation of their fathers. The strength of a lineage and its vitality were highly valued in Ruanda. To have numerous offspring ensured that the group ancestors would be honoured, traditions maintained, and legends transmitted.

Ambition for power may be a very fitting pursuit for people who do not have to worry about fundamental human needs such as food, shelter, &c. For the Hutu, the ultimate value was security which was achieved by getting for oneself the protection of a member of the superior caste. To secure this protection, one had to become a client, and therefore to be able to supply a lord with services in labour and goods. Consequently, it was essential to produce a surplus and not only what was necessary for the subsistence of the people living in the compound. Surpluses could be obtained only by work, and children were very important in this respect. As in most peasant societies, they were useful when still quite young in helping their parents in their work. Moreover, as in the case of the Tutsi, offspring could bring supplementary protection and wealth to the compound by their ability to obtain cattle and connexions.

The preceding account might give the impression that for the Ruanda children were just means to their ultimate value of power, fame, security. This would be very misleading as they enjoyed having children simply because they liked children. This is not to question the genuineness of their affection for their offspring. I want only to stress here the social functions of children in this particular society.

Ruanda biological knowledge of the processes of procreation was extensive. They knew that a single ejaculation could produce pregnancy, that there is a relation between menstruation and fertility, that conception is not prevented during the suckling period, &c. According to their theories, the man's participation in conception was more important than the woman's. The analogy with the sowing of seeds in a field is commonly used by informants. It was pointed out to me that if it is indeed necessary for the seed to be buried in the soil, strength and vitality are unquestionably in the seed rather than in the passive ground.[10]

This last theory is important in that it gives a biological basis to the patrilineage principle of descent and to the difference between

[10] Cf. Lestrade, 1955, pp. 85-86.

84 THE PREMISE OF INEQUALITY IN RUANDA

cross and parallel cousins. Lévi-Strauss's crucial assertion that parallel and cross-cousins 'from the point of view of the degree of biological proximity are strictly interchangeable',[11] would not be considered true by the Ruanda. For them any paternal cousin is *biologically* much closer than a paternal cross-cousin. The former, so to speak, originates from the same seeds as Ego, those of a common grandfather, whereas the latter comes from other seeds. This should be a relevant argument in the discussion of Lévi-Strauss's theory, since surely what matters here is not the biological conceptions of the anthropologist but those of the society which in this case differentiates parallel from cross-cousins.

Many characteristics of individuals were thought to be innate, a view coherent with the ideology of a caste society. Features were expected to be similar to those of the father (and, our informants say, this was the only way to be sure of who was the genitor). The complexion was supposed to be inherited from the mother. Psychological traits and temperament were said to come from the father, particularly in the case of his sons. Daughters were often regarded as more similar to their mothers.

The birth of a child was nearly always welcomed by a married woman, even if she were actually divorced. The only exception was in the case of twins of different sexes. This was regarded as caused by a particular intervention of Imana and as a sign of ill-luck. The diviner had to be consulted about it and often the only way to escape the evil consequences was to let one of the twins, usually the boy, die. If such a thing happened to cattle, the steer had to be killed. But a newly born baby was never unwanted. On the contrary, when it was not very clear to what group he belonged, the child was usually claimed by more than one.

The general rules were as follows: the husband was the pater of any child borne by his wife. The genitor had no right over the child even if he had been conceived in such circumstances as for instance during a very long absence of the husband in which there was no doubt about the genitor. A child borne by a divorced woman belonged to her father's inzu, though the genitor could pay a 'child-wealth' and have the child. This did not mean that he married the woman; he was redeeming the child from those who had rights in the mother's fertility. A genitor who was a married man could pay the child-wealth as well as a bachelor. If the

[11] Lévi-Strauss, 1949, p. 156.

MARRIAGE AND THE FAMILY

woman's divorce was not yet completely settled (i.e. if the exchange of marriage-gifts and counter-gifts had not taken place), the former husband was still regarded as a pater of the child and the genitor had to pay him the child-wealth, if he wanted to have the child.

My male informants affirmed not to know of any contraceptives and they did not think that women knew better. In Ruanda culture, they would probably have been used exclusively for premarital relations. One informant, however, stressed the fact that too many pregnancies were bad for very poor people not having enough cow-milk and goat-milk to give to their babies, who then often died from malnutrition or from intestinal diseases (goat-milk was regarded as vermifugal). A certain herb called *umuhoko* was known for its abortive effects and used sometimes by pregnant unmarried girls with the help of their mother.

(d) Socialization

The young Ruanda spent the first years of his life in his mother's compound. There the first stages of the long process of his socialization, which was completed only after he had achieved marriage and parenthood, took place.

In matters of education, as in others, the supreme authority in the compound was the father. The paternal uncle could discipline his nephews and nieces only when they were in his compound or when the father was not present. His role was that of a substitute for the father. The maternal uncle had no authority except where the bride-wealth had not been paid. The mother had no authority of her own and had to be backed up by the father. It is clear, however, that in everyday life and particularly when the children were young, the mother was a disciplinarian and the main agent of socialization.

The training for the different activities expected to be mastered by any member of his caste began early for the child. From weaning (when they were about two years old) to the age of five, children were supposed to be clean, quiet, and not to wander far from the compound. Not later than five years old, children began to collect wood, to carry water, to watch goats and calves. A ten-year-old boy was taught how to handle a hoe and worked with his father in the fields. A girl learned how to light a fire, to brush, and to carry out the household duties of a woman. Boys from twelve to

86   THE PREMISE OF INEQUALITY IN RUANDA

fifteen were in charge of cattle herds and were absent for several days and nights from the compound. They also hunted with their fathers.

Even before puberty, some socialization processes took place outside of the nuclear or polygamous family. Mythological tales about the material world, the origin of man and animal species, the arrival of the Tutsi in Ruanda, beliefs concerning *Imana*, the spirits of the dead and other beings from the invisible world, the history of the kings of Ruanda, of the military conquests, folk-lore and poems about cattle, and stories of the ancestors and the lineage heroes were transmitted to the younger generation by the grandfather. He was also the main agent of education in the modes of behaviour indicating what was to be done and what was to be avoided in order to gain social approval.

Between puberty and marriage the further education of Tutsi boys took place at the court of a chief or of the king. Hutu stayed in the paternal compound, mastering the different techniques of cultivation and also the attitude and abilities necessary for them to be appreciated by the lord. Sometimes the young man replaced his father in the service of the lord.

What has been said in this section up to now applied equally to each compound of the polygynous family. Children of different wives were not brought up together. In each compound the mother had a role very similar to that of the mother in a nuclear family. There was no head-wife. Usually one was preferred by the husband (*inkundwakazi*, the favourite one), but because of her qualities (obedience, tidiness, beauty, &c.), and not because she was the first married. But the fact that the eldest son of the first wife often succeeded to the father, gave her a particular importance and respect by the others because, after the husband's death, all of them would probably be dependent on her eldest son.

The mutual behaviour of wives and their children has been mentioned before. It may be summarized as: respect to the favourite wife and the first wife, and good 'fraternal' relations between all the wives and the children. This was the ideal behaviour which was often overtly maintained as long as the husband was living. But according to all our informants, the modal and covert behaviour was jealousy and hatred. A polygynous family was often designated by the word *amshali*, whose root *ishyali* means jealousy, and one wife used to refer to another as her *mukeba*, rival. In these

MARRIAGE AND THE FAMILY

conditions it was evidently impossible to socialize and to educate together all the children of the same polygynous family.

The father had very considerable authority to punish during the period of the educational processes, and could even go as far as to curse and disinherit his sons. He could not use such drastic punishments for daughters except in the case of a pregnancy of an unmarried one. Then she could be killed, but mainly because such an event was regarded as being unlucky for the whole lineage. This case has to be interpreted in connexion with those others in which the father could condemn a daughter to death for fear of her conveying ill-luck: these were should her breasts not develop or should she have no periods. The father could appeal to the inzu head when he was unable to discipline his children and the married children could appeal to him when they had been punished by sanctions they found too heavy.

(e) Ritual function

The inzu ancestor was honoured mainly in the compound of the patrilineage head. A small hut was devoted to him and on certain occasions all his descendants met to make offerings to him. Some of these occasions were fixed, others were decided only after consulting a diviner.

In each compound there was also a small hut dedicated to the spirits of the dead, where the ancestor of the patrilineage was honoured. The wife could not build there a hut for her own ancestors. Nearer forbears were honoured in the compound more than the inzu's ancestors: the husband's grandfather or great-grandfather. The husband introduced his wife to him saying: 'Here is the woman I have taken in order to beget children for you, to multiply your lineage.' The bull used for stud purposes was also presented to the great-grandfather's spirit. Not only forbears but other dead members of the patrilineage or the family were honoured, but less often.

Almost every day small offerings were made. A few drops of milk or of beer, or some beans or peas were thrown into the hut. Or a girl spent some time in the ancestor's hut to enable him to enjoy a woman. But sometimes the spirits required more.

We have mentioned earlier that they were often angry and could send illnesses, sterility, cattle-epidemics, and death. They were regarded as beneficial only in a negative way, i.e. when they did

88   THE PREMISE OF INEQUALITY IN RUANDA

not injure the living. Consequently the cult addressed to the *bazimu* (spirits of the dead) was essentially aimed at appeasing them. When an unfortunate event was ascribed to a dead relative's ire by the diviner, the spirit had to be placated by the immolation of a goat or even a bull.

These practices were symbolic. It was not implied that the *bazimu* really drank the milk, ate the meat, or slept with the girl. When a goat or a steer was offered, most of it was eaten by members of the family. Other practices are more difficult to interpret. It sometimes happened that water was given to the spirits and at the same time they were told very loudly that it was milk. The explanation given by most informants is that *bazimu* were regarded as rather stupid and that these mock offerings were not given to the ancestors who were respected but only to the collaterals who, as *bazimu*, were hated. To have feared powerful *bazimu*, however, and at the same time to have deceived them so grossly does not appear very coherent and requires, I think, further explanation.

Every fourth reign, there was an important ritual connected with the final burial of the fourth predecessor of the king. As all *bazimu* were thought to accompany the spirit of the king long ago deceased, their cult was abolished. The inzu heads, however, continued to be remembered.[12]

[12] Kagame, 1947, pp. 377-86.

CHAPTER IV

ECONOMIC PRODUCTION

As we mentioned earlier, it was by land cultivation and cattle rearing that the Ruanda satisfied their fundamental subsistence requirements. Consequently land, cattle, knowledge of agricultural and cattle-breeding techniques, implements, and ability to work were essential in the economic process of production.

Ruanda economy was primitive in the sense that every rugo was a unit which had to produce practically all that was necessary for the subsistence of its members. None of these units concentrated on certain crops and obtained other foodstuffs by exchange. Every family head was a producer. What access had he, then, to the different factors of production?

Knowledge of agriculture and cattle-rearing techniques was part of the common heritage of every Ruanda. The Hutu were more expert agriculturalists than the Tutsi, and though some Tutsi were probably more versed in cattle-rearing any Hutu had the knowledge necessary to a tiller and a herdsman. Equipment was not very elaborate, and hoes and bill-hooks were not scarce.

Access to the other factors of production, land, cattle, and labour, was more restricted. We shall now consider what were the opportunities of the individual family head from that point of view.

I. LAND TENURE

When Ruanda are asked who is the owner of the fields and pastures, some answer it is the king, others the land chief or the cattle chief, others the family head or the lineage head. All of them are right, which means that the question is wrongly phrased

The Ruanda did not conceive of ownership as a private and exclusive right to the various uses to which a thing may be submitted. They regarded each of the uses as the object of a particular right. It was not thought necessary that one person should be endowed with the sum of the rights affecting one object. On the contrary, it was usual that different persons could claim

90 THE PREMISE OF INEQUALITY IN RUANDA

different uses of the same thing. For instance, one person could have the right to sow a plot and to collect the harvest and another to use it for grazing purposes at another time of the year. Neither of them was considered as the owner letting somebody else use his property as a pasture or as a ground for cultivation.

On each pasture, cultivated plot or forest area, the king had a right very similar to the *dominion eminens* of Roman law, the kind of public ownership that a State has over the land within the borders. But he had also the right to prevent, if he chose to do so, somebody from using a particular tract of land in any way at all, which amounts to saying that the mwami had over land a right potentially superior to that of anybody else. The mwami's rights could be opposed to 'private rights'. In fact, the king very rarely insisted on this use of his rights and then only when he wanted to punish somebody who was guilty of disobedience or of some other crime.

The land chief's and cattle chief's rights to fields and pastures will be considered later in the section dealing with the administration. Suffice it to say here that these tax-collectors had the right to evict people for certain offences and to allocate land to newcomers in their districts.

The person endowed with rights on land for cultivation purposes was the head of a family (*rugo*). Mostly these rights came to him from his father's inheritance. Sometimes, however, it was a part of the bush that he had himself cleared. If he had not received enough from his father to support his family, he extended his plot in this way with the agreement of the political authority. If, because of a dispute with his brothers, he wanted to move elsewhere and the land chief could not allocate him a field already prepared at the place where he wanted to settle, he did the same. Such a plot was called *bukonde* as long as it was occupied either by the man who had cleared it or by his descendants. A third source of cultivation rights was the assignment by the land chief of a plot already prepared (*inkungu*). The former user of it had either to be evicted by the authority, or had left, or had died without heirs.

In the same way the family head had the right to use a certain area as pasture for his cattle either by inheritance, or by felling the trees of a tract of forest or by having it conceded by the cattle chief.

At the end of the nineteenth century the inzu had no collective

ECONOMIC PRODUCTION

rights over certain areas except in the north of Ruanda (Mulera, Rwankeri, Bushiru, Bigogwe) where the Tutsi occupation had been more superficial. I have been told that there the soil belonged to the patrilineage and that there was no land or cattle chief. From the point of view of the individual, however, the situation was very similar: he inherited a share of his father's tract. The difference was that, if the part were insufficient, he had to apply for more to the lineage head instead of to the land-chief, and a plot left without heirs returned to the patrilineage instead of the political authority.

The person entitled to the use of a plot could not sell his right but could let the tract. The rent was about one hoe every other year plus a jug of beer each harvest. The tenant was not permitted to settle by building a hut or planting banana trees.

The Twa resented very much the expansion of fields and pastures in the forests they regarded as their possession. The authority was not concerned with the way they divided it into hunting areas.[1]

2. RIGHTS OVER CATTLE

The rights over each head of cattle were also manifold. Property in the Western sense was split up into different aspects.

A global right existed over all Ruanda cattle, even sheep and goats, by which the king could claim actual possession of any of them. The mwami used this right more frequently, it seems, over cattle than over land. An important chief indulging in intrigues regarded as dangerous by the king might find himself dispossessed of all his cattle. The king's right over all the cattle of Ruanda was a constant threat which seems to have very effectively deterred the Tutsi of the ruling set from becoming too independent.

Another right was very similar to our bare ownership. The person who had it was not in possession of the cow but could at any time claim possession of the animal and the heifers and cows produced by that beast since the time when the possession had been transferred. This was the right of the lord (*shebuja*).

In contrast there was the usufruct right with respect to cattle. The person endowed with it could dispose of the milk, the male increase of the cattle, and the dead cows. This was the typical right of the client (*garagu*).

---

[1] For a more extended account of the land tenure system in traditional Ruanda, see Maquet and Naigisiki, 1957.

92 THE PREMISE OF INEQUALITY IN RUANDA

Sometimes these rights (bare ownership and usufruct) were possessed by the same person. The cattle concerned were then called *imbata*.[2]

3. INHERITANCE RULES

When the father died, the family unit of which he had been the head did not disappear as well. Some of the family functions had still to be carried on for some time: the younger sons had to be given a wife and the bride-wealth paid for them, the younger daughters had to be married, and perhaps young children had still to be taken care of by their mother for several years. In order that the family unit should be able to perform its tasks before its breakdown, it was necessary that the duties of the rugo head should continue to be fulfilled. Consequently the father chose one of his sons who could be trusted with that role (*umutware w'urugo rwa se:* head of his father's family). He was often, but not always, the eldest son of the first wife. The father could even choose a brother or one of his parallel cousins if he thought none of his sons was capable. The father's choice could always be reversed by the lineage head or the political chief or even the lord, if it appeared unwise to these authorities or if it was the cause of complaints from the other members of the family.

It was the father who was endowed, as we have just seen, with rights to land and cattle. The totality of these rights plus goods such as trees, huts, and household implements, constituted his patrimony.

If there was no declaration of will, custom determined the division of the patrimony according to the following rules.

The first heirs were the sons of the deceased, or, failing these, his brothers, then his paternal male parallel cousins, his grand-sons, the sons of his brothers and their male paternal parallel cousins, his paternal uncles. Then any male in the inzu or the umulyango. If there was no known kinsman left, the political authority (land or cattle chief) or the lord was the heir. In that case the patrimony might be divided according to the kind of rights left, for instance those over cattle went to the lord, those over land to the land chief. Or the more powerful authority was able to secure for himself the whole of the inheritance.

---

[2] See Vanhove 1941, pp. 48-59, for still other, but less important, rights over cattle.

ECONOMIC PRODUCTION 93

Nothing was definitely left to the wife, the daughters or the affines. But the wife had the usufruct of the rugo in which she had been living while she still had young children to care for. Even when all the children were married, it happened frequently among Tutsi that the wife remained in the rugo till her death. This was usual when the widow married one of her husband's consanguineal relatives, or did not marry again. If she married a man completely alien to her former husband's patrilineage, usually she had to leave the rugo.

The father, before he died, had already given a share of the inheritance to each of his married sons, at the time of the wedding. Consequently, what was left at the father's death had to be divided among the sons who had not yet received anything. In principle rights to cattle as well as to land were equally shared. When bare ownership of cattle was divided between the sons of a lord, the clients of the father became clients of the son to whom the bare ownership of a particular cow or herd of cattle had been ascribed. When usufruct on cattle had to be inherited, the successors became clients of the people who had the bare ownership of the same cattle. But the lord had to agree on the choice of his new client.

In a polygynous family the principle of equality of shares held good for each rugo. Consequently the shares of the sons of the same father could vary considerably if the number of sons of each wife was very dissimilar.

The son chosen as head of the rugo had a supplementary share (*ingarigari*) as he had more economic responsibilities. Normally he received it before his father's death. This was called *gukubita itoko*, to stroke the thigh, meaning to give a favour.

Debts owed by the deceased were divided between his heirs, but the family head had to meet a greater part than the others. Judiciary fines were cancelled by the death of the debtor. When the deceased was creditor, the debt had to be paid by the rugo head who shared it with his co-heirs.

The father could also make a will and usually did. He could alter the traditional procedure within rather narrow limits, and for reasons regarded as valid by the patrilineage head or sometimes the political chief or the lord. A son who had been cursed was *ipso facto* disinherited. A son could be punished in the same way

94 THE PREMISE OF INEQUALITY IN RUANDA

without having been cursed but by being guilty of some major disobedience or lack of respect towards his father, such as beating him. The father could also give a greater share to the sons he preferred, but this had to be justified on grounds other than his personal feelings. It had to appear as a reward for particular devotion or good behaviour. The father could not skip a category of traditionally defined successors and still less could he leave his rights to non-relatives. The persons who felt that they had been wronged could always appeal to the different authorities mentioned.

As may be expected, matters of inheritance were causes of suspicion, rivalries, and disputes among the sons. Each wanted to be favoured by his father. Even if there was no will, an equal division of goods and rights so different in kind was not easy to achieve, particularly in a society without money or any other standard of value.[3]

4. LABOUR

Much labour had to be expended on the soil and on the stock to produce consumer goods. It was, therefore, not sufficient for the producer to possess a certain amount of capital (land, cattle), he had also to control labour. What were his rights over the labour of various individuals?

The labour of wives, unmarried sons, and daughters belonged almost exclusively to the father, head of the rugo. He could make all these dependants work in the rugo fields and he could require his sons to give tribute labour to the political authorities in his stead or to carry out services for his lord.

The different political authorities had rights over the labour of their subjects. These rights were limited either to certain tasks (e.g. to build or to mend the chief's enclosure), or to certain periods of time (e.g. two days each week). The mwami, the supreme political authority, did not usually require more than a chief but in theory all the men of Ruanda belonged to him and he could demand all their labour as well as take their lives.

According to the 'agreement' by which the lord granted the usufruct on certain cows, the client had, in return, to give a not precisely limited number of days of work. These labour rights and duties were inherited with the bare ownership and the usufruct of the cattle.

[3] See also Bourgeois, 1954, pp. 344 ff.

ECONOMIC PRODUCTION

Servants' labour belonged completely to their masters. These servants (*abatindi* for men, *abaja* for women) were either war captives or simply very poor people (this is the first meaning of the word *abatindi*). Their payment consisted in receiving food, shelter, and clothing from their masters. Sometimes it was agreed that after a certain period of time (such as three years) the master would either pay the bride-wealth to provide the servant with a wife or would even give him his own daughter.

Family heads were the only persons who could dispose of their own labour resources, with the exception of that part required by the lord and the political authority.

*　　　*　　　*

Almost any Ruanda family head could command enough rights to capital goods and labour to make his rugo self-supporting, with a certain surplus for his chief and his overlord. But these rights were not finally his. The ultimate control of the factors of production was not his. Labour, land, and cattle, in that order, were increasingly slipping away from his control. Command of the factors of production and political power was so interwoven in Ruanda social structure that they are to be analysed together in the following chapter devoted to the political organization.

CHAPTER V

POLITICAL ORGANIZATION

I. DEFINITIONS

POLITICAL organization is a sector of the social structure not easy to define.

The phrase, widely used in everyday speech, immediately evokes the idea of government and rulers. That is to say, persons who deal with matters which are important because they concern the group as a whole and consequently the commonweal. Moreover, these persons are authorities, and are powerful; what they have decided will be carried out. Often they enjoy many privileges which they usually attempt to justify and which they try in any event to keep and to increase. Finally, they have relations with their counterparts in other groups: they discuss with them on an equal footing, sometimes they threaten them or are threatened by them and by opposing the forces of their groups they try to settle the dispute to their advantage.

The term 'political' thus suggests to us persons (chiefs, governing bodies), abstract ideas (authority, power), certain kinds of activities (which are called 'public'), a value which should be the aim of the action of the chiefs (the commonweal), the private interests of the rulers, diplomacy, and war. These elements are too numerous and varied for all of them to be included in a useful definition at the beginning of an inquiry.

A distinction must be made between the use of 'political' in an intragroup or intergroup context. Political relations between two groups have a completely different meaning from those existing between people belonging to the same group. Let us begin by an intragroup definition to use in the present inquiry.

(a) Intragroup political organization

A political organization is the totality of culturally patterned relationships between certain individuals who possess the legitimate use of physical force and all the others who inhabit a certain territory at a certain time.

The first words of this definition, *a totality of relationships*,

POLITICAL ORGANIZATION

indicate the level of reality we are dealing with. As any social system, political organization is a reality composed of relationships between men. What differentiates each system is how the human actors in the relationship are defined. A kinship system, for instance, is made of relationships between persons defined in terms of descent and siblinghood.

These relationships are *culturally patterned*. Political behaviour is not to be invented. Any well-socialized member of the group knows what is expected of him.

The two actors in a political relation are members of the *same group* which has a *territorial* basis. We follow here the majority of sociologists for whom a political organization must be linked to a territory. This certainly seems a necessary condition for the use of physical force, an essential part of the definition. As men are situated in space, it would not be possible for their rulers to inflict on them a physical coercion, or at least to threaten them effectively with it, if the rulers had not the control of a certain area where those who are to be submitted to pressure live. The *time* dimension is added. Indeed it is not necessary that the group inhabits always the same territory. For instance, nomads moving each season to new grazing land do not have a constant territorial basis, but they have a territory in the sense that their group has at any time the ultimate control of a certain area, even if that area is different every day.

Among members of the same group, what distinguishes the political relationship from others is that one of the actors possesses the legitimate use of *physical force*. This element of coercion has been stressed by many sociologists and anthropologists. For Oppenheimer, the origin of the state lies in the force used in conquest.[1] Max Weber speaks of 'that human association which within a definite sphere . . . successfully claims the monopoly of legitimate physical force'.[2] Lowie writes that 'the state embraces the inhabitants of a definite area who acknowledge the legitimacy of force when applied by individuals whom they accept as rulers or governors'.[3] Radcliffe-Brown, too, emphasizes the physical force component of a political organization: '. . . the organized exercise of coercive authority through the use, or the possibility of use, of physical force'.[4] MacIver and Page regard coercion or

---

[1] See Oppenheimer, 1922. [2] Quoted by Lowie, 1948, p. 156.
[3] Lowie, 1948, p. 317.
[4] Radcliffe-Brown in Fortes and Evans-Pritchard, 1940, p. xiv.

98   THE PREMISE OF INEQUALITY IN RUANDA

the threat of it as characteristic of the political law.[5] Such quotations can be easily multiplied.

It could be objected that some of the authors quoted above deal with the state rather than with political organization in general. The two terms are used here almost as synonyms. The only difference is that the word 'state' implies a greater emphasis on the stability and the permanence of the group which has the capacity to exert physical coercion.

Those in the dominant situation will be called rulers, superiors; the others, subjects, inferiors.

It is not necessary that compulsion be applied; it is sufficient that it could be made effective.

The term *legitimate* has no Western moral connotation here. It only means that the group regards physical coercion as a proper reaction when coming from some individuals. If it is admitted in a particular society that the chief has the right of life and death over all his subjects whether they have committed an offence or not, the suppression of anybody when ordered by the chief is legitimate. But when a thief steals valuables from somebody under the threat of harming him, the victim, in our society and probably in any other, is regarded as having been submitted to illegitimate coercion.

The preceding definition mentions neither the explicit aim nor the function of that totality of culturally patterned relationships. In his definition, Radcliffe-Brown includes the function of political organization which is, according to him, 'the maintenance or the establishment of social order'.[6] Herskovits mentions 'the regulation of affairs that concern the group as a whole'.[7] Indeed a functional definition is intellectually more satisfactory. But it should follow an analysis and not precede it. It is true that in any society certain social functions must be fulfilled if the group is to subsist and perpetuate itself (there must be a means to collect food, to distribute it, to obtain the security necessary to raise and educate children, &c.), and other functions may be fulfilled (such as the provision of the individual with certain comforts in the difficulties of life, with a world-view, &c.). But in spite of several attempts,[8] no satisfactory exclusive connexions have been established between these different functions and particular institutions

[5] Cf. MacIver and Page, 1949, p. 456.
[6] Fortes and Evans-Pritchard, 1940, p. xiv.   [7] Herskovits, 1948, p. 327.
[8] For instance, Malinowski, 1931, p. 645; 1944, pp. 91 f, pp. 125 f.

POLITICAL ORGANIZATION 99

which fulfil them. As we have seen previously, the Ruanda family organization had several functions (sexual, economic, reproductive, educational, ritual), some of which also belong elsewhere to other institutions. The same institution, religion for instance, may be a factor of social cohesion in one society, yet it may break the unity of another. Moreover, the same structure may have functions varying with time as the modern state which directly takes care of the welfare and health of the people living in its territory.

Consequently it seems better to distinguish clearly a social structure from the functions it may fulfil. By analysing an institution in a particular social context, we shall be able to determine what are its functions in the particular society studied.

(b) Power

Frequently what is political is identified with what concerns power. Lasswell has listed a series of social values and a series of institutions through which these values are formalized and shared among the members of a group. He indicates 'government' as the institution corresponding to 'power'.[9] This means that the political organization is the network through which power is distributed within a group. This conception does not seem to fit with Lasswell's own notion of power (which I entirely accept)—an interpersonal situation in which a severe deprivation may be inflicted by one person on another[10]—according to which power relations should be considered a *genus* of which a political relation is a *species*. Political relation is indeed power relation: to exert physical coercion against somebody, even if it is legitimate, is surely a way of inflicting severe deprivation on him. But all power relations are not necessarily political. An employer may threaten his employee to dispossess him of his livelihood. This is a power relation but it is not political.

(c) Social power

Another sort of power to be distinguished from political power is *social power*. It is an interpersonal relationship in which each of the human actors belongs to a different group or stratum of the same society; because of these different affiliations only, one person is able to exert pressure on the other.

---

[9] Lasswell, 1948, p. 17.
[10] Lasswell, 1948, pp. 10-14. See also Russell, 1938, pp. 35 f.

100 THE PREMISE OF INEQUALITY IN RUANDA

(d) Intergroup political relations

Intergroup political relations are essentially different. They do not imply inferiority and superiority. The opposite assumption is made: the two groups are supposed to be independent and equal. If by diplomacy or by war one succeeds in subduing the other, the subsequent unequal relations will be more similar to intragroup than to intergroup political relations.

If our definition of intragroup political organization be accepted, the word 'political' when applied to intergroup relations conveys a different and derivative meaning. Those who control legitimate coercion within a social structure are also those who are qualified to enter into intergroup relations. Subjects do not represent their own group, only rulers do. The ability to deal with intergroup relations results from a superior situation in internal political relations. In that sense, the political external relations may be said to be secondary. In the following account of Ruanda political organization the emphasis will be on the primary political relations, the internal ones.

*　　　　*　　　　*

In Ruanda, there were two types of relationships sanctioned by legitimate coercion on the part of the superior. Consequently we may distinguish within the political organization two structures which may be termed administrative and military. Another system of social relations was the clientage structure or the feudal organization. It occupied an intermediate position between the political and the private spheres. It was not purely political, but it was much more than a private agreement such as a loan. Consequently the feudal relations in Ruanda will be considered in close connexion with the administrative and military ones.

The three structures were interwoven and interconnected at each level. This was particularly the case at the top and at the bottom. The mwami held the supreme position in the three systems and the commoners were taxpayers, members of an army, and clients. In the intermediate levels it happened, too, that a superior and an inferior were linked by several ties: one could be at the same time the lord and the cattle-chief of an individual, and the client of one's army chief.

I shall describe and analyse each structure separately.

POLITICAL ORGANIZATION

2. DESCRIPTION OF THE ADMINISTRATIVE STRUCTURE

(a) Districts, hills, and neighbourhoods

From the point of view of territorial administration, the border zones were distinguished from the rest of the country. Border zones which were permanently threatened by foreign attack were administered by the chief of the army, the headquarters, and camp of which situated in the region. The centre of Ruanda and the regions which were close to a foreign territory not regarded as dangerous were divided into what we shall call administrative districts. There is an almost complete unanimity of informants (97 per cent.) on this.[11]

Unfortunately, there is confusion about the names applied to these areas. Five names were given by informants, with the following percentages: *igikingi* (3 per cent.); *igiti* (19 per cent.), *urugo* (12 per cent.); *umurwa* (7 per cent.); *ubukebe* (24 per cent.). Moreover, the three terms *igikingi, igiti, urugo* were all used, according to 2 per cent.; *igiti* and *urugo* according to 4 per cent.; *igikingi* and *igiti* according to 6 per cent.; *igiti* and *ubukebe* according to 8 per cent.; *igikingi, igiti,* and *ubukebe* according to 1 per cent. Finally, to add to the confusion, the same word was used to mean different but related units. For instance *igikingi* could mean a subdivision of a hill—according to 97 per cent.—and a hill was itself part of a district to which, as we have just indicated, 12 per cent. applied the term *igikingi*.

At all events the whole country was divided into administrative locations that may be designated as districts. Each of them was ruled by two chiefs, neither of them dependent on the other. Their authority extended over the same territory but from different points of view. The land-chief (*umunyabutaka*) took care of the dues from agriculture and the cattle-chief (*umunyamukenke*) of the dues from stock. According to 60 per cent. of our informants, the same person could not have the two charges. It was possible, however, according to 36 per cent. of the Tutsi asked. But the usual situation was to have two chiefs and not a single one.

The district was divided into hills (*umusozi*). At that level the

[11] As has been explained in the introduction, a hundred questions on the political organization have been put to three hundred informants chosen from all the regions of Ruanda (the interviews took place in seventy-four different places). The percentages to be found in that chapter refer to this sample. When the percentages included decimal fractions, the figures have been brought to the nearest unit.

102   THE PREMISE OF INEQUALITY IN RUANDA

cattle- and land-chiefs had only one subordinate, the hill-chief, *umutware w'umusozi*, whose counterpart in the present administrative organization is called sub-chief or *ibisonga*.

On each hill, there were usually several neighbourhoods. In each, one of the family heads living there was chosen as its head by the hill-chief. He was called *umukoresha*.

(b) Taxes

Tributes and dues for which the land-chief was responsible were: any kind of labour, usually agricultural; *uguhunika* (putting into the granary), which consisted of a certain number of baskets of beans, peas, and sorghum to be delivered at harvest time; *amavu* (bananas to be used for brewing beer). These tributes were due from Hutu. The person who provided these things was the family head who was considered as the individual producer of the rugo. But between him and the land-chief, there was a hierarchy of persons responsible for the carrying out of the levies: sometimes the lineage head (if he was living in the same neighbourhood), then the neighbourhood head, and finally the hill-chief.

Through the hill-chief, too (according to 68 per cent. of the informants), the cattle-chief obtained jars of milk from the Tutsi. Moreover, the latter had to provide (according to 88 per cent.) *inkuke*, cows kept by the beneficiary in order that milk could be consumed fresh.

These tributes were centralized in the royal residence of the district which was occupied by the king when he was travelling in the district. This residence was called *rugo*, the ordinary word meaning a compound dwelling. 95 per cent. of our informants remembered several names of royal district residences and 86 per cent. had not forgotten the name of the residence in the district where they used to live as children.

Revenues of a district were either reserved to the king himself or were granted to one of the king's wives. In the first case, the residence was called *ingaligali* and was administered by a king's concubine (*umuja*, girl-servant).

Administrative officers collecting tributes, had the right to keep a part for their own benefit. According to 95 per cent. of our informants, the hill-chiefs had the right to deduct some agricultural produce, of which they could keep about a third. Then the land-chief—according to 99 per cent.—could also keep a part of it,

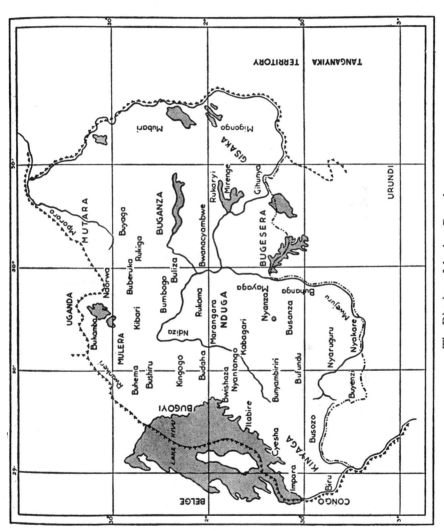

The Districts of Ancient Ruanda

POLITICAL ORGANIZATION 103

probably a little less than a third. For tribute labour, the hill-chief handed over to the residence the number of labourers requested but could have the others to work for himself.

According to respectively 92 and 91 per cent. of the Tutsi interviewed, neither the hill-chief nor the cattle-chief could deduct similar proportions from cattle dues. I have been told, however, that the cattle-chief required from the hill-chief more jars than the royal residence asked. It is very likely that the hill-chief imposed a similar obligation on those who had to bring the milk.

The land-chief acted as judge in disputes about rights over land between Hutu of his district.

Some places were not integrated into the district organization and were free from the cattle- and land-chief interferences. They were the domains belonging to *biru* and the royal funeral grounds. Biru, as we shall see later, were very important people keeping the secret traditions according to which the order of succession of the kings was determined, the ritual to be used in wars, the measures to be taken in times of famine, &c. In their privileged domains biru enjoyed powers similar to those of the king over Ruanda. 76 per cent. of our informants mention the name of a hill ruled by one mwiru (singular of biru) and 79 per cent. affirm that these domains were completely independent of the administrative chiefs.

The other privileged hills were those on which the royal corpses were laid. As the dead body of the king was believed to undergo different metamorphoses, it was not immediately buried, but mummified and left for a certain time in a wood, on the top of a hill. The corpse was watched by some chiefs and servants and finally buried. Even now 88 per cent. of our informants can mention the name of such a hill where a royal cemetery is to be found. One of the more renowned places is Rutare, not far from Kigali, which is mentioned by 71 per cent. 84 per cent. said that these hills were exempted from any tribute to the district residence.

3. ANALYSIS OF THE ADMINISTRATIVE STRUCTURE

Analysis of the different structures described here will be made from the point of view of the social function of these institutions. Social function is understood here as the contribution made by an institution, an association or a cultural trait to the working and the maintenance of a particular social structure. The contribution may

104 THE PREMISE OF INEQUALITY IN RUANDA

be negative or positive. It is to be distinguished from the aim explicitly stated in the charter (written or not) of the institution or the purpose of the association consciously conceived by its members.

Take, for instance, some of the religious ceremonies of a particular group. Their aim as known and admitted by every member of the group may be to honour the ancestral spirits, whereas their function, of which perhaps nobody in the group is completely aware, is to manifest and reinforce the *esprit de corps* of the group. Or an association whose explicit purpose is some philanthropic activity may have as its function the giving of certain political control to a particular set of people. Aim and function are not necessarily different. It may happen that the aim expresses one of the ways in which the institution is significant from the viewpoint of the perpetuation of the particular organization existing in that society.[12]

(a) Fiscal function

It is not difficult to determine the main social function of the administrative structure of Ruanda. It was identical indeed with its explicitly recognized aim in that society. Aim and function were fiscal: the country had to provide its rulers with consumption goods.

Tribute collecting was very methodically organized. Because of the division of the country into about seventy to ninety districts, the amount to be supplied was distributed in a way which did not favour one region more than another. Even parts of Ruanda which were far from the royal court had to provide dues for the local royal residence. The timing of the levies was also fortunate as the agricultural products were not demanded when the rulers needed them but at harvesting time. Tribute labour seems also to have been regularly required during the year.

Were these impositions heavy? It is very difficult to assess the proportion of foodstuff and labour required from each family head. I gathered from different informants that about a third of the labour of one individual was required from each family. It is important to stress the fact that only one person in each rugo had to fulfil this demand whereas there were usually several men able to give that tribute in each family.

[12] See Radcliffe-Brown, 1922, p. ix; 1940, p. 10; 1952, pp. 200 f; Maquet 1949a; 1954c, p. 65.

POLITICAL ORGANIZATION 105

It is still less easy to assess the relative importance of land and cattle taxes. Informants say that in the past they had to give a great deal, but such recollections of taxpayers do not mean very much. It is certain that if such a fiscal system has been maintained for numerous generations, exploitation has been kept within bearable limits. In Ruanda, as elsewhere, if the taxpayer is overburdened with dues and levies to such a point that he has not enough time and food left to go on producing, the source of impositions will dry up. Fifty years ago, after long practice, the Ruanda rulers had been able, it seems, by trial and error, to determine the exact amount of exploitation that the country could support. Yet if the group of taxpayers as such were not overexploited, it is certain that some individuals in the group have been very heavily taxed merely because those who had the power to impose taxes wanted to avenge a particular offence.

The taxpaying group was not restricted to the Hutu stratum since some tributes were due on cattle holdings. Agricultural dues and tribute labour however, were entirely provided by Hutu and as they constituted about ninety per cent. of the population, the total amount of their contribution was considerably higher than that of other groups.

Those who received benefit from this system were, first of all, the king and his spouses. They did not have to come and live in a district residence to have the use of the produce collected in that district. Goods were sent to the court or wherever the king wanted them. Other beneficiaries were the chiefs in charge of the collection: land-, cattle-, and hill-chiefs. About two-thirds of the impositions on agricultural produce was deducted by them. Were they all Tutsi? No, answered the Tutsi interviewed. According to ninety-two per cent. of them a Hutu could be appointed landchief. But he could not become a cattle-chief, according to ninety-one per cent. This is quite understandable, as the first had to deal with Hutu and the second with Tutsi. But were many Hutu in fact endowed with the profitable responsibilities of the land-chief or the hill-chief? 258 informants (eighty-six per cent.) were able to give the names of Hutu land-chiefs, but they mentioned only thirty-four different names. A Hutu land-chief, Ndarwubatse, was mentioned 180 times, another, Kanyonyomba, 109 times, and another, Segore, ninety-seven times. As our informants were scattered throughout Ruanda it is very probable that the cases of

106 THE PREMISE OF INEQUALITY IN RUANDA

Ndarwubatse, Kanyonyomba, and Segore were exceptional and that, in fact, Hutu were not very numerous among land-chiefs. The share of Hutu in political power was probably symbolic rather than quantitatively great. Hutu could also be hill-chiefs and sixty-nine per cent. of our informants were able to mention a few names. According to ninety-nine per cent. a Twa could be neither land-chief nor cattle-chief, unless he were ennobled. But in that case, he was not socially a Twa any more, but assimilated to a Tutsi. Twa could be hill-chiefs; sixty-five per cent. of our Tutsi informants mentioned the names of such Twa. Neighbourhood heads were frequently Hutu, but the advantages they drew from their office were minimal, if any.

(b) Maintenance of the central rulers in power

One may conclude that the very great majority of the beneficiaries of the fiscal function of the administrative structure were people of the Tutsi group.

A second function of the administrative structure was to enable those who enjoyed political power to keep it. The mwami and his wives centralized the means necessary to afford an important court. Moreover, by granting the profitable offices of land-, cattle-, and hill-chiefs, the mwami increased the number of his faithful dependents. For these chiefs of the administrative structure were appointed by the king. To the question 'who appointed the land- and the cattle-chiefs?' ten different answers were given, but if one adds up all the answers which named the mwami as the person or one of the persons who granted these official appointments, a majority of sixty-five is reached. The confusion in the answers seems due to the fact that different principles operated together in the nomination of such a chief. Firstly, one of the sons of the former office holder usually succeeded to his father, and the latter could often indicate his preferences, but this did not mean that the office was hereditary. Merely, it happened fairly frequently that the mwami liked to strengthen a man's loyalty on the understanding that if he was a good chief, the office could remain in his family. Secondly, the appointment could be made by the mwami following presentation of the candidate by an important chief, such as the army-chief. Consequently, it could appear that the latter was the one who gave the appointment. But the third principle remained: the king kept a complete control of these offices in the sense

POLITICAL ORGANIZATION 107

that no other authority had the final say in such appointments.

The danger of having some chiefs becoming more and more independent of the central government was avoided by the mwami's power to dismiss anybody and also by the curious duality of chiefs in each district. Increasing the control of the central government over its subordinates seems to have been the function of that duality. Tensions arose between these two chiefs who were neighbours and who exerted their prerogatives in the same territory yet were independent of each other. The mwami was always kept well informed by each of these chiefs of the exactions or suspicious activities of the other. Moreover, both chiefs had the same subordinate, the hill-chief. Consequently the mwami could be sure that if by chance the two chiefs were in agreement, it was very likely that if their common subordinate had some difficulty with one of his superiors, he would attempt and often succeed in getting the other on to his side: *duobus litigantibus tertius gaudens.* In addition, as conflicts of power were unavoidable in such a situation, the chief had to resort to the mwami as judge. In that way the links of the dependence of both of them on the mwami were tightened.

In this analysis it is not suggested that the duality of chiefs was conceived and put into being by a certain mwami in order to fulfil what we regard here as its function. It is possible that it happened in that way. But even if nobody ever thought of reinforcing the royal power by this dual organization, it was nevertheless its function in Ruanda society.

(c) Social cohesion

I have mentioned that the hill-chief required dues and tributes not from the individual taxpayer but from the lineage head when possible, and the latter demanded it from the family head. This way of reaching the individual through his kin group and family group enhanced the importance of the descent principle of of kin solidarity. Even in Ruanda where the political organization had taken over so many functions from descent groups, the individual as such was not yet recognized in very important matters like the contributions to the maintenance of the rulers. In this interpretation, the kinship and the administrative structures promote the social cohesion of the group as a whole.

To provide the central government with regular revenues, to

108 THE PREMISE OF INEQUALITY IN RUANDA

maintain its predominant and privileged situation, and to favour social cohesion, were the functions of the administrative structure. Moreover, as any authority in Ruanda, the land-chief was judge in the disputes concerning rights over land. The cattle-chief, however, had no judicial capacity because disputes about cattle were dealt with by the army-chief.

Impositions and taxes exist in all societies which have a centralized organization of political power. Rulers to maintain their dominant position need to be able to dispose of great revenues. The more centralized a government is, the larger is the amount of goods needed because the administrative officers are numerous.[13]

This political necessity of taxation has been justified differently according to the ideology of each culture.[14] Thus in modern democratic states, taxes are said to be the contribution of each citizen to the maintenance of services used by all members of the community, such as roads open to everybody, a police force which protects property and life against internal dangers, courts and tribunals for those who feel that they have been wronged and want to obtain reparation, an army which protects the community against an external threat, &c.

In Ruanda, tributes in labour and goods to the mwami were justified by the nature of the royal power. Kingship was divine. The first king of Ruanda, Nkuba (which means lightning), lived in heaven with his wife Nyagasani, their two sons Kigwa and Mututsi, and their daughter, Nyampundu. One day the three siblings fell from heaven and settled on a Ruanda hill. There Kigwa married his sister. Their descendents constituted the Abanyiginya clan. Mututsi, Kigwa's brother, married one of his nieces. Their descendents were the Abega. The two royal clans (usually the Abanyiginya married Abega girls) had thus a divine origin.[15] From this godlike nature of the mwami followed the justification of his absolute power and of the sovereignty of his rights over the people, the cattle, and the land of Ruanda. By virtue of that divine sovereignty, the king could require tribute. Because everything and everybody was his, he could confiscate any cattle or agricultural produce, and take the labour or even the life of anybody.

This was the theory. In fact the mwami did not use his prerogatives more than the rulers who were not divine but had the same means

---

[13] Maquet, 1952. [14] Maquet, 1954c, p. 65. [15] See Pagès, 1933, p. 491.

POLITICAL ORGANIZATION 109

of coercion at their disposal. If a mwami attempted to go beyond his effective power even without exceeding the limits of his divine rights, he exposed himself to the chance of meeting some obstacles. Nevertheless, he had sovereign as well as divine rights and his subjects were constantly reminded of these by the tributes they had to pay.

4. DESCRIPTION OF THE MILITARY STRUCTURE

Every Ruanda, Twa, Hutu as well as Tutsi, was affiliated to an army (*ingabo*). This is stated by ninety-nine per cent. of our informants. Although this military organization is obsolete at the present day—indeed it no longer exists—ninety-eight per cent. of the Tutsi interviewed can still give the name of the army of their paternal ascendants.

There were several armies. The name of each one had a military meaning. It was a challenge, a boast, the memory of a dynastic or historical event: for instance 'the tough ones' (*abashakamba*), 'the first to be praised' (*imbanzamihigo*), 'the fearless ones' (*inzirabwoba*), &c. At the beginning of each reign a new army was organized by the king. Moreover, a very important chief could be authorized by the mwami to raise an army.

(a) Recruitment

An army was recruited in the following way. The mwami asked his Tutsi clients to bring to the court their sons who had not yet had any military training. When about 150 to 200 young men were gathered, they constituted what we may call a company (*itorero*). During the reign, four or five companies were recruited in the same way and were added to the first one. According to ninety-six per cent. of our informants a man had to stay all his life in the company he had first entered. The young men (*intore*, the chosen ones) lived at the court of the king or of the chief who had been allowed to recruit an army. Under the direction of an officer called the chief of the king's residence (*umutware w'urugo rw'umwami*) or of its counterpart at a chief's court, they were trained for several years in military skills such as bow and arrow shooting, the use of the sword, spear, and javelin. They learned warlike dances, and to memorize and to recite the poems in which the high deeds of extraordinary bravery and boldness of the past warriors were exalted.[16] They were also taught how to compose

[16] See Kagame, 1949b; 1951.

110 THE PREMISE OF INEQUALITY IN RUANDA

poems in imitation of these great models. They attended evening sessions near the fire, in the kraal, where by sarcasm and humiliation, their capacity for self control was put to the test.

These few companies constituted the nucleus of a new army. It was completed by detaching a certain number of people from other armies to incorporate them in the new one. Except for this, armies existed indefinitely. When a king died and when a new army was formed, the previous army founded by him did not disappear. Only some members of the former armies joined the new one. These people were not incorporated individually but with their patrilineages, primary (*inzu*) or even secondary (*umulyango*).

Except for the *intore*, it seems more accurate to say that an army was made up of patrilineages rather than of individuals. Indeed 100 per cent. of our informants affirm that a man was not affiliated alone to an army but that he was in it together with his sons, married or not, his brothers and their sons, and his paternal uncles. It was a group of agnates indeed, as the sister's sons were not included in the group according to ninety-eight per cent. of our informants. In the army, the patrilineage remained a closed group under its inzu head. Our informants were unanimous (100 per cent.) that dues and services to which the army chief was entitled had to be asked for from members through the lineage chiefs. This rule did not apply to the *intore*. They entered alone into the army, although later their children would also join. According to 100 per cent. of the informants a man belonged only to one army. The army chief was called *umugabe* or *umutware w'ingabo*.

(*b*) *The warriors' section*

In any army, according to eighty-four per cent. of our informants, there were two sections—the warrior's section and the herdsmen's section (warrior: *ingabo*, herdsman: *umushumba*). The warriors' section was made up of the few companies of men who had received the *intore* training to whom were added their personal dependents who were also fighting. Warriors did not wear a uniform but had some special badges.

As mentioned in a preceding section, a certain number of warriors of an army camped near the borders threatened by neighbouring enemies. If an attack occurred, they called the other warriors who lived nearby and, while waiting for their aid, held

POLITICAL ORGANIZATION

the aggressors at bay. Army herdsmen also lived in the same region. Armies constituted during previous reigns were more likely to be localized in the interior of the country.

Expeditions against neighbouring countries were made. They were prepared by spies' reports. Military chiefs had at their disposal people named *abatasi*. They depended directly on the court and had taken an oath not to betray Ruanda. They were the only ones who could have connexions with foreign governments without committing an offence punishable by death.

There were two kinds of expedition: those planned by the king (*igitero*) and those planned by a military chief. The latter expeditions were short raids which could not last more than two days (*agateroshuma*). A very complicated ritual was observed in the choice of the leader of the expedition (*umugabe w'igitero*). This choice was made after divining operations by means of the viscera of steers and rams. During the battle, the general of the expedition would sit motionless in his headquarters; every move backwards of his would have resulted in his forces' flight.

Some of the warriors (*abakoni*, stick-bearers) had the special charge of capturing cattle. If the expedition was successful, it ended with a celebration lasting several days. During the festivities, rewards and badges of honour were granted, warriors marched off in triumph, and their deeds were hymned and praised in poems.

(c) *The herdsmen's section*

The section of herdsmen, as its name suggests, tended the army's cattle. A certain number of herds were regarded as linked to a particular army. The army-chief was also responsible for these cattle and in that capacity he commanded several head herdsmen (*umutware w'inka, umutware w'inyambo*).

An army's cattle did not constitute an homogeneous group from the point of view of the rights enjoyed over them by different persons. Four categories of an army's cattle may be distinguished according to the person who had the right of effective disposal of the cattle. By effective disposal is meant here the rights allowing one person to give cattle to another, who then becomes his client. A first category of the army's cattle comprises those of which the mwami had an effective disposal; the other three categories were those in which the rights belonged respectively to the army-chief,

112 THE PREMISE OF INEQUALITY IN RUANDA

a member of the warriors' section, and a member of the herdsmen's section.

The mwami could effectively dispose of the *nyambo* and *mabara*. *Nyambo* were cows which had some marked physical characteristics (as for instance long horns). The mere fact that beasts had such characteristics gave the king exclusive rights of disposal of them whatever may have been the previous rights of other people over them. Many lyrical poems were devoted to the praise of *nyambo* in which they are divided into two 'clans', the brown one (*ibihogo*) and the red-brown (*amagaju*) which were supposed to be in a permanent state of war.[17] A herd of *nyambo* numbered about fifty cows. There were not *nyambo* with every army. *Mabara* were ordinary cows, not fulfilling the *nyambo* qualifications, and of which the mwami had the effective disposal. One or several herds of *nyambo* and *mabara* were entrusted by the king only to certain armies.

The cows over which the army-chief had the rights of effective disposal were also considered, according to ninety-six per cent. of our informants, as army cattle and were tended by the army herdsmen.

Cattle at the effective disposal of each member of the herdsmen's section of the army were also regarded as army cattle. Here we have to distinguish between cattle possessed as a client and cattle not obtained from a lord (ninety-two per cent. of our informants said that one could have cattle which were not received from a lord). The former kind of cattle were linked to the lord's army and not to the client's army although the client had the right of usufruct and of effective disposal (as defined here) over that cattle. The latter kind of cattle was composed of cows obtained by exchange (*impahano*) which were regarded as army cows according to ninety-five per cent. of our informants; of cows given by the prospective husband to his father-in-law (*indogoranyo*) also according to ninety-five per cent.; of cows received as reward for brave conduct in war (*ingororano mu ntambara*) again according to ninety-five per cent.; of cows received as gifts (*inka z'ubuntu*) according to ninety-six per cent. Cows not kept by somebody as a client were called by the generic name of *imbata*, or, according to sixty-two per cent. of our informants, the mwami's cows (*inka z'umwami*), which is confusing.

[17] Kagame, 1947b, p. 792.

POLITICAL ORGANIZATION 113

Finally, the cattle that the warriors of an army could personally effectively dispose of were also considered as army cattle. There was a distinction between cows obtained from an overlord and *imbata*. Warriors' cattle, however, were linked to the army differently from herdsmen's: only the cattle of the latter were submitted to the different taxes I am going to examine now.

Each army had its own grazing grounds, particularly for the *nyambo*, *mabara*, and the chief's cattle as the other kinds were usually kept by those who had usufruct rights over them.[18]

(d) Tribute due by the army

Besides the personal services mentioned earlier (training, watching at the border, defending the country, foreign expeditions), each army had to provide the king, the court, and its chief with other benefits.

On a new king's accession, each patrilineage of the army had to give him a cow. This gift (*indabukirano*) showed the recognition of the authority of the person to whom it was offered. At the beginning of each reign there was also a ceremony called *murundo*, during which all the cattle of an army were numbered and presented to the king. A certain proportion was retained by him. Cattle raided by the stick-bearers (*abakoni*) of the army belonged to the king, according to eighty-seven per cent. of our informants.

Warriors and herdsmen of each army had the duty of keeping in order a part of the royal residence (*incyubagaba inkike*), according to ninety-three per cent. of our informants.

Each army was obliged to keep at the court a few cows to provide the king with fresh milk (*inkuke*). This herd was called *intamara* and was looked after by an officer, *umutware w'intamara*. According to ninety-eight per cent. of our informants, to provide *inkuke* was the duty of the herdsmen's section only. Besides they had to deliver daily to the court a certain number of milk jars (*igicuba*), according to ninety-nine per cent. A very important majority of Tutsi interviewed (eighty-nine per cent.) said that herdsmen had to supply the court with the necessary slaughter animals (*indwanyi*). Finally, each army had to provide the court with young steers used for divination purposes (*amamana*). According to fifty-five per cent. of our informants these had to be

[18] On this section, see Kagame, 1952.

114   THE PREMISE OF INEQUALITY IN RUANDA

provided by both sections of the army, according to forty-one per cent. by the herdsmen only.

All these services or dues were required only from Tutsi and from Hutu possessing cattle. Other Hutu replaced them by tributes consisting of agricultural produce (said ninety-two per cent. of our informants) and Twa by products from pottery or hunting.

The army-chief, too, could claim several dues from the army to his profit. When appointed to his charge, he was offered a cow (*indabukirano*) as a present recognizing his authority. According to a few informants, that present could consist of hoes or sheep for those who had no cattle, but ninety-two per cent. said such a present was necessarily a cow. As the king, the army-chief, when he was nominated to his office, had the right to have the cattle of his army numbered, presented to him, and a certain percentage offered to him (*murundo*). Ninety-six per cent. of our informants say that the presentation was always made at the same time as the recognition was offered. But certain informants indicate that the army-chief could not require the numbering to be done before a certain time had elapsed since the numbering for his predecessor. Moreover, according to eighty-three per cent. of our informants, the army-chief had to obtain the mwami's permission before summoning a numbering meeting. The cows kept by the army-chief were put at his effective disposal according to all informants. They were entrusted to the army herdsmen (according to eighty-eight per cent.), to army herdsmen only (according to thirty-five per cent.), and to them and *to inkomamashyi*, herdsmen alien to the army (according to fifty-three per cent.).

An army member, on certain occasions, principally when wanting to obtain a favour, used to give his chief a cow called *ituro*.

Finally, the army-chief could claim a certain part of the loot collected during an expedition in which his army had participated (*intorano*: cattle raided). Moreover, if the expedition had been a brilliant success, he received as a reward from the mwami a gift of several dozen cows.

(*e*) *Advantages for the members*

When in difficulty army members could ask for their chief's protection which could not be refused unless they had previously been disloyal to their chief. A chief could prevent a member of his

POLITICAL ORGANIZATION 115

army from being submitted to judiciary torture; he could be his surety if the member was unable to repay a debt. When one desired to obtain a favour, such as to be judged by the mwami, it was very useful to be accompanied by one's army-chief, said twenty-seven per cent. of informants. (Thirty-nine per cent., however, would have preferred to be accompanied by their lord and eighteen per cent. would have wished to have both of them.)

A client wanting to lodge a complaint against his lord requested his army-chief's intervention, according to fifty-three per cent. of the informants. (However seven per cent. thought that it was better to address the complaint to the lord's army-chief and eleven per cent. to the mwami.) A lord dissatisfied with his client could raise the question before his own army-chief according to fifty-three per cent. of the informants (thirteen per cent. would rather have gone to the client's army-chief and 9.3 per cent. to the mwami).

When a dispute concerning cattle arose between two Tutsi of the same army, it was judged by the army-chief, according to ninety-one per cent. of the informants. If the two litigants belonged to different armies, the case was settled by both army-chiefs, according to eighty-two per cent. of the informants.

The army-chief was chosen by the king and could be dismissed by him. Army members had the right to bring a charge against him at the mwami's, according to eighty-three per cent. In that case they sent delegates from the army to the court, said seventy-two per cent.

5. ANALYSIS OF THE MILITARY STRUCTURE

We are accustomed to regard an army as first 'the instrument of force in external relations'. It must defend the territory of the community against external threats and eventually attempt to expand the territory or to subdue alien groups. In Ruanda armies had other functions besides this.

(a) Warlike function

Permanent encampments established not far from the borders were defensive indeed, but they were also bases for expeditions into neighbouring territories. Whatever their frequency, it is certain that they were foci for strong feelings of admiration, pride, and emulation. Many features of these events exalted the spirit of

116   THE PREMISE OF INEQUALITY IN RUANDA

conquest: the procession of the victorious warriors, and the recitation of poems telling of the achievements of heroes. The whole country was mystically committed in the expedition through the king, the country's personification, who was magically taking part in it. The king and the queen-mother had (as the expedition leader) to sit motionless during the day of the battle (the army-chief in the field when deciding when to attack had to take into account the space of time necessary for a messenger to reach the court). The secrecy about the expeditions stressed their importance. Even after the battle was over, a messenger was sent to the court who could not tell anything about the expedition except that it was over. Then a few warriors were chosen by the army-chief to go and tell the king—and the king only—the story of the battle.

Ruanda was an aggressive neighbour. Its history, as it appears in the old traditions collected by Father Pagès for instance, is made up of numerous wars of annexation. The Abanyiginia dynasty started from about the centre of the present day Ruanda and expanded their domination progressively.

They were never permanently at peace with their neighbours, and when they had an alliance with some of them it was in order only to be free to concentrate their forces on others. They used any means that could ensure domination. In addition to direct attacks, they interfered in quarrels between smaller neighbours, helping one against the other and then overcoming both; they even murdered the chiefs and kings of small states.[19] Besides the territorial annexations they raided neighbouring countries for captives and cattle.

From the Ruanda point of view this policy of imperialism and looting did not require any rationalization. Their ethical obligations were limited to in-group relationships. One could not kill, steal from, or harm another Ruanda, but a foreigner was fair game. Ruanda people thought themselves to be quite different from people of other tribes, their land was the most important in the world and the country where Imana (the high god) came home every evening and spent the night. It was consistent with these beliefs to use out-group people for one's own purposes without the need for further justification.

The Ruanda military structure appears thus to have been in its

[19] See for instance Pagès, 1933, pp. 121 f.; pp. 298 ff.; pp. 554 ff.

POLITICAL ORGANIZATION 117

warlike role an organization for conquering and looting rather than for defence. But this warlike function was not its only one and perhaps not the most important in the appreciation of many Ruanda. Whereas almost all our informants (ninety-eight per cent.) still remember the name of the army in which their *inzu* had been incorporated first, only a smaller proportion is able to remember certain features concerning exclusively the warlike life. Only sixty-eight per cent. still know that *abakoni* were warriors whose task was to lay hold of cattle during the battle, sixty-nine per cent. that *umudende* was a badge of honour given to those who had killed seven enemies during a campaign; just fourteen per cent. can define *impotore* as the distinction granted to those who had killed fourteen enemies and merely eleven per cent. remember that *gucana uruti* (to burn the spears) was a ceremonial to honour warriors who had killed twenty-one enemies during an expedition. This less extensive knowledge of purely warlike aspects of the army is not to be accounted for merely by the fact that one does not organize raids now and that an opportunity to kill twenty-one enemies during an expedition does not arise frequently. As the whole military structure, even in its well-remembered aspects, became obsolete at about the same time as wars, the relatively poor knowledge of its warlike features suggests that the other functions of the armies were felt to be very important.

(b) Socialization

Every society is much concerned with socializing or 'encultural-izing'[20] the younger generation. Ways of life, common abilities, values, and beliefs of the group have to be inculcated into children in order to make them efficient and conforming participants of their own culture.

In Ruanda this process of socialization was formalized for Tutsi young men. During the years they spent at the court of the king or of a chief, they were systematically given education and instruction. Education is that part of a socialization process which aims at transmitting the bulk of knowledge and behaviour expected from any well-adjusted member of a group. Young Tutsi were taught the traditional sports and dances becoming to young noblemen, they were trained in poetry and the ability to carry on an eloquent and witty conversation. The great traditions of military

---

[20] Herskovits, 1948, pp. 33 ff.

118   THE PREMISE OF INEQUALITY IN RUANDA

courage of their forbears were made known to them, and the picture of the ideal Tutsi was impressed upon them.

The three main components of that ideal picture were *ubutware*, *ubugabo*, and *itonde*. *Ubutware* was the military courage so important in a group of conquerors. *Ubugabo* meant the quality of being a man (*mugabo*). This included trustworthiness in reference to promises, generosity in treating one's friends well, liberality towards the poor, moral courage to accept one's responsibilities. In a society where relations of inferiority and superiority were predominantly personal in the sense that authority was rarely abstract (a law, a principle) but generally identified with a person (chief, king, lord, &c.), emphasis was put on fidelity in all interpersonal relationships. *Itonde* could be translated by self-mastery. To lose one's temper, to manifest violent emotions was shameful. Anger, particularly, could not be violently expressed. The demeanour of a Tutsi was always to be dignified, polite, amiable, and a little supercilious. It was taken for granted that only vulgar persons showed off all their emotions. Hutu not being very self-controlled were much impressed by the external dignity of the Tutsi. There was in the *intore* companies a practical training in self-control. By jeers and scoffing, companions of the young Tutsi as well as older people, tried to make him angry and if he reacted emotionally, he was punished by further jokes. So finally he was able to remain apparently quiet and polite in any circumstances which would have elicited more violent reactions from people not thus trained.

Instruction aims at communicating a specialized knowledge and at teaching abilities in order to prepare certain individuals to fulfil the specialized tasks particularly useful to their group. The Ruanda armies instructed the young Tutsi in becoming experts in war and raiding. Some Tutsi are still proud of the superiority of their strategy over that of the Hima, pastoralists of related origin, who were living a more nomadic life in neighbouring territories.[21]

This socialization process, equipping personalities with qualities required of a nobleman, a courtier, and a warrior, was intended for Tutsi only. Hutu young men were not *intore* and did not become warriors, although Hutu were also members of the armies. But for them it meant being auxiliaries who carried the supplies

[21] On Hima, see Wilde, 1957.

PLATE 3

The late king, Charles Mutara Rudahigwa

PLATE 4

The queen-mother, Radegonde Nyiramavugo

POLITICAL ORGANIZATION 119

necessary to the warriors during the expeditions, and being liable for various services.

(c) Army and lineage

In its herdsmen's section, an army was constituted of patrilineages rather than individuals. According to 100 per cent. of the informants, the inzu head was the necessary intermediary between the army-chief and the army members of his lineage. He had the important task of apportioning the dues incumbent on the lineage between the different family heads. For instance when the numbering took place, he decided who was going to give, say, the three cows which were due by the lineage as such.

This connexion between the army, a group founded on a wide territorial basis, and the lineage, a group based on kinship, was very significant from two points of view.

Firstly, social cohesion was favoured and strengthened by the integration into one single structure of two systems which embodied different principles of grouping. In some other societies such systems remained independent. In Ruanda they formed a supple and strong network by which each Ruanda was tied to a political structure through a kinship structure.

Secondly, the authority of the inzu head over his kinsmen was limited by his incorporation in the military structure. In some circumstances an inzu member could ignore the authority of his inzu head and with the protection of his army-chief, remain independently in the army. At the numbering of cattle, for instance, he could present his own cattle separately from those of his patrilineage. This was, of course, advantageous for the chief who could claim a proportion of the cattle of the lineage plus a fraction of the cattle of the independent member. The lineage members could also bring a charge against their inzu chief before the army-chief, who could sometimes dismiss him. This limited the power of the lineage head and incited him to remain on good terms at the same time with his army-chief and the members of his inzu. This principle limiting the power of intermediary chiefs by the direct recourse of their subordinates to a superior authority had other applications in the Ruanda political organization. Its function was to reinforce the authority of the superior chief and to protect subordinates by giving them the possibility of resisting

120 THE PREMISE OF INEQUALITY IN RUANDA

their immediate superiors without endangering the principle of authority and social discipline.

From the point of view of social cohesion between the different strata of the population, it should be mentioned also that Tutsi, Hutu, and Twa were affiliated to the same army. But as the last two groups had only a secondary and not a fighting role in war, one cannot think that their association with the army was extremely important in this respect.

(d) Redistribution of wealth

Within Ruanda society, the main function of the army was that it acted as an agency for the redistribution of wealth, i.e. consumption goods and cattle.

Fresh milk provided by the *inkuke*, milk brought in jars, agricultural produce, spoils of the chase, pottery, butcher's meat, and steers utilized for divination purposes were consumption goods. Included in this category was statute labour (building and repairing royal enclosures). Most of these goods could not be kept for a long time and had thus to be provided regularly. This kind of tribute is characteristic of cultures which have neither a sufficient knowledge of the means of storing perishable goods nor a standard value of exchange permitting the dues to be collected in 'money'.

The beneficiary was the king. In this respect the army fulfilled a function very similar to that of the administrative structure.

A second category of wealth redistributed through the channel of the army was cattle. They constituted a special category of goods because of the particular significance of their possession in Ruanda society. Cattle, whatever their economic value, had a unique prestige value. One was as proud to be the owner of a beautiful herd of long-horned cows as, in some other societies, to possess race-horses. During the European Middle Ages, a noble had to have some landed property. Without going down in public estimation and losing his status, he could not have exchanged his real estate for gold and other goods of that kind even if they were 'worth' much more. Cattle in Ruanda were also noblemen's property. A Tutsi who did not own any cattle was still a Tutsi but a very poor one, dangerously slipping down in the social stratification, whereas a Hutu who possessed cattle was very near the aristocratic group and not infrequently could marry a Tutsi girl.

POLITICAL ORGANIZATION 121

The emphasis put on the social prestige bestowed by cattle ownership has sometimes led to the underestimation of a second meaning of their possession. Effective disposal of cattle was the main institutionalized means of achieving power. It certainly enables a person to secure labour and agricultural produce through the clientage structure. And at the present time, the disposal of cows gives more advantages than could be obtained by their counterpart in money.

Consequently, the redistribution of cattle operated through the army was extremely important and had much wider social implications than the dues paid in commodities.

Here, again, the mwami was the main beneficiary of the bovine tributes concentrated through the army. On his accession he received one cow as a recognition gift from every lineage, and a certain proportion of the cows presented at the numbering; after a successful campaign, the 'bow of the army' (cattle seized upon by the *abakoni*) was his. The king usually kept only the bare ownership of that cattle and granted its usufruct to important chiefs who then became his clients.

The army-chief was also much favoured in army cattle dues. He received a recognition gift on entering his office, a part from the herds presented and numbered, a certain proportion of the private booty of the warriors, rewards extended by the king after a victorious expedition, and gifts offered by army members. He had the effective disposal of these cows as long as he was in charge, that is to say, up to his death if he was not dismissed. He thus controlled a considerable amount of cattle, symbols of prestige and instruments of power. He could build up a wide clientage among army herdsmen as it was particularly among them that he chose his clients. But he could also grant his cows to non-army members (*inkomamashyi*), who then became army members.

In what measure was the ordinary army member affected by cattle? Firstly, whether warrior or herdsman, he was deprived of some of his own cows by the different payments to the king and the army-chief. Secondly, a member of the herdsmen's section could receive some cows as a client of the army-chief. Was it a real advantage? The question may be raised as the herdsman had to give cows to the chief. Obviously, there was an advantage only if he received the usufruct of more cows than he had given. This means that only a certain number of army members were very likely to

122 THE PREMISE OF INEQUALITY IN RUANDA

be favoured. This was a kind of redistribution of wealth among the lineages of the army made according to the preferences of the army-chief. Thirdly, the warriors as such did not receive cows from the army-chief (but they could be at the same time warriors and herdsmen). Their only privilege as warriors was to loot privately after the *abakoni* had laid hold on the 'bow of the army'. Moreover, if they had shown any particular gallantry, the mwami or the army-chief rewarded them with a gift of a few cows.

(e) Protection

When compared with the considerable benefits in cattle that the king and the army-chief derived from the military structure, the advantages of ordinary army members, particularly the warriors, seem to have been very meagre. The army tribute in goods and services were compensated for in a different way by the protection extended to his subordinates by the army-chief.

This protection could be asked for and received in all the difficult circumstances of life without being limited to any particular kind of circumstances. An instance frequently mentioned by our informants was the army-chief's support to one of his subordinates who was a party in a lawsuit. If the protection of a man of high standing appeared useful or necessary in such a situation one must suppose that judicial decisions were not taken only on the case's own merits, but that the respective power of the two protectors was weighed by the judge.

The army-chief's protection was diffuse and general, not limited to a few cases clearly defined. We have already come across such a characteristic of the superior's protection in respect of the chiefs of the administrative hierarchy. This suggests that power relations were emphasized in Ruanda and that the rights and properties of isolated men, that is to say those not identified in any respect with a powerful one, were insecure.

The judicial role of the army-chief must be related to his function of protection. In the disputes between two members of his army, he exercised a kind of paternal jurisdiction, as did any Ruanda authority. In contentions between members of different armies, the fact that the question was settled by the army-chiefs concerned suggests more a compromise in which each chief acted as a representative of one of the litigants, than a judgement based on pre-established norms.

POLITICAL ORGANIZATION 123

The army-chief's protection was not unconditionally granted to any army member. The chief could refuse to give support to one of his subordinates if he had been disobedient or disloyal. It was up to the chief himself to decide if his warrior or herdsman had an objectionable attitude. The fact that the chief was the only judge of the attitude did not, of course, give the subordinate the assurance of a fair treatment; however, the chief could not indulge often in arbitrary refusals of help because a member could always leave the army and join another if allowed to do so by the chief of this other army. Moreover, the principle of recourse to a superior authority against an intermediate authority was operative here also. If discontent was widespread in an army, the chief could be dismissed by the mwami. Consequently the chief had to take into account public opinion to some extent and could not be indifferent to his popularity. It is clear, however, that the means of pressure that a chief did have on his subordinates were more efficient than the ones subordinates had on him. They had thus to assume a submissive attitude and to gain the chief's favour by gifts and proper behaviour.

*   *   *

The different functions of the military structure of Ruanda were profitable mainly to the rulers: they contributed to the maintenance in power positions of those who were occupying them. Through that structure, the king secured, in addition to what he received from his tax collectors, an important amount of commodities (necessary for the upkeep of a numerous court), more cattle (consequently the possibility to increase the number of people personally bound to him), and a more complete control of all the chiefs under him (by the possibility of a direct recourse of the subordinates to the royal supreme authority). The ruling position of the army-chiefs was also consolidated by their increase of control on cattle.

The preceding analysis has also disclosed how the army was an important instrument of domination for the Tutsi caste. Warriors being recruited only among Tutsi, organized physical force was exclusively theirs. They alone had in their hands the ultimate basis of political power. Moreover, by the serious training of the *intore*, the aristocratic values and virtues so well adapted for domination were inculcated into the new generations.

The army organization was also a factor for maintenance of the

124   THE PREMISE OF INEQUALITY IN RUANDA

social order by the protective function of the army-chiefs. A minimum of individual security must be granted to every member of a society. The support of the army-chief secured partly that minimum of security. The protection against incursions of enemies was also provided by the army as such. Finally, the participation of Hutu and Twa in foreign expeditions, although extremely restricted, certainly contributed to the formation of a Ruanda 'national' feeling.

6. THE CENTRAL GOVERNMENT

In the administrative and military structures, the king was the supreme political authority of Ruanda. Very closely associated with him was the queen-mother, who had an official role in the political sphere. Next, the highest dignitaries of the kingdom were the *biru*, guardians of traditions concerning the important events of the collective life of Ruanda. Finally, there was the council of the great chiefs. These four institutions may be regarded as having constituted the main element of the central government of Ruanda.

(a) *The king*

The theory of the Ruanda kingship was that the mwami was an absolute monarch in the fullest sense. There was no stated limit to his powers over the inhabitants, cattle, land, and even commodities of his country. His powers were not delegated by any authority and thus he had not to render an account of them to anybody. He was the supreme judge: his sentences were without appeal. He was the legislator having the right to change customs.

This theory of the king's powers was founded on their divine origin as mentioned earlier. The bami (plural of mwami) were very careful not to let their subjects forget their heavenly origin. Many rites stressed that they did not participate in the common nature of other men. This was also the reason why special words were used to indicate their common activities and the everyday objects they used (as for 'to get up', 'it is raining on the king's hut', 'his bed', 'his house', etc.). It was thus emphasized that in spite of their appearances, these activities and objects were fundamentally different from what they were for ordinary people.[22]

In fact the king's powers were of course limited. He had to respect the vested interests of important Tutsi lineages, he had to

[22] Pagès, 1933, pp. 491 f.

POLITICAL ORGANIZATION 125

refrain from decisions which could have impaired the economic production of the country, such as requiring tributes which were too heavy, or which could have lowered the level of personal security to such an extent that people would have preferred to flee abroad.[23] Moreover, profound legislative modifications would have roused the resistance of the *biru*. Nevertheless, his powers were still extremely great. A fact which reinforced and consolidated them was the tradition of the long past of the dynasty. The present mwami, Mutara III Rudahigwa is regarded as the fortieth king of Ruanda. Even if the first twenty names are considered as legendary, three or four centuries is a considerable past for a dynasty. The Abanyiginya clan has indeed been able to keep the kingship of Ruanda as long as kings are remembered.

The mwami was not only of divine origin but he was Ruanda personified. This mystical identification with the country resulted in numerous avoidances and a very careful behaviour was expected from the mwami. What happened to him would reverberate, as it were, over the country. He should not bend his knees, for instance, lest Ruanda's territory would shrink.

Royal succession was not completely fixed by custom. The heir was chosen by the king from among his sons. He was generally one of the youngest because the strength of Ruanda was magically connected with the king's strength. The name of the chosen one was kept secret. Even the future mwami did not know it. It was revealed only after the king's death by the three most important biru whom the mwami had entrusted with his decision. The other sons and their mothers generally did not agree willingly to the choice and there was often a period of unrest, even of civil war, before the new mwami became an effective ruler.[24]

A new name was given to the new king, one of the five royal names which were chosen according to the same sequence: Cyrilima, Kigeli, Nibambwe, Yuhi, Mutara. The kings named Cyilima, Yuhi, and Mutara were called 'peaceful bami'. They were not allowed to cross the Nyabarongo, a river which runs in the centre of the country, not far from Nyanza, the capital, and this symbolized the fact that they should not send their armies abroad. This rule very wisely allowed the country to recuperate and to assimilate new territories conquered during a preceding warlike reign.

[3] Maquet, 1955.   [24] See Gluckman, 1954, p. 8.

126 THE PREMISE OF INEQUALITY IN RUANDA

The symbol of kingship was Kalinga, the sacred drum. To possess this drum meant to be king. Kalinga was regularly sprinkled with the blood of the animals used for divination. Around Kalinga were hung the genitals of Ruanda enemies killed by the bami. Kalinga was never beaten but other drums were beaten in its honour as they were beaten for the king.[25]

(b) The queen-mother

It was essential that the role of queen-mother (*umugabekasi*) should always be fulfilled. If the mwami's mother's death occurred when her son was still living, he had to be given another 'mother'. The queen-mother had no special task, but she shared the royal prerogatives. She lived at the king's capital where she had her own court, and her protection was eagerly sought. She had herds of cattle and clients. But her role should not be regarded as independent of that of the king.

It can be said that the same kingship was realized by two persons at the same time, without any division of responsibilities or privileges. This was expressed by the term often used to designate together the mwami and his mother: the kings (*abami*). In that partnership the king, however, kept a predominant position: when he died, his mother completely lost her powers.

(c) The biru

The *biru* did not constitute a council or a board. They were dignitaries with different tasks and very strictly ranked in a fixed hierarchy. Their activities, however, in common were concerned with the preservation of ritual knowledge and the accomplishment of ceremonies essential to the existence of Ruanda and its government. This knowledge and activities were kept secret from everybody who was not a *mwiru* (singular of *biru*).

Biru were under the king's authority in the sense that he could create new offices of *mwiru* and he could dismiss one of them who had been disloyal. The royal control was limited to this. It was really the minimum without which *biru* would have been completely independent of the mwami. The offices were hereditary and even when a *mwiru* had been dismissed one of his sons succeeded him. As we have seen previously, their domains were exempt from any interference of the land- or cattle-chief.

[25] Vanhove, 1941, pp. 88 f. See the series of photographs in Maquet, 1957.

POLITICAL ORGANIZATION 127

The most important *biru* were the three to whom the king communicated the name of his successor and the recommendations he wanted them to transmit to the new king later. There were about a dozen main *biru* offices. These important *biru* had assistants from their lineages, prospective successors whom they gradually trained in order that the oral traditions should not be lost.

Biru had to memorize secret rules, governing for instance the order according to which queens would be chosen from different descent groups, the ritual to observe in case of spreading of cattle disease, lack of abundance of rain, warlike ceremonies, celebrations of the sorghum harvests, &c.

The *biru* institution safeguarded the interests of the great Tutsi descent groups. This function appears clearly in the determination made for several reigns in advance of the secondary lineages and clans from which the queens should be successively chosen. The *biru*, as representatives of their kinship groups had, as it were, established the order in which the interests of different clans and lineages would be favoured in turn.

No one *mwiru* knew the entire body of customs. That knowledge was divided into parts, the remembering of each being entrusted to a *mwiru*, that is to say a descent group, as the office was hereditary. In this way it may be said that the exclusive knowledge of a part of the most important Ruanda ritual had become almost the property of each great Tutsi descent group.

A second function of the *biru* institution was to secure the continuity and the prevalence of the tradition which could have been endangered by the very considerable powers of the king. That traditional body was not unlike a constitution in a modern state and the *biru* institution could be said to have had a role similar to that of a supreme court judging whether a new rule is compatible with the fundamental charter of the country. Of course they had explicitly neither such a task nor such institutionalized means to prevent the mwami from establishing new rules, but the disapproval of an innovation by the *biru* was not to be taken lightly as they represented the great Tutsi kinship groups.

To assess more exactly the function of this institution, one should know more about it. The present day *biru* are still very reluctant to provide information and still less to let it be published, in spite of the encouragement to do so that they receive from the king.[26]

[26] See Kagame, 1947a.

128 THE PREMISE OF INEQUALITY IN RUANDA

(d) *The council of the high chiefs*

The most important chiefs were called *batware w'intebe*, which means chiefs with a stool. Sometimes, especially in times of crisis, the king summoned them and they were consulted on the situation.[27]

It seems that the patterns of behaviour in the face-to-face relationships with an authority, particularly the supreme one, were such that an opinion opposed to that of the mwami was very unlikely to be voiced. Consequently, the main use of that council appears to have been for the king to explain what he wanted to do and to elicit suggestions on the means of carrying it out.

One of these chiefs was called the 'favourite counsellor' and acted as a sort of prime minister to the king. Besides the tasks he fulfilled by helping the mwami in administering the kingdom, the favoured counsellor's role included the most useful function of taking the blame for what the mwami did wrong. As the king was divine and essentially good, he could never be criticized even by those who suffered from one of his decisions. To relieve the tensions raised by an arbitrary action of the king, however, it was better that the responsibility for it could be imputed to somebody else. The favourite counsellor was that scapegoat: the victims of a royal decision and their friends could go on saying that the king was good but that his favourite counsellor was very bad and cruel and responsible for what they had suffered. This aspect of the favourite counsellor's role was no small contribution to the feelings of trust that Ruanda had for their ruler.

[27] Maquet and Hertefelt, 1959, chap. 1.

CHAPTER VI

THE CLIENTAGE STRUCTURE

I. DESCRIPTION OF THE *BUHAKE* INSTITUTION

T HE *buhake* is an institution to which anthropologists who have studied Ruanda social structure have devoted a great part of their attention, if not the greatest. The name is not easily translated. *Buhake* comes from *guhakwa*, a verb meaning 'to pay one's respects to a superior in his court'.[1] It has been called cattle-lease (*bail à cheptel*),[2] recommendation (in the sense of the mediaeval latin *recommendatio*),[3] and contract of pastoral servitude.[4]

The *buhake* denoted the relation which existed between a person called *garagu* and another called *shebuja*. That relationship was created when an individual, Hutu or Tutsi, who had an inferior social prestige and who was less well provided with cattle, offered his services to and asked protection from a person whose status was higher and whose wealth was greater. The following sentences were usually, but not ritually said by the man offering his services, after he had given a jug of beer or hydromel to the other: *urampe amata* (I ask you milk), *urankize* (make me rich), *uramenye* (always think of me), *urambere umubyeyi* (be my father), *n'ange nzakubera umwana* (I shall be your child).

If the offer was accepted, the man in the superior position bestowed on the other one or several cows. From that time on, they were in the institutionalized relation of *shebuja* (which I translate 'lord' or 'patron') and *garagu* ('client').

(a) The client's rights

The rights the client enjoyed over the cattle granted to him were those of usufruct: he had full rights of ownership over milk, the male increase of the cattle, and the meat and skin of a cow which had died or had had to be slaughtered. The female increase of the cattle remained at his disposal under the same conditions as the original cows given to him by the *shebuja*. Cows received

---

[1] Sandrart, 1930, p. 151. [2] Vanhove, 1941, p. 48; Bourgeois, 1958.
[3] De Lacoer, 1939, vol. I, p. 45. [4] Kagame, 1952, p. 18.

130 THE PREMISE OF INEQUALITY IN RUANDA

from a patron could be granted by the client to somebody else by another *buhake* agreement in which the original client became a lord.

The protection granted by the patron included support in lawsuits (*kulengera*): according to thirty-nine per cent. of our informants, it was usual and very useful to be accompanied by one's *shebuja* if one wanted to be judged by the mwami. Moreover the patron extended help to his client if the latter was in a state of poverty. For instance, he gave milk for the *garagu*'s children if their father's cows did not yield enough; he contributed to the payment of the bride-wealth if the client and his lineage could not meet the expenses; he provided his Hutu *garagu* with a hoe when it was needed; he granted meat and hides to his client if, on certain occasions, they were badly needed. When the *garagu* committed an offence, his lord had to help him out of his predicament by paying the fine or the compensation to the victim (*kugura*).[5] If the client was murdered and his lineage was too weak to do anything about it, the *shebuja* had to demand justice from the mwami or even avenge his death by blood feud (*kumuhorera*). Finally, if, after the *garagu*'s death, his widow and children could not be taken care of by his brothers or parallel cousins, the lord had to help them (*kumuremera*).

(b) The client's obligations

On the other hand, the client had to go and pay his respects to his lord. This included personal service which required the presence of the client at the patron's rugo for a certain time. Some obligations were common to Hutu and Tutsi *garagu*. They were: to accompany the *shebuja* when he was travelling, for instance when he went to the king's court or participated in a military expedition (*kumutabaraho*); to carry the lord's messages (*gutumwa*); to build or repair a part of the *shebuja*'s rugo (*kubak' inkike*). It was advisable also for clients, Hutu as well as Tutsi, to offer from time to time to their patron, some presents such as jugs of beer. If the lord happened to lose his herds, the *garagu* had to provide him with cattle and jars of milk. Some services were imposed only on Hutu clients, such as working in the *shebuja*'s fields (*kutanga imibyizi*), or joining the night watch in the lord's enclosure (*kurarira*).[6]

[5] Cf. Vanhove, 1941, p. 77s.
[6] Cf. Sandrart, 1930, p. 152; Vanhove, 1941, p. 75s.

THE CLIENTAGE STRUCTURE 131

The measure of the different obligatory gifts and services (number of days, &c.), was not fixed. It depended on the *shebuja*'s temper, his requirements, the number of cows granted to the *garagu*, and on the client's expectations. Moreover, each client was usually not requested to fulfil all the obligations we have just mentioned. The patron, particularly if he had many *garagu*, frequently gave to each of them a precise task in which the client was particularly competent (to brew beer, to cook, to mind the cattle, &c.). Even now, in spite of the limitations added by the native courts to the clients' obligations (for instance the building and repairing of the enclosure cannot be claimed by the lord more than once a year; not more than a month a year may be required by the patron for all the household services, &c.), we are still far from having a list of precisely defined duties and claims standard for the whole of Ruanda.

(c) *End of the* buhake *relation*

The *buhake* relationship was perpetuated even after the death of both parties. The *shebuja*'s heirs inherited their father's relations of *buhake*, *vis-à-vis* his clients and the client's heirs kept the cows (and/or their progeny) granted to their father. But the *shebuja* had the right to refuse to recognize as a successor of his client a person without the proper qualities to be a good *garagu*. The lord could then designate another heir of his client, or end the relationship and take back the cows. The person receiving an important number of clients by inheritance (several dozen, for instance) could require them to present him with all the cows which were then numbered, as in the case of the army-chief's *murundo*; he could then choose a certain number of them, usually the best ones, which he took away from his clients either to keep the usufruct himself or to endow other people with them.

The *buhake* relation could be ended when both client and patron or only one of them wanted this. But the person who initiated the breaking off usually gave some reason for it, such as the non-fulfilment of a particular obligation by the other party. At all events the *shebuja* could not oblige his client to stay in his service and the client could not prevent his patron from dismissing him.

What happened to the cows in such a case? As mentioned earlier, all the cows a client effectively controlled were not necessarily received from a patron, that is to say they were not all *inkazibiti*

132 THE PREMISE OF INEQUALITY IN RUANDA

when the client was Hutu and *ingabane* when he was Tutsi. A *garagu* could have cows from another source (called *imbata*) such as those received as bride-wealth, as a reward for bravery or acquired by exchanging other goods. In the case of a Hutu client, who possessed both *inkazibiti* and *imbata* at the time when his relation with a *shebuja* was broken off, there are two opinions with regard to the cows' ownership. According to the first, the *imbata* possessed by the client before he entered in the *buhake* relation were regarded as *inkazibiti* and consequently the lord had the same rights over them as over those he had given to the client as cows of *buhake*. Moreover, the cows which the client eventually acquired when he was already *garagu*, and which in other circumstances would have been regarded as *imbata*, were also added to the cows received from the lord. The result was that at the breaking off of the *buhake* relation, the patron could take all his client's cows, *imbata* as well as *inkazibiti*. The other opinion is that the *imbata* acquired by the client before or after the *buhake* relation began, remained definitely *imbata* and that the lord had no claim on them.

It seems that both opinions are accurate, but that they refer to different periods. The second probably expresses the most ancient rule which had been prevalent up to about 1920. The practice of merging *imbata* and *inkazibiti* (or *ingabane*) in favour of the lord is likely to have been introduced only during the last forty years. This would be due to the fact that the chiefs of the administrative divisions (recognized by the Belgian authority under the names of *chefferies* and *sous-chefferies*) assumed at the end of the reign of king Yuhi Musinga (who was dismissed from his royal charge by the Belgian Administration in 1931) an undue importance, because their powers were no longer counterbalanced by those of the chiefs of the other hierarchies. Army chiefs did not enjoy their former authority, as the military structure had received no official recognition; Musinga, isolated in an attitude of indifference and hostility towards Europeans, was left without much effective power. Administrative chiefs who were important lords are said to have taken advantage of this situation, and to have modified the custom to their own advantage by establishing the principle of the merging of the cows received from the lord with those acquired independently of any *shebuja*.

It was not impossible, though it was rare, to be the client of

THE CLIENTAGE STRUCTURE   133

more than one lord, I was told. Firstly, the services required were such that it was not easy for the same person to perform them twofold. Secondly, a lord did not like to enter into *buhake* relations with somebody who was already the client of another *shebuja*, because such an arrangement was very likely to result in a considerable lessening of each lord's control on his client.

2. ANALYSIS OF THE CLIENTAGE STRUCTURE

(a) *Notion of feudality*

If the term 'feudal' is to be legitimately applied to the social structure described in the preceding section, it must be understood as a notion covering more than the historical sense of that term as used when referring to the Western Middle Ages. Feudality is here an 'ideal-type' in the Weberian sense.

Feudality is a particular ordering of certain human relations. This organization is based on an agreement between two individuals who unequally partake in the symbols of wealth and power culturally recognized in their society. The person who, in that respect, is inferior to the other, asks the other for his patronage, and, as a counterpart, offers his services. This is the essence of the feudal régime which must be found in any social system qualified by that term. Feudality is manifold in its modalities. The latter differ in many respects. For instance, obligations of each party may vary and be more or less definite in measure; the symbols and proofs of the feudal relation may be very dissimilar. Thus, in the European Middle Ages, the symbol and the proof of the feudal agreement was the tenure of a tract of land granted by the man in the superior position to the other. That piece of land was called a fief and the parties concerned became suzerain and vassal as soon as the tenure had been granted and accepted.

It seems that the qualification 'feudal' may be applied to the organization of social relations between a *shebuja* and a *garagu* described in the preceding section. At the root of that relation, there are two individuals having a different social status. From one of these individuals, there is a demand for aid and protection, and from the other a promise of assistance in counterpart of services. Granting the usufruct of a few cows to the man of inferior status is the symbol and proof of the agreement.

The word 'agreement' is employed here rather than 'contract' which is more frequently used in this connexion. I do not consider

134   THE PREMISE OF INEQUALITY IN RUANDA

that the kind of covenant in which the bond *shebuja-garagu* originated can be said to be a contract in the sense given to that term of Roman law and legal systems which are derived from it. There are three main differences between a contract and the *buhake* agreement.

Firstly, the freedom not to enter into such an agreement was socially illusory. In a society such as that of Ruanda, it was most inadvisable to be found without a patron. As a proverb put it, 'a dog is not feared for his fangs, but for his lord'. To live without a lord was to invite trouble.

Secondly, the lord and the client faced very different situations when *buhake* relationships had to be ended. When he wanted to break off the relation, the *shebuja* either did not give any reason or more frequently accused the *garagu* of a breach of the agreement because in that case, even if there was no merging of *imbata* and *inkazibiti* cows, he could take one or two more cows as a sort of fine. Then he recovered the cows that he himself or one of his ascendents had granted to the client. Sometimes a client accused of a breach could manage to obtain protection elsewhere, and to bring the case before a court, whereas the *shebuja* was under no obligation to present the proof of his client's misdemeanour before punishing him by seizing the cows. He was thus in a very favourable situation if, for one reason or another, he coveted some of his client's cows, or if he merely wanted to harm him. Nevertheless, informants say that a lord could not take too much advantage of his capacity to punish and despoil his clients without incurring implicit social sanctions. If he got the reputation of being a bad *shebuja*, people who were considering a *buhake* agreement were led to choose another lord.

In the reverse situation, when a client wanted to terminate the *buhake* relation with his lord, he certainly could do so, but he incurred the risk of being deprived of some of his *imbata* and if he had grievances against his lord, it was certainly not easy for him to obtain redress. Here again, however, the situation could be corrected by the interplay of the safeguards that an able and cunning man did not fail to secure. Supported by his army-chief, his lineage head or his cattle-chief, he could obtain more favourable results. But even if these counterbalances had some efficacy, it remains that the lord and the client, because of these very different conditions, did not enjoy that equal freedom to end the

PLATE 5

The dynastic drums, with enemies' trophies

PLATE 6

A Hutu diviner

THE CLIENTAGE STRUCTURE 135

relationship which should be enjoyed by both parties according to the classical definition of contract.

A third way in which *buhake* was different from the Western conception of contract lay in the vagueness and uncertainty in the measure of the reciprocal obligations. The patron could be more or less generous in the number of cows he granted, more or less exacting in the services he required; the client could be more or less prompt and zealous in his service. If there was a dispute about these differences in the execution of the agreement, there was no charter one could refer to for an assessment of rights and duties.

(b) Caste structure

To understand the functions of the feudal system in Ruanda society, one must first clarify some important features of that society.

As our descriptions and analysis of Ruanda proceed, it becomes more and more certain that there was there a caste structure or something very similar to it. Sociologists usually define a caste society as one composed of several graded groups, each of which is endogamous and practising an hereditary occupation, membership of which can be obtained only by birth.[7]

Birth was, indeed, the usual way in which one became a Tutsi, a Hutu or a Twa. This does not mean that the three strata were 'racial' units, but that an individual was a Tutsi, a Hutu or a Twa when his father was a Tutsi, a Hutu or a Twa. In the same way was his father a Tutsi, a Hutu or a Twa. But in order to avoid such expressions, which could go on *ad infinitum,* a definition other than an hereditary one should be found. But it does not seem that there is any other than that a Tutsi, a Hutu or a Twa is a person who regarded himself, and was regarded by all those who knew him, as a Tutsi, a Hutu or a Twa, the usual way for a person to fulfil this social definition being to realize the hereditary one. In some cases, however, it was possible to be socially recognized as a Tutsi without having been begotten by a Tutsi father. For instance a Twa who had been ennobled or the son of a rich Hutu cattle owner and of a Tutsi woman, was sometimes regarded as a Tutsi. But these were exceptional cases and we may say that the caste criterion of membership by birth held in general for all the three Ruanda groups.

The same may be said of the criterion of endogamy. We saw

[7] Cf. Lowie, 1948, pp. 10, 273.

K

136 THE PREMISE OF INEQUALITY IN RUANDA

previously that marriages between Hutu and Tutsi were not banned but that they were neither favoured nor frequent. Marriages between Twa and the two other groups were prohibited.

Since cattle rearing, agriculture, and hunting, with pot making, were the main activities characteristic of our three strata, the criterion of hereditary occupation was certainly realized in Ruanda.

The fourth criterion, the hierarchy of the groups within the society, was certainly to be seen in Ruanda. We must, however, consider more closely what kind of ranking existed between the castes.

Social power has been previously defined as an interpersonal relation in which each of the human actors, because he belongs to a different group or stratum of the same society, is able to exert pressure on the other. One occupies a postition of power over somebody, not because of personal qualities or the specific social role one fulfils or one's wealth, but only because one is a member of a certain group. The two human terms of the relation do not stand on their own personal merits but as representatives of their groups. Personal characteristics do not matter, only the identification with a group.

This notion of social power which operates in interpersonal relations is based on social power regarded from the collective point of view. Collectively, social power is the intergroup relation in which one of the two groups may inflict on the other a severe loss. It is the pressure exerted by one group as such on another.

The three Ruanda castes were in a hierarchic order, then, from the standpoint of social power, both collective and individual. The Tutsi caste could as a group inflict severe deprivations on the Hutu or Twa castes, and any individual Tutsi could exert strong pressure on any Hutu or Twa irrespective of their personal qualities and possessions.

Let us now turn to the function of the feudal system in Ruanda.

(c) Protection by identification

To live in a society where several castes very unequal in their social power coexist, frequently puts the individuals of the weaker groups in a very difficult position. Indeed, anybody may be at any time confronted with an exacting demand made on him by somebody possessing higher social power. To be protected against such

THE CLIENTAGE STRUCTURE 137

a demand, it is indispensable for the person submitted to it to increase his own social power. It is impossible to do this directly as he cannot, except very rarely, enter into the upper caste, but he may obtain it indirectly by succeeding in identifying himself with a person endowed with great social power. Feudality is an institutionalization of that identification of an individual socially weak, with another, socially powerful, who secures for the former the necessary protection against other socially powerful individuals.

Is it not possible, in a caste society, to protect the persons enjoying little social power by other means than a clientage system?

The political power of the superior group could be limited by preventing that group from using the pressure of legitimate physical force. For instance, it could be made illegal for a person of the upper group to force somebody to work for him under the threat of having him imprisoned or beaten if he refused. This solution was aimed at in the nineteenth-century Western liberal state. There the groups were not castes but classes, defined both by amount of wealth and the type of its usage (capital investment versus consumer goods buying). The difference between classes and castes is irrelevant at this stage of our argument. According to its Marxist critics, that solution has not succeeded in preventing the domination of the economically weak group by the economically powerful one. If, they said, a rich man is not allowed to force another one to work for him under the threat of police, he may force him as effectively by the threat of taking his livelihood from him. Consequently, the Marxists proposed another solution to make the economic power of all individuals equal.

It is clear that both solutions attempt to solve the problem of the protection of socially weak individuals by changing the hierarchic structure of the society. In the liberal solution the dominant group is stripped of its political privileges, which makes it weaker as a superior group; in the Marxist solution, it is deprived of its preponderant social power, and completely disappears. It seems that a clientage institution is the only means permitting the protection of socially weak individuals without destroying the unequal participation of the groups in social power. In that system the groups continue to be endowed with an unequal collective social power, whereas the range of variability in individual social power

138 THE PREMISE OF INEQUALITY IN RUANDA

is made narrower in order to give everybody the opportunity of obtaining sufficient personal security.

Such was, it appears, the first function of the *buhake* system in Ruanda. In that society where it was advisable to go into court accompanied by socially powerful persons, and when a Hutu possessing some wealth but no protector was risking the loss of his possessions, the feudal organization, by institutionalizing the identification of the Hutu client with the Tutsi lord, secured the necessary protection and security for the socially weak. With a few exceptions, the Twa were outside that feudal system. Their caste occupations were not compatible with cattle-rearing and made available to them other means of obtaining the personal protection of upper caste people. On the other hand, their small number made that kind of protection very effective.

(d) Social cohesion

A second function of the feudality in Ruanda was its contribution to the cohesion of the society.

In this respect we have to distinguish the feudal agreements in which clients were Hutu from those in which they were Tutsi. Let us first take the former. In order that two castes whose interests were so often divergent or opposed could constitute a stable unitary structure, it was necessary that they should not remain merely juxtaposed but should show some solidarity. Through the feudal relations economic currents flowed between Hutu and Tutsi: the land tillers had at their disposal some cattle; the pastoralists consumed agricultural produce and had fields cultivated by their servants and clients. In this way the economic system of production in Ruanda was mixed, made up of techniques, abilities, and wealth brought by the two groups. Through *buhake*, Hutu participated in the Tutsi values. They valued cattle very highly and entered the prestige system based on bovine possession. They assimilated some Tutsi alimentary habits, such as drinking milk. Feudality proved a very effective instrument for the constitution of a culture common to all Ruanda.

When there was a feudal agreement between two Tutsi, the *buhake* had another relevance to social cohesion. It may be said that any Tutsi client was also a lord and any Tutsi lord was also a client. The mwami was the only patron who was nobody's client. His *garagu* were the great Tutsi chiefs, the lords of less important

THE CLIENTAGE STRUCTURE 139

Tutsi, who themselves were patrons of still less important Tutsi, and so on. In this way the Tutsi consituted a homogeneous unit of individuals linked to one another by bonds of fidelity and protection. From that point of view, *buhake* contributed to the unity and the solidarity of the aristocratic caste.

(e) Maintenance of caste privileges

Besides the protection of socially weak individuals and the promotion of social cohesion, a third function was fulfilled by the feudal system: the maintenance of the social *status quo* and the perpetuation of Tutsi privileges. This function seems somewhat opposed to the first two. Let us see how all these functions have been combined by the *buhake* system.

In a stratified society where control of a category of goods or a type of ownership is characteristic of the superior layer, the access of the members of other groups to these goods or to the particular rights of ownership constitutes an active factor of social mobility. It is the reason why the aristocracy frequently keeps exclusively for itself these goods and these rights. Thus in Ankole the Hima pastoralists bar Iru cultivators from the ownership of productive cows. They may possess only barren cows and bull calves.[8]

Ruanda Tutsi did not impose such severe rules but by the *buhake* system they obtained very much the same results. They allowed Hutu to have cattle at their disposal—which in exchange provided Tutsi with labour and agricultural produce—but at the same time prevented them from gaining independent ownership rights over these cattle. Those who had the final control of cattle were always Tutsi. As the Hutu had been granted only usufruct rights over cattle which were different from those enjoyed by the lords who were Tutsi, there was no chance that the group of cattle owners could be invaded by Hutu.

By definition the client's possession was precarious. This uncertainty in the duration of the disposal of cattle was further emphasized by the circumstances mentioned above. The breaking off of the *buhake* relation was almost always favourable mainly to the lord and could often be disastrous for the client. It may even be said that when the practice of merging the *buhake* cows (*inkazi-biti*) with the cows not received from a lord (*imbata*) was regarded as customary, all the Hutu cattle were precariously held and under

[8] Oberg, 1940, p. 130.

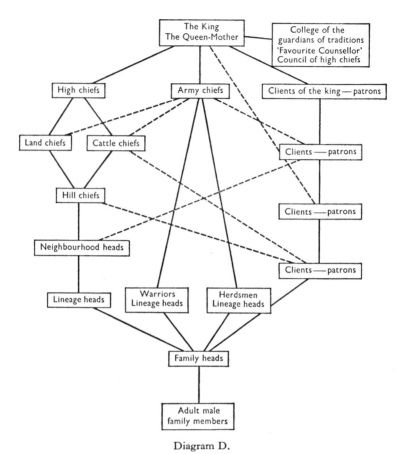

Diagram D.

This diagram suggests the complexity of Ruanda social relations if it is remembered that an individual generally has several political roles. Thus a high chief was very often also an army chief as well as a client of the king, and all the chiefs of the two premier hierarchies had their places in the system of feudal relations as clients and patrons. The broken lines indicate some of these possible pluralities of relationships.

THE CLIENTAGE STRUCTURE 141

Tutsi control. A Hutu who in exchange for labour or agricultural goods had been able to acquire a few cows had necessarily to ask for the protection of a lord in order that his cows should not be seized upon under some pretence by a socially powerful neighbour. Then he received cows from his lord and they were merged with his own *imbata*. Consequently, if the agreement had to be ended, the lord could take away besides the cows he had granted, those which had previously belonged to the client.

The two political structures benefited most those among the Tutsi who were rulers. The feudal structure, by granting only a precarious possession of cattle to the clients, left in the hands of the Tutsi the ultimate control of cattle, symbol of social prestige and instrument of power. On the other hand, by the same *buhake*, Tutsi were obtaining the advantages of being provided with labour and agricultural produce. From that standpoint, the Ruanda feudal system granted a minority the means to live—and to live better than the bulk of the population—without having to participate in the manual labour of economic production, by the moderate and clever exploitation of the majority.

In order that an aristocratic structure may perpetuate itself without change as long as it is profitable to the superior caste, it is not sufficient to prevent an invasion or even an infiltration of members of inferior groups who, by modifying the proportion between exploiters and exploited, would completely disturb the smooth working of the system. It is also necessary that all those who are by birth members of the upper caste should live according to the standards of their group. It is most unusual for an upper caste to regard the falling off of some of its members without uneasiness and dismay. This is particularly true when the group position of power is rationalized in terms of innate superiority. Some modern governments in Africa, for example, are much concerned about the 'poor whites' because their decadence threatens the myth of the white racial superiority.

The Tutsi had a similar pretence to a natural superiority as has been pointed out already. Consequently, if one of them was unable to support himself in a way becoming to his caste and seemed on the point of slipping down into the group of those who work manually, it was regarded as a shocking situation that should at once be put right. The remedy was to become the client of a richer Tutsi. The cows thus received, allowed him to subsist in

142   THE PREMISE OF INEQUALITY IN RUANDA

such a way that he could become the patron of a few Hutu who would work for him and cultivate his fields. On the other hand, while the lord of such a Tutsi would not get many material advantages from him, his social prestige was enhanced by an increase in his following, and by being advised by a trusty Tutsi he was able to exert a greater influence in the different intrigues which played such an important part in his life.

(f) Feudal and political structures

We have said earlier that the Ruanda clientage system occupied an intermediate position between the public and private spheres. It must now appear more clearly why *buhake* was not just a private agreement between two persons, such as a loan. The element of pressure, although not going usually as far as the use of physical force, was certainly an important aspect of that relationship. There was also a constant interplay of the feudal structure of the two political ones (administrative and military). When, as frequently happened, one was at the same time administratively subjected to and a client of one's hill-chief, a client's obligations were not merely added to a subject's tribute: the total amount was reduced. This was a very favourable situation for the subject-client. All the great political chiefs were also rich lords. Their political offices helped them to increase their clientage, as is particularly evident in the case of the army-chief who could require cows from the army members merely in order to be able to gain more clients. On the other hand their wealth helped them to obtain important offices and to keep them.

It would be impossible, for these reasons, to describe adequately the working of the two political structures in Ruanda without describing the feudal system as well. It might even be said that the *buhake* is more fundamental in the sense that many political relations have been patterned on the client—lord relation. For instance, the army chief was really a lord for the members of the herdsmen's section of his army.

In spite of the psychological and perhaps historical precedence of the feudal system, it has been described after political organization because, as I wish to focus attention on the political organization, it seemed that the role of the feudal system in that respect would emerge more clearly.

CHAPTER VII

THE PROBLEM OF TUTSI DOMINATION

AT the beginning of this century, after an historical development of which we can at the most have only a glimpse,
Ruanda society appeared to be composed of two main
strata, the Hutu and Tutsi castes. The latter was dominant in
social power and used it to exploit economically the former and to
retain political power exclusively.

This system of the social domination of a caste and of the
political domination of a group within that caste seemed to be
successful and stable at the beginning of the twentieth century.
How did the Tutsi achieve the difficult task of keeping such a
large caste kingdom a working concern? Before considering the
social structural factors which were operative one must take into
account the frame in which and the background against which the
problem of domination had to be solved. By frame and background,
is understood here the totality of circumstances which appeared to
the Tutsi, and were for them, unalterable. Tutsi had to adapt
their pattern of domination to these circumstances as they were
in any event beyond their control. These circumstances were
very numerous, pertaining to physical environment (ecological),
to human biology, and even to the culture of the group. What
these very various elements had in common was that, at the time
referred to in this study, they set limits to the action and ways of
life of the group. Some of these limits were not immutable in
themselves but they were so none the less for the Tutsi at the
beginning of the twentieth century.

From this vast congeries of natural, biological, and cultural
factors, I shall review only a few which appear most significant
from the present point of view: that of the conditions of domination.

I. FRAME AND BACKGROUND OF THE DOMINATION SYSTEM

A first relevant background fact was that, apart from the
ultimate control of a most valuable resource, namely, cattle (a
subject which will be discussed later), the difference between the
equipment of Tutsi and Hutu was not very considerable. It is

144 THE PREMISE OF INEQUALITY IN RUANDA

possible that when Tutsi first came into the country, the difference was greater than at the beginning of this century. It was not, however, to be compared with the difference existing, for instance, between the material culture of the Europeans in Central Africa and of the Africans during the nineteenth century and at the present time. A large and complex material culture is one of the most important factors not only in conquest but also in the maintenance of a dominant group's superiority. Motor vehicles, dwellings in permanent materials, electric power, European kinds of food are so fundamentally different from the traditional Central African means of transportation and habitat that it is easy for those who have the almost exclusive use of them to maintain high prestige and great power.

Except for cattle, Tutsi material equipment did not allow them to impress on Hutu minds, to a comparable extent, the idea of their superiority. Certainly they had more spacious compounds, they were better dressed than the Hutu, they drank better beer, and when travelling, instead of walking, they were frequently carried on a litter by Hutu or Twa servants. All these differences, important as they were, were only, however, differences of quantity and degree, characterizing two strata which had not the same access to the good things of life, rather than essential differences. By 'essential' is meant here that the Tutsi equipment did not include elements such as steam-machines, electricity or gun-power, which, when possessed exclusively by a group, are sufficient to secure an easy domination. Tutsi power did not rest on a superiority in material culture.

Another relevant background factor was the ratio between Tutsi and Hutu. As was previously stated, it is not possible to know that ratio very accurately. It is very likely, however, that it was never greater than ten or fifteen per cent. This fact was extremely important, because an economic exploitation of land tillers for the benefit of cattle-raisers would have been impossible if the Tutsi had numbered much more than this percentage of the total population. If, for instance, the Tutsi had constituted fifty per cent. of the population, the Hutu would not have been able to provide them with the foodstuffs and labour necessary to comfortable subsistence. Oberg makes similar comments on the ratio between pastoralists and agriculturalists in Ankole.[1]

[1] Oberg, 1940, p. 126.

THE PROBLEM OF TUTSI DOMINATION 145

One may wonder whether this demographic factor appeared to the Tutsi as a purely natural fact completely beyond their control, or whether they tried to maintain that fortunate proportion. We know that they made it difficult for a Hutu to enter their caste, but it does not seem that they favoured a restriction in the number of their group and an increase in the Hutu group. They shared with the Hutu a very high valuation of fertility and appreciated families with numerous offspring. It should not be forgotten that if a decrease in population would have contributed towards giving each member of the Tutsi caste a greater share in the wealth of the group in an imperceptible degree, for the individual, to have many children was a way to obtain also a greater share of wealth in a very perceptible manner. I suspect that the latter consideration was much clearer than the former for any Tutsi. It is also questionable if the bringing about of the first situation would have been psychologically compatible with the attitude of self-assertion of a domineering caste of warriors. At all events the demographic situation of Ruanda has been a factor favouring, even making possible, the economic exploitation of a majority by a minority.

A third factor which made the second so crucial was the type of economy of the country. Because of the relatively poor soil, the irregularity of the rains, and the methods of cultivation, there was not a very considerable surplus. Having to subsist on a very limited national income, the rulers had to cope with an economic problem in the fundamental meaning of the term—that is, they had to organize a way of life with means insufficient to meet needs. This emphasized the capital importance of compulsory labour and tributes, of regular and efficient collection, and of an apportionment of levies which did not let any prospective taxpayer escape.

A limited character of national resources is certainly a circumstance adverse to the centralization of a government. Indeed, a very centralized government needs a complex machinery: agencies, army, messengers, civil servants, local delegates, &c. Such an organization had been built up in Ruanda in spite of the small economic surplus.

A biological element also has been significant in the establishment and maintenance of Tutsi power in Ruanda. This was the difference in physical appearance between Tutsi and Hutu. Whatever may be the objectivity of physical caste characteristics,

146   THE PREMISE OF INEQUALITY IN RUANDA

it is certain that there were (and still are) Tutsi and Hutu physical stereotypes socially recognized. Such characteristics regarded as significant were, for the Tutsi, to be slender, tall, and light skinned; for the Hutu, to be short and stout with coarse features. To conform to one of these types was not sufficient to make of a man a Tutsi or a Hutu. Indeed there were some Tutsi and Hutu who did not possess the physical characteristics of their caste.

Sociological and psychological studies devoted to racial problems, and particularly to anti-semitism, have stressed the importance of the physical stereotypes of groups. It is immaterial whether the stereotypes are verified in the majority of cases, or only quite rarely. What *is* important is that they provide a basis on which many moral, psychological, and occupational characteristics are crystallized and form a simple picture. This picture, haunting the imagination of those it is supposed to represent as well as of the others, makes everyone extremely conscious of his group participation and of the differences that separate his group from the others.

The fact that a group is characterized by a physical type differentiating it from the others is a factor which may act both ways from the standpoint of social and political power. A minority endowed with a stereotyped physical appearance will have a very great social visibility. If that minority is at the bottom of the hierarchy, its members are constantly despised, and develop attitudes characteristic of those who are looked down on by those with whom they have to live. Consequently, they are hopelessly confined to their group and enjoy almost no opportunity to increase their power. This was the case of the Twa. Their physical stereotype stressed all the features which could be interpreted as ape-like.

If, on the contrary, that physically stereotyped minority is at the top of the power structure, it avails itself of its appearance, regarded as 'beautiful', to support its claims to an innate superiority. Consequently, it is an asset to its power.

Tutsi have been able to use the three different stereotypes of the physical characteristics of the Ruanda castes as a confirmation of their superiority: they have convinced all Ruanda that to be slender and light skinned is much better than to be stout and dark (this was even aesthetically translated in the patterns used in the ornamentations of baskets: they manifested a preference for elongated slim forms). They used the stereotypes also as a proof

THE PROBLEM OF TUTSI DOMINATION 147

of their different nature which entitled them to rule and as a guarantee against social mobility: because a Hutu was usually not endowed with the Tutsi physical characteristics he could not easily pass the line.

Two other important elements related to the political power system of Ruanda were its extent and its orographic configuration. The country was not very large, about 100 miles from north to south and 140 from west to east. But its relief was that of a maze of hills, many of them very steep, separated by deep valleys. Moreover, it was traversed, from north to south, by a chain of mountains which separate the Congo and Nile basins and is covered with very dense forests inhabited by elephants, leopards, and buffalo.

A centralized government requires good communications. The king must remain, as much as possible, in constant contact with all the regions of his country; tribute must reach the capital regularly, armies must arrive rapidly in any place threatened by an external enemy; local authorities must not be left isolated lest they become too independent. The small extent of Ruanda was indeed an asset from this point of view but this was largely neutralized by the relief which made communications extremely difficult. Notwithstanding these unfavourable physical factors, the mwami had been able to establish and maintain his political network connecting all the subordinate authorities of Ruanda to himself.

These five elements are among those which more significantly affected the domination system of the Tutsi. They are the only ones. Three of them refer to the social power of the Tutsi caste (type of material culture, Tutsi-Hutu ratio, physical appearance), while two others (economy with a small surplus, area, and relief) were operative rather in the sphere of political power. Only two of these background facts (demographic ratio and physical type) were favourable to the domination pattern whereas one (absence of a different material equipment apart from cattle) was neutral and two (lack of a great surplus, geographic configuration) were obstacles.

2. THE SOCIOLOGICAL PROBLEM OF DOMINATION

Within the limits set by these conditions external to the social system, Tutsi had to adapt their organization in order to keep the dominant position for their caste and its rulers. Their problem

148 THE PREMISE OF INEQUALITY IN RUANDA

was: how to monopolize social and political power to their benefit without preventing a Ruanda society from existing and functioning as a unity? How to realize an equilibrium between the necessities of any social life and the necessities of a permanent dominion of a group? This fundamental problem may be analysed into three antinomies: maintaining a caste society and promoting the cohesion of the society as a whole; exploiting and protecting the lower stratum; delegating powers to subordinate authorities and establishing a centralized and absolute government. How were these antinomies solved?

(a) Caste society and social cohesion

In order that the members of a dominant and hereditary group may keep their privileges, it is necessary that what gives prestige remains exclusively under their control. We have seen that in Ruanda the basis of social power and prestige lay in the effective disposal of cattle. As indicated earlier, the feudal system permitted the Tutsi to keep complete control of all Ruanda cattle, as the whole of a client's cattle was always liable to be confiscated by the lord under any pretence. Moreover, outside the *buhako* structure, the king kept the pre-eminent right over all Ruanda cattle. Even if he did not use frequently his rights against Hutu, they were not forgotten: the very cows which were not received from a lord but acquired by one's own efforts and over which the possessor had usufruct plus bare ownership, were called 'king's cows' (*inka z'umwami*) as often as *imbata*.

Usually, an upper caste shows its superiority by, among other things, its leisure and pleasant life. It has to enjoy a greater share of the good things of life than the commoners and it has to get this apparently without effort, rather as a right than as a reward for specific tasks. It was again the *buhake* which made it possible for the Tutsi caste to enjoy 'gracious living' becoming to its high social status. The man in control of a few head of cattle could, through the clientage institution, live without having to participate in the manual work of the production processes.

A third requirement for the maintenance of a caste identity is the preservation of the group's *esprit de corps* and traditions and their handing on by one generation to the next one. This was done in the kinship groups mainly by the grandparents, particularly by the paternal grandfather. There, lineage values and particular

THE PROBLEM OF TUTSI DOMINATION   149

traditions were transmitted. But a multiplicity of kinship group agents cannot be entrusted with a function as important for the caste as the socialization of its young members and their training in the qualities and virtues which had permitted their forbears to obtain power. Consequently, in Ruanda some formal institutes of education and instruction were set up. The *intore* companies in which every young man of the Tutsi caste spent several years, fulfilled these functions.

In order to avoid the dogma of the innate superiority of the upper layer being questioned if one of its members had to be cast out because he was unable to live up to the standards of his group, the clientage system acted as an institutionalized means of rescuing such people. It should be mentioned that the rescuer was not losing anything, as the Tutsi saved from social death could give him in return what was mainly expected from any Tutsi client: his attendance and his councils.

The tendency which leads a powerful group to constitute a closed caste, to maintain jealously its advantages, and to try to increase them, cannot be left without something to counterbalance it. Each caste, as Linton says, is a society in itself.[2] If the caste accentuates too much the characterististics which make it a socially complete group, isolated in the society of which it is only one layer, the cohesion of that society may be destroyed. Consequently, powerful factors of cohesion are needed to check the tendency towards social disintegration that exists within any caste structure. I have described solidarity factors already, but they may be summarized here.

First, there are certain groupings in which Tutsi and Hutu were to be found together. Names of the Tutsi and Hutu clans were similar. This suggested a certain solidarity among the bearers of the same clan name, however minimal it was. A comparable kind of Hutu participation existed in the armies. It is possible that the fact of having been commonly associated in dangerous circumstances gave a deeper feeling of unity to Hutu and Tutsi. The Ryangombe sect was open to Hutu and Twa as well as to Tutsi. Ryangombe himself is said to have addressed his invitation to join to every Ruanda, explicitly calling the Tutsi, the Hutu, the Twa, the men and the women.[3] As initiation ritual took place among kinsmen, however, there was no real inter-caste mingling in the

[2] Cf. Linton, 1936, pp. 130 f.   [3] De Lacger, 1939, vol. I, p. 257.

150   THE PREMISE OF INEQUALITY IN RUANDA

ceremonies. We may say that clan, army, and sect were 'national' only nominally and superficially. Notwithstanding, these associations between Hutu and Tutsi had probably some limited significance from the standpoint of social cohesion.

In that connexion, *buhake* is a much more important factor. By that agreement, almost any Hutu was linked to a Tutsi, and partook in the social power of the upper caste by identifying himself with a protector who was a member of the dominant group. He obtained for his disposal some cattle, the symbol of artistic values, and he entered into exchange relationships with the nobility. Through the clientage institution, Ruanda constituted a unified economic system which distributed agricultural and pastoral products among the totality of the population. The personal bond with a privileged caste member and access to possession, however precarious, of cattle, seem to have been essential from the point of view of national solidarity.

A third integrative factor was social mobility, even as limited as it was in Ruanda. It is certain that the number of Hutu and Twa assimilated to Tutsi because of their holding of political offices or because of their wealth, has always been tiny.

The possibility of being accepted into the superior group even if it is illusory for almost all the members of the inferior group has had in many societies a very great integrative influence. It is well known that in the United States, during the first quarter of this century, the fact that a few men among the wealthiest of the country had been born poor, greatly contributed to the psychological solace of a considerable mass of men and women who had personally no opportunity to achieve such brilliant successes. In addition to individual comfort, the belief that there was no intrinsically insuperable obstacle (such as having been born outside a closed hereditary group) helped Americans to feel that they were all members of the same nation regarded as not significantly stratified.

I do not imply that the social ascent of a few Hutu has played a similar part in Ruanda. Firstly, there was no egalitarian ideology which makes almost unbearable the fact that one is obliged by birth to live in an inferior social group; secondly, cases of inter-caste mobility were extremely rare in Ruanda. Nevertheless, these cases were a proof for Hutu that, although not belonging to the upper stratum, they were members of the Ruanda nation as

THE PROBLEM OF TUTSI DOMINATION   151

well as Tutsi. They did not feel that they were out-group people.

A fourth factor which counterbalanced the socially disintegrative influence of the caste system was the plurality of the structures in which any Ruanda was affiliated.

Through several structures, subjects were much more efficiently bound among themselves and to their rulers than in a unique hierarchy. In the latter case, indeed, if the individual can extricate himself from that hierarchy, he becomes absolutely unattached. In Ruanda, even if one link was broken, the subject did not escape from his superior chiefs. Indeed, he was linked to them, particularly to the mwami, by more than one tie. Almost any Ruanda was dependent on the king through two hierarchical channels: *via* his hill-chief (who himself was subordinated to the cattle- and land-chief) and *via* his army-chief. In addition, the feudal system integrated him into a set of personal loyalty relations such that the person occupying the superior position in one of these relations is himself an inferior in another relation.

It should be mentioned also that any Ruanda was a member of three kin groups: primary and secondary patrilineages and clan. Of course kinship affiliations as such did not cut across caste lines (except for the clan name), but as many of these kinship groups had been for so long established in Ruanda territory, they were certainly a supplementary link between the individual and his country.

The network of relations woven by the political and clientage systems was particularly important in a country where there were no clear-cut groupings based on co-residence. This has led some observers to believe that Ruanda were living in a kind of social vacuum. On the contrary, a Ruanda was never isolated: his social links connected him with the authorities and were ramified, if not in the whole territory, at least in a large area of it.

The last factor of social cohesion to be mentioned here was the ideology developed around the monarchic institution. The mwami was regarded as the king of all Ruanda and not only of the Tutsi. His divine origin keeping him separate from men, bestowed on him an authority which no commoner thought to question. He was closely connected with Imana, conceived as a supreme god rather remote but benevolent. The mwami, representative of Imana, was the father and protector of all Ruanda. Was it not enough to assume towards him a filial attitude and to feel one's

152 THE PREMISE OF INEQUALITY IN RUANDA

dependency upon him? As in many cultures in which a king is a paternal and divine image, the Ruanda monarch certainly contributed towards the creation in Ruanda individuals of a feeling of belonging to a unit which presented some similarities to a family.

This was, it seems, how the Ruanda political and feudal structures, by their complexity, succeeded in keeping an equilibrium between, on one hand, the tendencies towards social disintegration that a caste system necessarily produces and, on the other, the minimal cohesion necessary to the maintenance of a social unit such as a nation.

(b) *Exploitation and protection of Hutu*

The Tutsi were confronted with the dilemma that all conquerors must solve when they settle on a new territory with the intention of staying permanently: are they going to draw upon the natural resources of the country themselves, using their own labour and equipment, and to remove from the area the aboriginal inhabitants by pushing them further on and even by exterminating them as a people, or are they to let them stay and use them by having them working for their benefit? Europeans who settled in North America adopted the first solution, they did not attempt to use Indian labour and they expelled the native population from their hunting areas and began to cultivate their country. The second method has been chosen in most parts of Africa south of the Sahara where Europeans have settled.

Whether Tutsi have explicitly considered this problem is immaterial here. In fact they have adopted the solution which was most advantageous to them. Being pastoralists and not numerous (in comparison with the Hutu peasants), they had no interest in expelling them. If this had been done, they would have had either to till the land themselves or to dispense with beer, peas, sorghum, &c. It was preferable for Tutsi to adopt what Oppenheimer calls the bee-keeper's policy (as opposed to the bear's policy who for the purpose of robbing the beehive, destroys it),[4] that is to say, to keep in the country peasants in order permanently to exploit their productive work. Those who control territory are not a dominant group; it is upon men that power is exerted.

We have seen how, through the political and feudal structures, the country's surplus resources were drained and concentrated in

[4] Oppenheimer, 1922, pp. 65 ff.

THE PROBLEM OF TUTSI DOMINATION 153

Tutsi hands. From that point of view, we have to distinguish here two categories. In the first, we put the mwami, the court, the intermediary military and administrative chiefs, whom we call the rulers; in the second, the ordinary Tutsi. The rulers received tributes and labour through the military and administrative channels; the second got fewer consumption goods directly, but mainly labour by the *buhake*. Thus the satisfaction of the needs of the superior caste was not obtained by economic means but by social pressure.

Were these services in labour and in kind heavy for the Hutu caste? It seems that it was not a too painful obligation for about nine-tenths of the population to secure the whole of the agricultural produce of the country. But we should not forget that it was an economy based on rudimentary techniques and which did not yield a considerable surplus. Moreover, the standard of life of the dominant group was much higher than that of the inferior castes; one may thus safely assume that Tutsi consumed much more than a tenth of the total production. Such an assessment is not very precise but it does not seem possible to obtain a more accurate one.

What is certain is that the social power enjoyed collectively by the Tutsi caste was so great that it must have been a permanent temptation for them to increase their demands on the Hutu group. Such a situation was indeed at the same time both advantageous and dangerous as it carried in itself the seeds of its own destruction. For if the measures of the impositions were exceeded (and the technological and environmental circumstances made the margin very narrow), the subordinate group would be weakened and its productivity would diminish. Eventually, it might be led to leave the territory. To prevent such detrimental occurrences was all the more difficult as each Tutsi was endowed with so much individual social power that he might be inclined to misuse it.

How did the Tutsi deal with this threat? Firstly, by a universal distribution of the levies obtained through the military and administrative structures. Every familial unit of production was obliged to contribute—certainly not equally, but the mere fact of having universal impositions tended to prevent very considerable differences, because a sufficient return was secured and rules were established. These rules were not as fixed and publicized as the fiscal laws in a Western society, yet the mere fact of their existence

154   THE PREMISE OF INEQUALITY IN RUANDA

made for certain guarantees. For the *buhake* services, what each client had to give or do was less clearly determined and depended more on the *shebuja*'s wishes. There were also in that sphere, however, some traditionally admitted limits.

Universality and regulation of dues as such do not prevent the exactions committed by socially powerful individuals and those who required payment of taxes were powerful. Another more efficient obstacle to an exaggerated exploitation was the fact that the political and clientage structures gave to any individual of ability the opportunity to secure for himself a defender and a protector. This opportunity resulted from the plural character of the Ruanda hierarchy.

When one belongs to a single structure, there is only one immediate superior. Consequently, everything must be obtained from him and is owed to him. In a plural system, there are several immediate superiors of approximately equal rank and who are not interdependent. Consequently, it is possible to have the support of one chief (or his complicity even) when resisting another.

This is what happened in Ruanda. An example will show how the plurality of chiefs could be used. Suppose a Hutu had inherited cattle granted by a lord to his grandfather who had also received cows from his army-chief, and who had acquired other cattle by exchange of goods (*imbata*), and because his present lord was too exacting, our Hutu wanted to change and become the client of another important man. He knew that his lord would try to seize all his *imbata* and to choose the best cows among his other cattle. By some gifts, he obtained the support of his army-chief. Before entering into discussion with his lord, he and his army-chief had agreed that all the best cows he had at his disposal and all his *imbata* would be said to have been received from the military chief. They were removed and put on grazing grounds directly protected by the army-chief. Then when the lord claimed more cows than his client wanted to return to him, he had to settle the matter not with a man of very limited power but with the army-chief.

Of course this required clever handling of the situation, but when it succeeded it secured efficient protection against extortion.

It should be added that the recourse of a subject to a higher authority within the same hierarchy was approved and even encouraged in Ruanda. This was another means of putting a check on the exorbitant demands of immediate superiors. This, however,

THE PROBLEM OF TUTSI DOMINATION 155

did not play an important part in the feudal system because there were no socially recognized ties between a client and his lord's lord. Feudality was not a ranking system in the same sense as were the political structures. Each lord had his personal following; he was not as such the representative of a higher authority.

To sum up, the political and clientage structures at the same time secured the economic exploitation of the Hutu and protected them against an exaggerated pressure which could have led to disaster for the upper caste.

(c) Delegation and centralization of political power

Before the European occupation the kingdom's population was already numerous, probably around 1,700,000 inhabitants. The orographic configuration of the country made communications rather difficult. In that non-literate culture, an efficient collection of tributes required almost a face to face acquaintance between the subject and his ruler. These circumstances necessitated a delegation of authority to many intermediary chiefs who would be the local representatives of the rulers.

But such an unavoidable system was very dangerous for the central government. Its subordinated agents having frequently authority over a rather numerous population which could provide them with abundant supplies (if nothing was sent to the court) could be tempted to isolate themselves completely from the capital and become independent. Such a course of action would have been facilitated by the military structure and the feudal system.

Some important chiefs were, indeed, authorized to raise an army. Moreover, any military chief whose army was encamped near the border, in a district far from the capital, could gain such ascendancy over his warriors as to win over their allegiance to himself.

The *buhake* was perhaps still more dangerous because, as in any feudal system, it created personal bonds of allegiance between the client and his lord. As such, that bond of loyalty did not extend beyond the lord. One had to obey one's lord because he was one's lord and not because he was a mwami's representative. This is why any feudal system has always been so dangerous for a central government. Independence and revolt against the king have been recurring events in the areas where a feudal system existed.

Ruanda rulers were able to check successfully these tendencies

156   THE PREMISE OF INEQUALITY IN RUANDA

towards the fragmentation of the political unity of their country, first, by the ritual character of the royal power.

To revolt against the king, identified with Ruanda and supported by Imana, was a sacrilege and a profanation. It is not claimed that such a theory was sufficient to secure the kings with effective power indefinitely. Elsewhere similar ideologies of absolute and divine power of the monarchs have not prevented some of them from being stripped of their real authority, whereas their divine prerogatives were still respected. The ritual sanction does not seem to have had a primary importance in the maintenance of submission to the Ruanda kingship. In 1896 or 1897, a young mwami, Mibambwe IV Rutalindwa, was assailed and eventually lost his life in a revolt instigated by the brother of the queen-mother. That queen-mother was not the mother of the mwami but another wife of his father. Her clan, the Abega, wanted a son of hers as mwami.[5] This shows that when the king lost effective control of power, ritual sanctions were not an effective safeguard for his prerogatives, or even for his life. This is why it has not been thought necessary to expand on the ritual aspect of the Ruanda kingship. But it certainly was a factor which contributed to the obedience of the Ruanda nobles.

Another check was that the king kept at his disposal the coercive force of the armies. Even if the rebel had the support of one or two armies, the king had all the others.

But the main factor which I think prevented local authorities from asserting their independence from the central government, was the plural character of the political and feudal organization. In connexion with the maintenance of the effective power of the central government, this plurality of structure was a very effective means of maintaining misunderstanding, hostility, and jealousy among the subordinate chiefs. It is certain that the *shebuja* of our example in the preceding section, would have been only too glad to denounce to the mwami the army-chief if the latter was indulging in suspicious manœuvres. The co-existence of chiefs of almost the same rank who were constantly induced by their subjects to take sides in disputes was sufficient to create mistrust among themselves. Moreover, conflicts were numerous, particularly when two chiefs had the same territorial power (as in the case of the cattle- and land-chiefs). To settle conflicts they had to resort to the

[5] Pagès, 1933, pp. 195-206.

THE PROBLEM OF TUTSI DOMINATION 157

superior authority's judgement and this increased the ruler's power over his subordinates.

This applied not only to the political organization but also to the feudal structure, which had potentially the most disruptive action on a centralized government. Indeed, the subject-client had often to ask protection and support from his political chief against his lord and from his lord against his political chief. Consequently, between the important lords, even those who were not themselves prominent in the political hierarchies, and the political chiefs, relations were often very tense. Moreover, as the very important lords who could have attempted to resist the central government held at the same time political offices, they were directly enmeshed in rivalries and jealousies.

Engendered by the hierarchic plurality, the mistrust which prevented the subordinate chiefs from uniting against the central government, which led them to spy on each other and to inform the king of anything suspect, was the main check against tendencies towards local autonomy in Ruanda. Even if that hostility between important Tutsi happened to express itself openly and violently, the central government was not very anxious to restore peace as long as troubles remained localized and did not threaten the regular collection of taxes and the authority of the king.

3. THE FUNCTION OF THE POLITICAL ORGANIZATION IN RUANDA

At the beginning of this study, in order to delimit the social phenomena we wished to study, political organization in an intragroup context was defined as 'the totality of culturally patterned relationships between certain individuals who possess the legitimate use of physical force and all the others who inhabit at a certain time a certain territory'. This definition did not include the function of a system of political relationships because, it was stated, it is only through analysis that the function fulfilled by a set of institutions in a particular social context, may be ascertained.

In the preceding chapters, the different political structures have been analysed from a functional point of view. It will be sufficient to summarize what has been said to grasp the function of the Ruanda political organization as a whole. Here we shall consider together the feudal as well as the administrative and military systems.

158 THE PREMISE OF INEQUALITY IN RUANDA

At the beginning of this century, Ruanda political organization was an instrument of social immobility. It was not a force of expansion meant to increase the Tutsi dominion over the country, but a machinery which succeeded in maintaining a difficult equilibrium between the antinomic tendencies I have reviewed. Any institution in which divergent tendencies meet and are kept balanced bears in itself the principle of its own disintegration. But in Ruanda the equilibrium problem had been so efficiently solved that it seems that an optimum point had been reached. The political organization that sustained the domination system could have been perpetuated as long as forces external and internal to the system itself remained constant. The external influence which modified the political organization has been the contact with the Europeans, another conquest group entering Ruanda history around 1900. But apart from such a consequential event, internal phenomena such as a modification in the demographic ratio, the introduction of new agricultural techniques, the impoverishment of the soil, &c., could have been sufficient to destroy the equilibrium maintained by the Tutsi political organization.

What was 'immobilized' by the political organization was the Tutsi's caste's and rulers' almost exclusive control of power. They used it for exploitation, by which is meant here the satisfaction of needs not by economic production but by pressure. I follow here closely Oppenheimer's distinction between economic and political means. Both have the same end, he writes, the satisfaction of needs. But when this end is obtained by one's labour and the equivalent exchange of one's own labour for the labour of others, one may speak of 'economic means' while the unrequited appropriation of the labour of others is 'political means'.[6] This should, however, be qualified in the *buhake* where the client received the usufruct of cattle.

It would, of course, be completely misleading to assume that Ruanda political organization had for its only function the preservation of Tutsi exploitation. Through the political structure, as has been shown, the inferior castes enjoyed security. Collectively, peasants were protected against raiding expeditions of neighbours and against an unlimited and too arbitrary exploitation. Individually, in the difficult or dangerous events of life, a Hutu could rely upon the protection of his lord, of his army-chief, and

[6] Oppenheimer, 1922, p. 25.

THE PROBLEM OF TUTSI DOMINATION

of his administrative chiefs if he could not or did not wish to ask his lineage's aid.

Should one, then, speak of a counterpart and interpret the Tutsi privileges as a retribution for the care of the commonweal and public order? No, political organization in Ruanda fulfilled different functions. It cannot be said that one function is the counterpart of the other merely because it benefited different groups. It just so happened that two different functions were fulfilled by the same set of institutions.

To sum up, this political system was a means of maintaining a certain social order in which the group of rulers and their caste appropriated to their consumption a considerable part of the country's goods without having to use their labour in the productive processes.

CHAPTER VIII

THE PREMISE OF INEQUALITY

I. DEFINITIONS

THERE is in a culture much more than can be observed (artifracts, behaviour) or known by direct questions (myths, religious beliefs, &c.). There are conceptions concerning the place of man in the world, his destiny, his main values, his attitudes to his fellow men, the meaning of the invisible world, &c. That covert part of a culture is partly or totally implicit in the sense that these fundamental conceptions and values remain for the culture bearers unexpressed or even unconscious. They are thus reached by induction, some by immediate inference from observation, some by a process encompassing several states of abstraction.

Some elements of the covert culture are particularly fundamental because they underline different cultural phenomena which hitherto might have appeared unrelated. They act as a principle in the logical order from which a set of conclusions may be deduced. This is why the word 'premise' has been preferred here to others such as 'configuration',[1] 'sanction',[2] and 'theme'.[3]

On the other hand, the word 'premise' should not be thought to imply that the relationships between the cultural principle and its cultural consequences obey the strictest laws of rational logic. This relationship may be said to be logical only in a very broad sense. Or more accurately, we must clearly distinguish between 'logical' and 'rational'. There are relationships which are meaningful although they express a sequence which is emotional or 'psychological' or even unconscious rather than rational. Such relationships, however, may be said to be 'logical' in the sense in which we speak of a logic of sentiments or emotions. This simply means that we expect them, 'understand' them.[4]

To make the point clear, let us take an example of a logical but not rational relationship between two social phenomena. In the past, a positive correlation has been noted between low economic

[1] Kluckhohn, 1941, 1943.   [2] Herskovits, 1948, pp. 222 f.
[3] Opler, 1945.   [4] Maquet, 1951, p. 165.

THE PREMISE OF INEQUALITY 161

indices and the lynching of Negroes in the Southern States of the Union. There is evidently no rational means for the whites of the south to impute the responsibility for the lack of rain—which was then the cause of the poor cotton crops—to Negroes. This typically irrational behaviour, however, becomes comprehensible if we accept the frustration-aggression sequence. In this sense, it can be said that the relation between the two phenomena, economic crises and lynching, is a logical relation.[5]

Ruanda political relations disclose one of the premises of that culture. Underlying the political and feudal structures there was a general assumption about human relations. In order to formulate it as accurately as may be possible, I shall first consider more closely the social roles of the superior and inferior in the field of political and feudal relations. In the following section the words 'ruler' and 'subject' refer to superiors and inferiors in the administrative, military, and clientage structures.

2. THE RULER'S AND SUBJECT'S SOCIAL ROLES

The analysis of the political organization of Ruanda indicates that the ruler was expected to assume a complex role towards his subject. The two poles of it were protection and profit. The subordinate was somebody whom one protected: he was also a resource from which it was normal to draw some advantage.

Protection was not restricted to a certain field of action, but potentially encompassed the whole of the subject's life. When the inferior needed some help, any help, he was expected to apply to his ruler even if the issue was completely alien to the sphere of the main relations between the ruler and the subject. A client could ask his *shebuja* for aid in matters not pertaining to cattle and *buhake* services. It was even thought proper for the ruler to interfere in difficulties which his subject through his own misdemeanour had run into as, for instance, when an inferior had been caught stealing from somebody. When protection was refused, it was not because the question was not the ruler's concern, but on other grounds, such as disloyalty.

The extent of that protection was not strictly defined. It did not constitute for the ruler a set of particular and fixed obligations. The subordinate had a general right to be protected but very few claims to particular advantages. In *buhake*, when one offered one's

[5] Dollard, 1939, p. 44 (quoted by Maquet, 1951, p. 166).

162   THE PREMISE OF INEQUALITY IN RUANDA

services to a lord in order to become his client, one was entitled to receive usufruct of his cattle. But the number of cows was not determined. It could be one or twenty or fifty or even more.

It was up to the ruler to decide if any protection was to be granted and to what extent. Of course the pressure of public opinion obliged him not to refuse aid to his subordinate unless he had some socially accepted reason to do so (such as the subordinate's disobedience), but the measure of the protection depended on his own will and pleasure.

These characteristics of the protective attitude (care of the whole of the subordinate's life, its very variable extent being left to the superior's judgement) allow us to apply to it the qualification of 'paternalistic'. Paternalism is understood here as 'the principle of acting in a way like that of a father towards his children. Because of the total dependency of the human offspring, during their first years, on those who nurse and educate them—and they are usually their parents—the latter's authority ranges over the whole of the life of the child. In everything he needs his parents, in everything they have to direct and control him. Moreover, parents sovereignly judge what they are going to give their children. Undoubtedly, their social groups force them to secure for their children the protection they need to live and develop but the children may not require such or such a particular service. Parents decide without further ado what is suitable for the child and think that better than he they know what is 'best for him'.

A paternal relation does not exclude profit. In describing the Ruanda's father's role towards his sons, I mentioned that the father's interests were usually thought to be predominant in respect of the children's interests. When inferiors were not the superior's children but his subjects or clients, that aspect of profit was much more emphasized. All those who occupied the inferior position in the relations of the political and feudal structures had dues to give and tribute labour to perform for the profit of their superiors, and some of these obligations were heavy. It did not appear at all unusual to Ruanda that power brought many privileges to those who had it. If one is a chief, is it not fitting to draw advantages from one's situation? Here, again, the extent of the subject's obligations was left within very broad limits to the superior's discretion.

The ruler's role seems to have been that paternalistic blend of

THE PREMISE OF INEQUALITY 163

protection and profit. Of course, that role was not always perfectly fulfilled. Chiefs who have been more exploiters than protectors are remembered. It was by comparison with that ideal picture that their behaviour was judged and blamed.

The subject was expected to have a role complementary to the one we have just described. He was supposed to assume an attitude of dependency. Inferiority is the relative situation of a person who has to submit to another in a well delimited field. Dependence is inferiority in the whole of life. When the ruler gives an order, he has to be obeyed, not because his order falls within the field over which he has authority, but because he is a ruler.

It could be objected that in Ruanda this attitude of dependence was not in principle unlimited. We saw that cattle- and land-chiefs could not require as many dues as they liked, that subjects could resort to higher authorities against their immediate chiefs, and that it was possible to oppose one chief against another. This does not change the fact that the dependent attitude was the only one socially expected of the subject. Indeed it was impossible to be considered a 'good' subject if one asserted independence of one's superior. A claim of independence, even limited, obliged one to leave the superior, to ask for the support of another and to assume towards the latter an attitude of complete compliance. This appeared clearly in the feudal relation. A lord could not be refused what he asked (even at the present time a shop assistant who is obliged by the law to sell only for cash, will find it very difficult not to sell on credit to his lord). He could only be deserted for another.

3. FORMULATION OF THE INEQUALITY PREMISE

When paternalism and dependence define the permanent roles expected from two persons, much more is implied than when they express the transitory roles of a father and his young son. In the latter case it is known that the son will grow up and one day, even if he has to wait till after his father's death, will be equal to what his father was when the latter was young. But when paternalism and dependence are linked in permanent reciprocal roles, the assumption is that there is a fundamental inequality between the two persons. The subject will never grow up, he will never 'reach his majority'. It is implied without any doubt that there is between the ruler and his subject a difference so fundamental that it never can be suppressed. This fundamental inequality of men is the

164 THE PREMISE OF INEQUALITY IN RUANDA

cultural premise underlying the social roles of the ruler and the subject.

We have seen that Ruanda society is made up of three hereditary groups with a very different participation in social power and that these differences were explained in terms of innate qualities. On the other hand, in a very great proportion of the political and feudal relations, the superior and the inferior belong to different castes. This indicates in what sense Ruanda feel men to be unequal.

This was not an inequality founded on differences in individual qualities or possessions. Of course, a very clever and artful man, a very wealthy possessor of great herds of cattle, could exert much greater influence, could have access to many more amenities of life and would command much more respect than a not very intelligent or a not very wealthy man. But these differences were not regarded as entailing such a significant inequality between them if they belonged to the same caste. Caste affiliation was mainly what made men unequal.

Several stories expressed the differences between the three castes and the qualities which were thought characteristic of them.[6] I mentioned above physical stereotypes. To them, moral qualities were added. Tutsi were said to be intelligent (in the sense of astute in political intrigues), capable of command, refined, courageous, and cruel; Hutu, hardworking, not very clever, extrovert, irascible, unmannerly, obedient, physically strong; Twa, gluttonous, loyal to their Tutsi masters, lazy, courageous when hunting, without any restraint. These stereotypes, admitted with only minor qualifications and slight differences and emphases by all Ruanda, Hutu and Twa as well as Tutsi, were thought to be essentially linked to caste affiliation. When asked if a Hutu brought up with Tutsi, and as a Tutsi boy, could not develop the Tutsi qualities, Hutu and Tutsi informants answer that such a training could change the boy to some extent, but not completely; the differences pertain to nature.

Caste status was, of course, not founded on a difference of qualities, objective or assumed, in the sense that if a particular Hutu was recognized as intelligent and courageous as a Tutsi, his status remained nevertheless unaffected. What mattered primarily indeed was not to have the qualifications of the upper caste, but to have been born in it. This was sufficient to determine a very

[6] Cf. for instance Sandrart, 1930, p. 139; Hurel, 1922.

THE PREMISE OF INEQUALITY 165

different share in social power and fundamentally different rights.

The Ruanda principle of inequality could be expressed in the following terms: people born in different castes are unequal in inborn endowment, physical as well as psychological and have consequently fundamentally different rights.

That premise, closely connected with the caste structure, is suggested by the analysis of the political and feudal structures. Indeed, when a principle of inequality exists in a society with respect to a certain type of relations, it does not fail to spread to other relations more or less similar. In Ruanda, the inegalitarian premise of inter-caste relations has permeated the intricate relations which could be regarded as analogous in certain respects. A Tutsi who was lord over another Tutsi was thought to be superior over his client in a way comparable to the manner in which he was superior over his Hutu clients. Of course significant differences remained between inter- and intra-caste relationships of superiority, but the latter tended to be patterned on the former ones.

The extension to intricate relations of the premise of inter-caste inequality made it a principle of integration with a very wide bearing as it could, and did, in fact, pervade all the human relations in which a superiority of one actor over the other was implied. It could be the relation between a mother and her young child, a father and his son, a man and his wife, an old man and a youngster, a craftsman and an apprentice, &c. These relations constituting the texture of social life, the impact on collective living of the premise of fundamental inequality, cannot be over-estimated.

4. THE THEOREMS

In order to understand better how the inequality premise influenced the whole of Ruanda social life, the different aspects of that influence must be made explicit. They will be expressed as a set of theorems, by which is meant general propositions or statements which are not self-evident.

Theorem One

When two persons are involved in any kind of social relation, it is their mutual hierarchical situation which is regarded as the most relevant element of the relation.

Superiority and inferiority were *foci* of the Ruanda social structure to such an extent that as soon as they entered as a

166 THE PREMISE OF INEQUALITY IN RUANDA

component in the content of a social intercourse, other components were regarded as less important and were coloured by the hierarchical situation of the two actors. In Euro-American culture, relationships of inferiority are defined not only as regards the people taking part in them but also as regards the matters concerned. A business executive may give orders to one of his employees only within very well-defined limits of competence and time, but he cannot oblige him to accept his views on for instance artistic or political questions. In Ruanda, on the contrary, when one of the persons involved in a dyad was superior to the other from a certain point of view, the superiority was diffused, as it were, through the whole relation. For his subject, a chief was always a chief in whatever matter.

This first theorem is a consequence of inequality conceived as essential. When two persons are considered unequal by nature, the superiority of one over the other cannot be limited to a certain sphere. Obedience in everything must be required: there is no field in which a father could be wrong and his son right.

Theorem Two

As in almost any human relation there is some superiority of one actor over the other, as that aspect is always stressed and as inferiority relations are patterned on inter-caste relations, paternalistic, and dependent attitudes were to be found in almost every human relation in Ruanda.

The only exceptions were relations between people who were equal from any point of view, as for instance young men of about the same age, belonging to the same caste and whose families were about at the same level of wealth.

This is very noticeable today, even in relations with Europeans. A clerk usually assumes towards the European he assists, a dependent attitude different from the behaviour of a European employee. The clerk expects from his employer a behaviour similar to the paternalistic attitude of the Ruanda superiors and he is puzzled and disappointed if the employer does not assume such an attitude.

Theorem Three

There is no private sector in the life of the inferior *vis-à-vis* his superior. The superior has the right to control the whole of his

THE PREMISE OF INEQUALITY   167

subordinate's activities. This is not resented by the inferior as unbearable meddling. On the contrary, it is expected by the inferior who feels that such interference is a proof of the interest his superior extends to him. When a European employer avoids intruding into the privacy of a Ruanda subordinate, the latter not infrequently tends to interpret it as a withdrawal from the protective role expected from any superior.

If a subordinate were to refuse his Ruanda superior's interference on the grounds that he should not be concerned with his private affairs, such a pretension would be regarded as at least a definite lack of respect.

Theorem Four

Strictly contractual relations are not possible. To enter into a contract implies that the intended parties are previously independent of one another. If one is submitted to the other for the whole of his life, how could he freely commit himself to give the other certain services? And how could the other promise to secure his inferior a counterpart that the latter can legally claim? When entering into contractual relations, it is necessary that each prospective partner should be a person independent of and equal to the other in that context. In the Western world, admittedly, it frequently happens that an agreement which verifies the juridical forms of a contract is entered into by persons who are not independent and equal. Circumstances may exert such a pressure that freedom to accept or refuse a particular obligation is purely illusory. Conditions of independence and equality, however, are often realised. In ancient Ruanda such a situation could almost never have happened as it was rare for two persons who might otherwise be related by a contract, not to be already involved in paternalistic and dependent relations.

Moreover, after the contract has been concluded it is necessary that each partner should be able to defend himself against any demand of the other which would exceed the terms of the covenant, and that he should have the means to oblige the other to fulfil what the latter has agreed to give or to do. This implies again that one part is not completely dependent on the other. Now, as I mentioned earlier, the extent of the superior's obligations is left, in Ruanda, to his will and pleasure. Consequently, it was unthinkable for the party who was at the same time in a position

M

168   THE PREMISE OF INEQUALITY IN RUANDA

inferior to the other to claim some particular fulfilment of the agreed promises from the other.

This appears clearly in the difficulties Ruanda often meet when they have to adjust themselves to European labour contracts. They are sometimes confused by the fact that the employer requires from them at the same time less and more than they expect. Less because the employer does not ask for more services, for longer office hours for instance, than what has been stipulated, and more because he is very exacting in the execution of what has been undertaken, for instance in matters of punctuality.

Theorem Five

With such socially accepted conceptions about inequality, those who occupy the superior positions in most of the social relations in which they are involved, tend to develop a permanent authoritarian behaviour. This is characterized by a propensity to command, to be self-assertive, arrogant, protective, and compassionate.

Chiefs, rulers, and other superiors try to extend not only the size or range of their power (the number of people controlled) but its density (the degree of control of the subordinates).[7] Any independence manifested by the inferior will be resented as rebellious.

This leads to intolerance. The superior's opinions should never be opposed by the inferior who is always and everywhere expected to manifest his dependence by attitudes of compliance. Even today this conduct tends to prevail. Some years ago a Ruanda deliberative assembly of people of standing was asked its opinion on a contemplated reform. After the most important person present there had given his opinion, everybody voted for his proposal. But after the meeting many expressed privately their divergent opinions. At the time of the vote, they had considered it improper and impolite not to agree with the superior.

Theorem Six

Even if the caste system and political and feudal institutions have succeeded to a large extent in moulding personalities in such a way as to make inferiors self-effacing, submissive, compliant, and dependent, the conditioning has not been perfect. Often the inferior wants to disagree with his superior's opinions, to avoid executing an order or obeying his commands. A straight refusal

[7] Cf. Russell, 1938, pp. 165 f.

THE PREMISE OF INEQUALITY 169

being regarded as insulting, disrespect or revolt, the only way out for the inferior is to appear to behave always as expected: to fall in with any desire of his superior while concealing his own opinion, never to say no to any order but to find clever excuses for not doing it. Consequently dissimulation is very highly thought of and a skill necessary to master for someone wanting to live more or less securely under such a political régime.

Many stories and proverbs give evidence of the frequency of covert disobedience to the rulers and of the appreciation in which an astute excuse and a 'good lie' were held. This was the only way to adapt oneself to such a situation.

Theorem Seven

It is commonly accepted in the Western tradition that truth has a high value and that language is the medium used to express 'truth', that is to say, 'what reality appears to be to the person who speaks'. Undoubtedly, in Western practice, language is used, even in the cognitive sphere, for many other purposes than to express what the speaker thinks. Moreover, most of the scholars who, in recent years, have studied the problem of the origin and function of language, bring qualifications to the traditional view. In the almost unanimous opinion of the carriers of Western culture, however, the ideal verbal behaviour must express 'truth' and not what is useful to the speaker. This is, for example, what is inculcated into children in schools.

In a society in which human relations are imbued with some cultural premises as the one being considered in this chapter, 'truth' cannot be recognized as a dominant value. Indeed, one is supposed to use language not to say what is thought to conform to reality but what is thought to conform to the ruler's opinion. Nobody, the ruler included, entertains many illusions on the sincerity of what is said, but submission has been expressed at the right time and this is felt to be most important.

This theorem could be formulated in this way: the verbal behaviour towards a superior must express dependence rather than 'truth'.

Theorem Eight

Once it is taken for granted that in hierarchical relations, behaviour must conform to the superior's expectations even to the

170 THE PREMISE OF INEQUALITY IN RUANDA

point of agreeing with all his opinions, a similar attitude tends to spread to other fields. Each time there is a conflict between what is useful to the speaker or expected from him and what he thinks, he is apt to say rather what is useful or expected.

Thus a dependent attitude in hierarchical relationships favours the extension to all social relations of a utilitarian usage of language.

5. ORIGIN OF THE INEQUALITY PREMISE

We have read the premise, as it were, into the Ruanda political and feudal organization. But this does not solve the question of their mutual priority. Had the political organization of Ruanda, as it existed at the beginning of this century, been built in order to express a belief deeply buried in the psyche of those who have slowly formed and shaped it? Or, on the contrary, is it that the premise of inequality and its sequels have been evolved from the political organization as an ideology and a set of attitudes which fitted the political situation well?

To raise such a question is certainly legitimate in the sense that it expresses a genuine problem which, if it could be solved, would add significantly to our knowledge of the working of social systems and of cultural premises. But there are certain facts crucial to the solution of that question that we are not likely ever to know, such as a good knowledge of the Tutsi culture and its premises before the pastoralists reached Ruanda. It seems possible, however, to make some comments on this problem.

Tutsi came into Ruanda as conquerors. Even if their arrival into the country inhabited by Hutu looked rather like a peaceful infiltration, it was nevertheless a conquest. They wanted to settle in the country and they built a permanent system of economic and political relations with the Hutu whereby they established themselves definitely as masters and exploiters. That is to say, a caste society evolved from their will to stabilize the conquest situation with all its advantages. Now, the more obvious rationalization of a caste structure is the belief that there are inborn and fundamental differences between the members of different castes.

This is not meant to be a schematic view of the historical origin of the Ruanda inequality premise. It is possible that Tutsi had previously to their arrival in Ruanda such a belief, perhaps already embodied in their social organization, or in their external relations with surrounding peoples, and that quite naturally they

THE PREMISE OF INEQUALITY 171

shaped the new Ruanda situation according to their ideology. Again, it is possible that some themes and types of organization of the Hutu cultivators were particularly capable of being used in the formation of the Ruanda ethos as I have described it. But a conquest evolving into a caste structure is sufficient to account for an inegalitarian premise. Even if prior to the conquest each of the two groups concerned has an egalitarian ideology, the establishment of hereditary groups, whereby the status of vanquishers and vanquished is perpetuated, suffices to give birth to a theory of inequality.

I am of the opinion that such a theory is a necessary 'superstructure' (in the Marxist sense) of a caste system. Undoubtedly, a body of inheritance laws, opportunities for a certain kind of education restricted to the wealthiest, a difference in languages, &c., may maintain for some time a high social power in the hands of the conquerors' descendents, even if the cultural ideology is that all men are born equal. But such a lack of internal coherence ('all men are born equal' versus 'political and economic power is restricted to those who are descendants of the conquerors') is very likely to result rapidly in an evolution from a caste system to a class society. A 'racial' theory seems the only ideology perfectly consistent with a caste structure. It is very probable that conquerors adopt it not only for consistency's sake, but because it is more efficient, more easily understood and accepted, particularly when different physical traits are characteristic of each caste.

It should be understood that when we speak of 'the adoption of an ideology by the conquerors', it is not meant that one day the conquerors made a conscious choice among various possible ideologies. Rather, once a caste system operates, the patterns of political domination and of economic exploitation require people to behave as if the upper caste members were by nature different from that of the lower caste members. When the 'idea behind' these behaviours is made more or less explicit, as in tales and proverbs, it is rationalized in terms of fundamental and inborn inequality.

If there is such a necessary link between caste systems and the premise of inequality, then to know whether the conqueror's ideology, prior to the conquest, was egalitarian or not is only an historical question; when the vanquisher settles and establishes a caste system, the inegalitarian ideology is produced, as its corollary.

172   THE PREMISE OF INEQUALITY IN RUANDA

The question of the previous premise of the conquerors' culture, however, remains very important in another connexion: to what extent does an anterior egalitarian ideology deter the conquerors from establishing a caste system? Is the conqueror, if imbued with an ethos of egalitarianism, inclined to admit that his principles are valid also in his relations with the vanquished group? Or does he think that obviously the conquered groups are different people? Because of our ignorance of the Tutsi cultural premises before they entered into Ruanda, these questions have to be left unanswered in the case of ancient Ruanda.

APPENDIX 1

Translation from Ruanda of the questionnaire on political organization.

1. (*a*) Name of informant.
   (*b*) Son of . . . .
   (*c*) Is he a Tutsi, a Hutu, a Twa?
   (*d*) What is or was his occupation, office, title?[1]
   (*e*) What is your 'territoire' (Belgian administrative division)?
   (*f*) What is your 'chefferie' (*igihugu*)?
   (*g*) What is your 'sous-chefferie' (*umosozi*)?
   (*h*) Give the name of your patrilineage (*umulyango*).
   (*i*) Give the name of your clan (*ubwoko*).
2. Give the name of your patrilineage head.
3. Where are people more numerous, in the *inzu* or in the *umulyango*?
4. Were all the members of your *umulyango* under the command of a single army-chief or were you scattered in different armies?
5. Give the name of the chronologically first army to which your *inzu* was affiliated.
6. Has your *inzu* been affiliated to armies other than the first one?
7. Have you been trained as an *intore*?
8. Was every Ruanda (whether Tutsi, Hutu or Twa) a member of an army?
9. Was a man ever under the command of two army-chiefs?
10. When an army-chief wanted to recruit *intore* or to require services, could he request it from any individual directly or had he to ask the patrilineage head?
11. Could a young man be incorporated into two *intore* companies?
12. Do you know anybody who has been in that situation? Give his name.
13. When somebody was a member of an army, was he usually the only person of his kin group in that army?
14. Or was he with his married sons?
15. With his unmarried sons?
16. With his brothers?
17. With his brothers' children?
18. With his sisters' children?
19. With his paternal uncles?
20. With his clients?
21. Was it possible for somebody who had never received any cows from a lord to have cows that belonged to him and did not depend on any lord?
22. Were the cows acquired by somebody's independent economic activity regarded as army cows?

[1] The preceding questions were usually answered by the investigator, not directly by the informant. To the following the informant's reply was recorded.

174   THE PREMISE OF INEQUALITY IN RUANDA

23. Was a married man who was left without any living member of his *inzu*, regarded as an *inzu* head and had he the same obligation towards his army-chief?

24. Was it the same or was it different to be a client and to be commanded by an army-chief?

25. Were the cows called 'cows of the king' received from a lord?

26. Could all the members of an army be required to perform services concerning cows and war or were they divided into two groups, one of warriors and one of herdsmen?

27. When a new army-chief was appointed, had all the army members the obligation of numbering the cows (*murundo*) and of giving him a cow as recognition of his authority (*indabukirano*)?

28. Was the army member who had no cows obliged to give another recognition gift?

29. Had the army-chief an effective disposal of the cows taken by him during the *murundo*?

30. Could the army-chief order the numbering by himself?

31. Who minded the cows taken during the numbering?

32. When two Tutsi members of the same army and living on the same hill had a dispute about cattle, who had to judge the case?

33. If the two Tutsi were members of different armies, who had to judge the case?

34. When a client wanted to complain about his lord, to whom did he bring the case?

35. When a lord wanted to complain about his client, to whom did he bring the case?

36. When somebody wanted his litigation to be judged by the king, by whom was it advisable to be accompanied?

37. Could anybody, whether Tutsi, Hutu or Twa, appeal to the king if he did not want to accept the previous judgement of another authority?

38. If somebody wanted to appeal to the king and was prevented from doing so by some pressure, what happened if the king knew of it?

39. Could army members who were dissatisfied with their chief do anything to have him dismissed?

40. If it was possible, what did they do?

41. What section of the army had to give to the court the cows supplying fresh milk (*inkuke*)?

42. The service of jugs of milk (*igicuba*)?

43. The foodstuffs (*amakoro*)?

44. The bulls to be slaughtered (*indwanyi*)?

45. The steers for divination purposes (*amamana*)?

46. The service of the maintenance of the enclosure?

47. Were all these services and dues given by the patrilineage head or severally by every member of the army?

48. Did the king command the whole country directly or was it divided into several districts?

APPENDIX ONE

49. What was the name of these districts?
50. What was the name of the royal residence of the place where you lived?
51. Do you remember the names of other royal residences or districts?
52. What is the meaning of *umunyamukenke*?
53. What is the meaning of *umynyabutaka*?
54. Who collected the sorghum tribute (*urutete*) for the court?
55. In addition to the judgs of milk and other *inkuke* sent by the royal residences to the court, were there other jugs of milk and other *inkuke* requested by the tax collectors and sent to the residence?
56. Who required these additional jugs of milk from the hill chief?
57. Which cattle provided the milk?
58. What is the meaning of the word *abakoni*?
59. For the benefit of whom were the cattle seized during military expeditions?
60. What is the meaning of the word *umudende*?
61. Could you give the names of five persons who had *umudende*?
62. What is the meaning of the word *impotore*?
63. Could you give the name of five persons who had *impotore*?
64. What is the meaning of the words *gucana uruti*?
65. Could you give the name of five persons for whom the *gucana uruti* ritual has been performed?
66. Who granted the *umudende* badge?
67. Who granted the *impotore* badge?
68. Who performed the ritual of *gucana uruti*?
69. Did the army cattle include only *nyambo*?
70. Were the army-chief's herds regarded as army cattle?
71. Were the cows given as rewards to the warriors for bravery regarded as army cattle?
72. Were the cows received as bride-wealth regarded as army cattle?
73. Were the cows given to an army member regarded as army cows?
74. Were the cows received by exchange by army members regarded as army cattle?
75. Who granted the hill-chief his office?
76. Who was the superior of the hill-chief?
77. What was the difference between *ibikingi* and *umusozi*?
78. Was any *ibikingi* depending directly on the royal court?
79. Who appointed the heads of these royal *ibikingi*?
80. Had the cattle-chief authority over them?
81. Could the land-chief require tribute labour from the people living on these royal *ibikingi*?
82. Were those who had received these *ibikingi* from the king under the authority of the army-chief?
83. Was the cattle-chief allowed to retain a part of the milk he sent to the court?
84. Was the hill-chief allowed to retain a part of the milk he sent to the cattle-chief?

176 THE PREMISE OF INEQUALITY IN RUANDA

85. Was the land-chief allowed to retain a part of the foodstuffs he sent to the court?
86. Was the hill-chief allowed to retain a part of the foodstuffs he sent to the land-chief?
87. Give the name, if you can remember it, of a hill on which there was a royal cemetery.
88. Were the people living on such hills obliged to pay taxes (in agricultural produce) to the court?
89. Do you remember the name of a place under the authority of a *mwiru*?
90. Was such a place submitted to the authority of the cattle- and the land-chiefs?
91. Was it possible for the same person to be at the same time land-chief and cattle-chief?
92. Was the office of the cattle-chief granted only to Tutsi or to Hutu as well?
93. Was the office of land-chief granted only to Tutsi or to Hutu as well?
94. Give the names of Hutu you know, who have been land-chiefs or cattle-chiefs.
95. Give the names of Hutu who have been hill-chiefs.
96. Give the names of Hutu who have been army-chiefs.
97. Could a Twa be appointed hill-chief?
98. Give the names of Twa who have been hill-chiefs.
99. Without being ennobled, could a Twa be appointed cattle-chief or land-chief?
100. When a Twa or Hutu was appointed chief, did the Tutsi living under his authority have to obey him?

APPENDIX 2

Computation of answers given to the Questionnaire by a sample of 300 Tutsi.

			Absolute figures	*Per- centages*
1.	Is there a difference between *umulyango* and *uwoko*?	yes no	274 26	91·3 8·6
2.	Do they know the name of their *umulyango* head?	yes no	278 22	92·6 7·3
3.	Is there a difference between *inzu* and *umulyango*?	yes no	295 5	98·3 1·6
4.	Was your family under the authority of one or several army-chiefs?	one several	248 52	82·6 17·3
5.	Do they know the name of the first army to which their *inzu* belonged?	yes no	295 5	98·3 1·6
6.	Has your *inzu* belonged to other armies?	yes no	90 210	30·0 70·0
7.	Have you been *intore*?	yes no	187 113	62·3 37·6
8.	Was any Ruanda a member of an army?	yes no	298 2	99·3 0·6
9.	Was it possible to be a member of two armies?	yes no	1 299	0·3 99·6
10.	Could the army-chief require dues directly from anybody or only through the lineage head?	direct lineage head	0 300	0·0 100·0
11.	Could a man be incorporated into two *intore* companies?	yes no	13 287	4·3 95·6
12.	Do they give the name of somebody who has been in such a situation?	yes no	13 287	4·3 95·6
13.	Was an army member usually the only person of his kin group in the army?	yes no	0 300	0·0 100·0
14.	Or was he with his married sons?	yes no	300 0	100·0 0·0
15.	With his unmarried sons?	yes no	300 0	100·0 0·0
16.	With his brothers?	yes no	300 0	100·0 0·0
17.	With his brothers' children?	yes no	300 0	100·0 0·0

178 THE PREMISE OF INEQUALITY IN RUANDA

		Absolute figures	Per-centages
18. With his sisters' children?	yes	5	1·6
	no	295	98·3
19. With his paternal uncles?	yes	300	100·0
	no	0	0·0
20. With his clients?	yes	22	7·3
	no	277	92·3
	DK[1]	1	0·3
21. Was it possible to have cows not granted by a lord?	yes	277	92·3
	no	17	5·6
	DK	6	2·0
22. Were the cows acquired by independent economic activity regarded as army cows?	yes	256	85·3
	no	42	14·0
	DK	2	0·6
23. Was a married man, the only member left of his *inzu*, regarded as a lineage head from the army point of view?	yes	293	97·6
	no	0	0·0
	DK	7	2·3
24. Was it the same to be a client and to be commanded by an army-chief?	yes	3	1·0
	no	297	99·0
25. Were the 'king's cows' *imbata*?	yes	185	61·6
	no	4	1·3
	DK	111	37·0
26. Did they distinguish in any army two sections (warriors and herdsmen)?	yes	251	83·6
	no	1	0·3
	DK	48	16·0
27. When a new army-chief was appointed, were *murundo* and/ or *indabukirano* obligatory?	*mur.* only	0	0·0
	ind. only	10	3·3
	both	288	96·0
	DK	2	0·6
28. If one had no cows, was one obliged to give a recognition gift?	yes	24	8·0
	no	275	91·6
	DK	1	0·3
29. Had the army-chief the effective disposal of the *murundo* cows?	yes	300	100·0
	no	0	0·0
30. Could the army-chief order the numbering by himself?	yes	14	4·6
	no	269	89·6
	DK	17	5·6

[1] The symbol DK denotes not only the avowed ignorance of the informants. It has been used also when an answer had to be discarded for other reasons such as its irrelevance indicating that the informant did not understand it, or when it appeared clearly in the interview that the informant was giving any answer for answer's sake, or was answering what he thought the anthropologist wanted.

APPENDIX TWO

		Absolute figures	Percentages
31. Who minded the cattle taken in the *murundo*?	*abashumba* only	106	35·3
	inkomamas only	0	0·0
	both	158	52·6
	a warrior	1	0·3
	DK	35	11·6
32. A dispute between two Tutsi of the same army and the same hill was judged by:	their army-chief	274	91·3
	their land-chief	6	2·0
	DK	20	6·6
33. A dispute between two Tutsi from different armies was judged by:	one army-chief	19	6·3
	both army-chiefs	245	81·6
	their land-chiefs	7	2·3
	DK	29	9·6
34. With whom had a client to lodge a complaint against his lord?	client's army-chief	158	52·6
	lord's army-chief	20	6·6
	king	34	11·3
	DK	88	29·3
35. With whom had a lord to lodge a complaint against his client?	client's army-chief	39	13·0
	lord's army-chief	159	53·0
	land-chief of both	1	0·3
	king	28	9·3
	DK	73	24·3
36. If one wanted one's litigation to be judged by the king, it was advisable to be accompanied by:	one's lord	117	39·0
	one's army-chief	82	27·3
	both of them	54	18·0
	DK	47	15·6
37. Could everybody appeal to the king?	yes	266	88·6
	no	26	8·6
	DK	8	2·6
38. Were those who prevented somebody from appealing to the king punished?	yes	149	49·6
	no	82	27·3
	DK	69	23·0
39. Could army members have their army-chief dismissed?	yes	248	82·6
	no	44	14·6
	DK	8	2·6
40. Who brought the case to the mwami?	all army mem.	5	1·6
	a delegation	215	71·6
	DK	80	26·6
41. What section of the army had to provide the court with *inkuke*?	*abashumba*	295	98·3
	warriors	1	0·3
	DK	4	1·3

180 THE PREMISE OF INEQUALITY IN RUANDA

		Absolute figures	Per- centages
42. What section of the army had to provide the court with jugs of milk?	*abashumba*	296	98·6
	warriors	0	0·0
	DK	4	1·3
43. With foodstuffs?	*abashumba*	3	1·0
	warriors	11	3·6
	Hutu army mem.	277	92·3
	DK	9	3·0
44. With bulls to be slaughtered?	*abashumba*	268	89·3
	warriors	2	0·6
	both sections	8	2·6
	DK	22	7·3
45. With steers for divination purposes?	*abashumba*	123	41·0
	warriors	2	2·6
	both sections	166	55·3
	DK	9	3·0
46. What section of the army had to maintain the enclosure?	*abashumba*	11	3·6
	warriors	2	0·6
	Hutu army mem.	4	1·3
	all army mem.	278	92·6
	DK	5	1·6
47. All these services and dues were given by:	lineage head	294	98·0
	each member	2	0·6
	DK	4	1·3
48. Was the country divided into several districts?	yes	290	96·6
	no	7	2·3
	DK	3	1·0
49. What were the names of these districts?	*igikingi*	10	3·3
	igiti	58	19·3
	urugo	36	12·0
	umurwa	22	7·3
	ubukebe	72	24·0
	igikingi, igiti, rugo	5	1·6
	igiti, rugo	11	3·6
	igikingi, igiti	17	5·6
	igiti, ubuheke	25	8·3
	igikingi, igiti, ubuheke	3	1·0
	DK	41	13·6
50. Do they know the name of the royal residence in the place where they lived?	yes	258	86·0
	no	28	9·3
	DK	14	4·6

APPENDIX TWO 181

		Absolute figures	*Per-centages*
51. Do they remember the names of other such residences?	yes	283	94·3
	no	16	5·3
	DK	1	0·3
52. Do they understand *umunyam-ukenke* in the sense of cattle-chief?	yes	277	92·3
	no	7	2·6
	DK	16	5·3
53. Do they understand *umunyab-utaka* in the sense of land-chief?	yes	283	94·3
	no	6	2·0
	DK	11	3·6
54. Who collected the *urutete* for the court?	land-chief	267	89·0
	army-chief	11	3·6
	both of them	3	1·0
	another person	6	2·0
	DK	13	4·3
55. In addition to milk and *inkuke*, which other cattle dues were sent to the residence?	milk only	0	0·0
	inkuke only	30	10·0
	both	233	77·3
	neither of them	32	10·6
	DK	5	1·6
56. Who required these additional jugs of milk from the hill-chief?	cattle-chief	204	68·0
	another person	70	23·3
	DK	26	8·6
57. Which cows provided that milk?	indep. acquired	1	0·3
	abashumba's cows	247	82·3
	others' cows	33	11·0
	DK	19	6·3
58. Do they understand *abakoni* in the sense of those who seized cattle in expeditions?	yes	203	67·6
	another meaning	49	16·3
	DK	48	16·0
59. For whose benefit were the cattle seized by *abakoni*?	army-chief	6	2·0
	mwami	261	87·0
	DK	33	11·0
60. *Umudende* means:			
badge for having killed 7 men		206	68·6
badge		74	24·6
something else or DK		20	6·6
61. How many names do they remember of warriors having worn *umudende*?	five or more	114	38·0
	less than 5	140	46·0
	none	46	15·3
62. *Impotore* means:			
badge for having killed 14 men		42	14·0
badge		133	44·3
something else or DK		125	41·6

182 THE PREMISE OF INEQUALITY IN RUANDA

		Absolute figures	*Per-centages*
63. How many names do they re-member of warriors having worn *impotore*?	five or more	12	4·0
	less than five	78	26·0
	none	210	70·0
64. *Gucana uruti* means:			
	ritual after having killed 21 men	32	10·6
	a military honour	213	71·0
	something else or DK	55	18·3
65. How many names do they remember of warriors having received that honour?	five or more	5	1·6
	less than five	108	36·0
	none	187	62·3
66. Who granted the *umudende* badge?	oneself	16	5·3
	army-chief	2	0·6
	king	245	81·6
	DK	37	12·6
67. Who granted the *impotore* badge?	oneself	5	1·6
	king	164	54·6
	DK	131	43·6
68. Who performed the ritual of *gucana uruti*?	oneself	146	48·6
	army-chief	1	0·3
	lord	2	0·6
	king	89	29·6
	DK	62	20·6
69. Did the cattle army include only *nyambo*?	yes	23	7·6
	no	267	89·0
	DK	10	3·3
70. Did the army cattle include the army-chief's herds?	yes	287	95·6
	no	3	1·0
	DK	10	3·3
71. Did the army cattle include the cows given to the army warriors as rewards for bravery?	yes	284	94·6
	no	5	1·6
	DK	10	3·3
72. Did the army cattle include the cows received as bride-wealth by army members?	yes	286	95·3
	no	4	1·3
	DK	10	3·3
73. Did the army cattle include the cows received as gifts by the army members?	yes	287	95·6
	no	3	1·0
	DK	10	3·3
74. Did the army cattle include the cows received in exchange with the army members?	yes	286	95·3
	no	4	1·3
	DK	10	3·3

APPENDIX TWO

		Absolute figures	*Per-centages*
75. The hill-chief received his office from:	land-chief	5	1·6
	cattle-chief	8	2·6
	army-chief	26	8·6
	king	97	32·3
	cattle-chief, army-chief	17	5·6
	land-, army-c., king	1	0·3
	army-c., king	68	22·6
	cattle-c., army-c., king	21	7·0
	land-c., king	1	0·3
	cattle-c., king	9	3·0
	DK	47	15·6
76. The superior of the hill-chief was:	land-chief	7	2·3
	cattle-chief	30	10·0
	army-chief	77	25·6
	lord	1	0·3
	another person	63	21·0
	cattle-c., army-c.	38	12·6
	cattle-c., king	2	0·6
	army-c., king	7	2·3
	DK	75	25·0
77. The area of the *umusozi*, when compared to that of the *ibikingi* was:	larger	290	96·6
	the same	8	2·6
	DK	2	0·6
78. Were there *ibikingi* depending directly on the royal court?	yes	294	98·0
	no	4	1·3
	DK	2	0·6
79. Who appointed the heads of these *ibikingi*?	king	296	98·6
	somebody else	1	0·3
	DK	3	1·0
80. Had the cattle-chief authority over them?	yes	101	33·6
	no	192	64·0
	DK	7	2·3
81. Could the land-chief require labour from those living on these royal *ibikingi*?	yes	64	21·3
	no	232	77·3
	DK	4	1·3
82. Were those who had received these *ibikingi* from the king under the army-chief's authority?	yes	171	57·0
	no	128	42·6
	DK	1	0·3

184 THE PREMISE OF INEQUALITY IN RUANDA

		Absolute figures	*Per- centages*
83. Was the cattle-chief allowed to retain a part of the milk he sent to the court?	yes no DK	18 273 9	6·0 91·0 3·0
84. Was the hill-chief allowed to retain a part of the milk he sent to the cattle-chief?	yes no DK	16 276 8	5·3 92·0 2·6
85. Was the land-chief allowed to retain a part of the foodstuffs he sent to the court?	yes no DK	296 0 4	98·6 0·0 1·3
86. Was the hill-chief allowed to retain a part of the foodstuffs he sent to the land-chief?	yes no DK	285 8 7	95·0 2·6 2·3
87. Do they know the name of a hill on which there was a royal cemetery?	yes Rutare no DK	263 214 30 7	87·6 71·6 10·0 2·3
88. Were the people living on such hills obliged to pay agricultural dues to the court?	yes no DK	13 251 36	4·3 83·6 12·0
89. Do they know the name of a *mwiru's* place?	yes no DK	229 55 16	76·3 18·3 5·3
90. Was such a place submitted to the authority of the cattle- and land-chiefs?	yes no DK	3 237 60	1·0 79·0 20·0
91. Could the same person be at the same time cattle- and land-chief?	yes no DK	107 180 13	35·6 60·0 4·3
92. Could a Hutu be cattle-chief?	yes no DK	18 273 9	6·0 91·0 3·0
93. Could a Hutu be land-chief?	yes no DK	275 21 4	91·6 7·0 1·3
94. Do they know the names of Hutu cattle-chiefs?	yes no	14 286	4·6 95·3
95. Do they know the names of Hutu land-chiefs? Do they know the names of Hutu hill-chiefs?	yes no yes no DK	258 42 207 83 10	86·0 14·0 69·0 27·3 3·3

APPENDIX TWO

		Absolute figures	*Per-centages*
96. Do they know the names of Hutu army-chiefs?	yes	167	55·6
	no	130	43·3
	DK	3	1·0
97. Could a Twa be appointed hill-chief?	yes	201	67·0
	no	96	32·0
	DK	3	1·0
98. Do they know the names of Twa who have been hill-chiefs?	yes	195	65·0
	no	101	33·6
	DK	4	1·3
99. Could a Twa be appointed cattle-chief or land-chief without being ennobled?	yes	0	0·0
	no	297	99·0
	DK	3	1·0
100. When Tutsi lived under the authority of a Twa or Hutu chief, did they have to obey him?	yes	284	94·6
	no	7	2·3
	DK	9	3·0

APPENDIX 3

Bibliography

Adamantidis, D., 1956, *Monographie pastorale du Ruanda-Urundi*. Bruxelles.

Adriaens, E. L., et Lozet, F., 1951: 'Contribution à l'étude des boissons fermentées indigènes du Ruanda-Urundi', *Bulletin agricole du Congo belge*. Bruxelles. pp. 933-50.

Arian, A. d', 1954: 'Une enquête pilote sur l'alimentation des indigènes du Ruanda-Urundi', *Zaïre*. Bruxelles. Vol. viii, 4, pp. 339-51.

Arianoff, A. d', 1951: 'Origine des clans hamites du Ruanda', *Zaïre*. Bruxelles. Vol. v, 1, pp. 45-54.

—— 1952: *Histoire des Bagesera, souverains du Gisaka*. Bruxelles.

Arnoux, A., 1912-13: 'Le culte de la société secrète des Imandwa au Ruanda', *Anthropos*. Vienne. T. vii, pp. 273 ff., 529 ff., 840 ff.; t. viii, pp. 110 ff., 754 ff.

—— 1918: 'La divination au Ruanda', *Anthropos*. Vienne. T. xiii, pp. 1-57.

—— 1931: 'Quelques notes sur les enfants au Ruanda et à l'Urundi', *Anthropos*. Vienne. T. xxvi, pp. 341-51.

—— 1948: *Les Pères Blancs aux sources du Nil*. Paris.

Baumann, H., et Westermann, D., 1948: *Les peuples et les civilisations de l'Afrique*. Paris.

Biche, Y., 1956: 'Le problème de l'élevage du bétail au Ruanda-Urundi', *Le Ruanda-Urundi, ses ressources naturelles, ses populations* (Les naturalistes belges, ed.). Bruxelles. pp. 60-71.

Borgerhoff, R., 1928: *Le Ruanda-Urundi*. Bruxelles.

Bourgeois, R., 1954: *Banyarwanda et Barundi: La coutume*. Bruxelles.

—— 1956: *Banyarwanda et Barundi: Religion et magie*. Bruxelles.

—— 1957: *Banyarwanda et Barundi: Ethnographie*. Bruxelles.

—— 1958: *Banyarwanda et Barundi: L'évolution du contrat de bail à cheptel*. Bruxelles.

Close, Jean, 1955: *Enquête alimentaire au Ruanda-Urundi*. Bruxelles.

Coulborn, Rushton, ed., 1956: *Feudalism in History*. Princeton, N.J.

Coupez, André, 1956: 'Deux textes rwanda: initiation au culte de Ryangombe', *Kongo-Overzee*. Anvers. T. xxii, 2-3, pp. 129-51.

Coupez, André, et Kamanzi, Thomas, 1957: 'Rythmes quantitatifs en poésie rwaanda', *Folia Scientifica Africae Centralis*. Bukavu. T. iii, 3, pp. 58-60.

Czekanowski, J., 1911: *Forschungen im Nil-Kongo-Zwischengebiet*, Dritter Band. Leipzig.

—— 1917: *Forschungen im Nil-Kongo-Zwischengebiet*, Erster Band. Leipzig.

Delmas, P., 1930: 'La vache au Ruanda', *Anthropos*. Vienne. T. xxv, pp. 945-52.

APPENDIX THREE 187

Delmas, P., 1950: *Généalogie de la noblesse du Ruanda*. Kabgayi.

Dessart, Charles, et Cayet, J., 1953: *Ruanda-Urundi*. Bruxelles.

Dollart, J., and others, 1939: *Frustration and Aggression*. New Haven, Conn.

Dresse, P., 1940; *Le Ruanda d'aujourd'hui*. Bruxelles.

Dufays, F., 1912: *Wörterbuch Deutsch-Kinyarwanda*. Trier.

Dufays, F., et De Moor, V., 1939: *Les enchaînés au Kinyaga*. Bruxelles.

Evans-Pritchard, E. E., 1940: *The Nuer*, Oxford.

Everaerts, E., 1947: *Monographie agricole du Ruanda-Urundi*. Bruxelles.

Fortes, M., and Evans-Pritchard, E. E., eds., 1940: *African Political Systems*. London.

Gabriel, Fr., 1929: *Étude du Runyarwanda*. Gand.

Gerkens, G., 1949: *Les Batutsi et les Bahutu: Contribution à l'anthropologie du Ruanda et de l'Urundi, d'après les mensurations recueillies par la mission G. Smets*. Bruxelles.

Gevers, Marie, 1953: *Des mille collines aux neuf volcans*. Paris.

Götzen, G. A. von, 1899: *Durch Afrika von Ost nach West*. Berlin.

Gourou, Pierre, 1954: *La densité de la population du Ruanda-Urundi*. Bruxelles.

(Gouvernement du Ruanda-Urundi), (1956): *Historique et chronologie du Ruanda*. (Usumbura).

Guillaume, H., 1956: 'Les populations du Ruanda et de l'Urundi', *Le Ruanda-Urundi, ses ressources naturelles, ses populations* (Les naturalistes belges, ed.). Bruxelles. pp. 109-53.

Gusinde, M., 1949: *Die Twa-Pygmaën in Ruanda*. Wien.

Halley, Lord, 1957: *An African Survey Revised 1956*. London.

Harroy, Jean-Paul, 1954: 'La lutte contre la dissipation des ressources naturelles au Ruanda-Urundi', *Civilisations*. Bruxelles. Vol. iv, 3, pp. 363-74.

Herskovits, Melville J., 1926: 'The Cattle Complex in East Africa', *American Anthropologist*. Menasha, Wisc. Vol. 28, 1, pp. 230-72; 2, pp. 361-88; 3, pp. 424-528; 4, pp. 633-64.

—— 1948: *Man and His Works*. New York.

Hertefelt, Marcel d', 1959: 'Huwelijk, familie en aanverwantschap bij de Réera van noordwestelijk Rwaanda', *Zaïre*. Bruxelles. Vol. xiii, 2, pp. 115-47; 3, pp. 243-78.

Heusch, Luc de, 1958: *Essais sur le symbolisme de l'inceste royal en Afrique*. Bruxelles.

Hiernaux, Jean, 1952: 'La pression sanguine des indigènes du Ruanda-Urundi', *Annales de la société belge de médecine tropicale*. Bruxelles. T. xxxiii, 4, pp. 379-88.

—— 1954a: 'Influence de la nutrition sur la morphologie des Bahutu du Ruanda', *Actes du IVe Congrès international des Sciences anthropologiques et ethnologiques, Vienne, 1952: Anthropologica*. Vienne. pp. 157-62.

—— 1954b: *Les caractères physiques des populations du Ruanda et de l'Urundi*. Bruxelles.

188 THE PREMISE OF INEQUALITY IN RUANDA

Hiernaux, Jean, 1956a: 'Note sur une ancienne population du Ruanda-Urundi: les Renge', *Zaïre*. Bruxelles. Vol. x, 4, pp. 351-60.

—— 1956b: *Analyse de la variation des caractères physiques humains dans une région de l'Afrique centrale (Ruanda-Urundi et Kivu)*. Tervuren.

Hurel, E., 1920: *Grammaire Kinyarwanda*. Alger.

—— 1922: *La poésie chez les primitifs*. Bruxelles.

—— 1934: *Dictionnaire Français-Runyarwanda et Runyarwanda-Français* (2e éd.). Kabgayi.

Inforcongo, eds., (1958): *Ruanda-Urundi*. (Bruxelles).

Jentgen, P., 1957: *Les frontières du Ruanda-Urundi et le régime international de tutelle*. Bruxelles.

Kagame, Alexis, 1947a: 'Le code ésotérique de la dynastie du Ruanda', *Zaïre*. Bruxelles. Vol. i, 4, pp. 363-86.

—— 1947b: 'La poésie pastorale au Ruanda', *Zaïre*. Bruxelles. Vol. i, 7, pp. 791-800.

—— 1947c: 'La voix de l'Afrique', *Africa*. London. Vol. xvii, 1, pp. 41-46.

—— 1950: 'Les poètes du Ruanda et la famine', *Jeune Afrique*. Elisabethville. No. 9, pp. 5-13.

—— 1951: *La poésie dynastique du Ruanda*. Bruxelles.

—— 1952: *Le code des institutions politiques du Ruanda précolonial*. Bruxelles.

—— 1954: *Les organisations socio-familiales de l'ancien Ruanda*. Bruxelles.

—— 1956: *La philosophie bantu-rwandaise de l'être*. Bruxelles.

—— 1959: *La notion de génération appliquée, à la généalogie dynastique et à l'histoire du Rwanda des Xe-XIe siècles à nos jours*. Bruxelles.

Kamanzi, Thomas, et Nkongori, Laurent, 1957: *Proverbes du Rwanda*. Tervuren.

Kandt, R., 1921: *Caput Nili*. Berlin.

Kiendl, H. 1935: *Ruanda und die Nilgiris, ein geographisch-völkerkundlicher Vergleich*. Hamburg.

Kluckhohn, Clyde, 1941: 'Patterning as Exemplified in Navaho Culture', *Language, Culture and Personality* (L. Spier, A. I. Hallowell and S. S. Newman, eds.). Menasha, Wisc. pp. 109-30.

—— 1943: 'Covert Culture and Administration Problems', *American Anthropologist*. Menasha, Wisc. Vol. 45, 2, pp. 213-27.

Lacger, L. de, 1939: *Ruanda: Le Ruanda ancien, le Ruanda moderne* (2 vols.). Namur.

Ladd, John, 1957: *The Structure of a Moral Code*. Cambridge, Mass.

Lasswell, H. D., 1948: *Power and Personality*. New York.

Lebrun, J., 1955: *Esquisse de la végétation du Parc National de la Kagera*. Bruxelles.

—— 1956: 'La végétation et les territoires botaniques du Ruanda-Urundi'. *Le Ruanda-Urundi, ses ressources naturelles, ses populations* (Les naturalistes belges, ed.). Bruxelles. pp. 22-48.

APPENDIX THREE 189

Lestrade, A., 1955: *La médicine indigène au Ruanda et lexique des termes médicaux français-urunyarwanda*. Bruxelles.

Leurquin, Philippe, 1957: 'La vie économique du paysan ruanda. L'exemple de Karama, Nyaruguru', *Zaïre*. Bruxelles. Vol. xi, 1, pp. 41-67.

—— 1958: 'Economie de subsistance et alimentation au Ruanda-Urundi. Quelques cas concrets', *Zaïre*. Bruxelles. Vol. xii, 1, pp. 3-35.

Lévi-Strauss, Claude, 1949: *Les structures élémentaires de la parenté*. Paris.

Linton, Ralph, 1936: *The Study of Man*. New York.

Loupias, 1908: 'Tradition des Batutsi sur la création du monde', *Anthropos*. Vienne. T. iii, 1, pp. 1-13.

Louwers, O. P., 1935: 'La conquête du Ruanda-Urundi', *Bulletin des séances de l'Institut Royal Colonial Belge*. Bruxelles. Vol. vi, 1, pp. 167-78; 2, pp. 372-8.

Lowie, Robert, 1948: *Social Organization*. New York.

MacIver, R. M., and Page, C. H., 1949: *Society*. London.

Malinowski, Bronislaw, 1931: 'Culture', *Encyclopaedia of Social Sciences*. Vol. iv, s.v.

—— 1944: *A Scientific Theory of Culture and Other Essays*. Chapel Hill, N.C.

Maquet, Emma, 1957: 'Le potier Semusambi', *Jeune Afrique*. Elisabethville. No. 24, pp. 19-21.

Maquet, Emma, et Thys, Robert, 1955: 'Le tréfilage du cuivre et les bracelets en fil de cuivre au Ruanda et au Buhunde', *Anthropos*. Fribourg. T. 50, 4, pp. 434-7.

Maquet, Jacques J., 1949a: 'L'unité de l'anthropologie culturelle', *Bulletin de l'Institut de recherches économiques et sociales de l'Université de Louvain*. Louvain. Vol. xv, 5, pp. 3-37.

—— 1949b: *Sociologie de la connaissance*. Louvain.

—— 1951: *The Sociology of Knowledge*. Boston.

—— 1952: 'Le problème de la domination tutsi', *Zaïre*. Bruxelles. Vol. vi, 10, pp. 1011-6.

—— 1953: 'Les groupes de parenté du Rwanda ancien', *Africa*. London. Vol. xxiii, 1, pp. 25-29.

—— 1954a: 'The Kingdom of Ruanda', *African Worlds* (International African Institute, eds.). London. pp. 164-89. (Reprinted in Maquet, 1958).

—— 1954b: *Le système des relations sociales dans le Ruanda ancien*. Tervuren, Belgique.

—— 1954c: *Aide-mémoire d'ethnologie africaine*. Bruxelles.

—— 1955: 'Les pasteurs de l'Itombwe', Avec le concours de Denyse Hiernaux-L'hoëst. *Science et nature*, Paris. No. 8, pp. 3-12.

—— 1956: 'Ruanda-Urundi: Lands of the Mountains of the Moon', *Les Beaux-Arts*. Brussels. Special issue. pp. 15, 38.

190 THE PREMISE OF INEQUALITY IN RUANDA

Maquet, Jacques J., 1957: *Ruanda. Essai photographique sur une société africaine en transition.* Avec la collaboration de Denyse Hiernaux-L'hoëst. Bruxelles.

—— 1958: 'The Religion of the Kingdom of Ruanda', *Reader in Comparative Religion: An Anthropological Approach* (Lessa, William A. and Vogt, Evon Z., eds.). Evanston, Illinois. pp. 523-32. (Reprinted from Maquet, 1954a).

—— 1959: 'Ruanda-Urundi: The Introduction of an Electoral System for Councils in a Caste Society', *From Tribal Rule to Modern Government* (Raymond Apthorpe, ed.). Lusaka. pp. 57-68. (Mimeographed.)

Maquet, Jacques J., et Hertefelt, Marcel d', 1959: *Elections en société féodale. Une étude sur l'introduction du vote populaire au Ruanda-Urundi.* Bruxelles.

Maquet, Jacques J., et Naigiziki, Saverio, 1957: 'Les droits fonciers dans le Ruanda ancien', *Zaïre.* Bruxelles. Vol. xi, 4, pp. 339-59.

Meinhard, H., 1947a: *Provisional Outline of the Ethnographic Provinces of East Africa.* (London). (Mimeographed.)

—— 1947b: *The Interlacustrine Bantu. A Survey.* (London.) (Mimeographed.)

Meisel, James H., 1958: *The Myth of the Ruling Class.* Ann Arbor, Michigan.

Merriam, Alan P., 1953: 'Les styles vocaux dans la musique du Ruanda-Urundi', *Jeune Afrique.* Elisabethville. No. 7, pp. 12-16.

—— 1953b: 'African Music Re-examined in the Light of New Material from the Belgian Congo and Ruanda-Urundi', *Zaïre.* Bruxelles. Vol. vii, 3, pp. 244-53.

—— 1953c: 'The Game of Kubuguza among the Abatutsi of North-East Ruanda', *Man.* London. Vol. 53, art. 262, pp. 169-72.

—— 1954: 'Banyaruanda Proverbs', *Journal of American Folklore.* Lancaster. Vol. 67, 265, pp. 267-84.

—— 1957: 'Yovu Songs from Ruanda', *Zaïre.* Bruxelles. Vol. xi, 9-10, pp. 933-66.

Mineur, G., 1945: 'Le mwami peut-il modifier la coutume?', *Servir.* Astrida, 6e année, 1, pp. 50-52.

—— 1948: 'Le divorce en droit coutumier', *Bulletin des juridictions indigènes.* Elisabethville. 16e année, 12, pp. 361-3.

Ministère des Colonies, 1922a-57a: *Rapport sur l'administration belge du Ruanda-Urundi.* Bruxelles. (Published annually.)

—— 1951b: *Plan décenal pour le développement économique et social du Ruanda-Urundi.* Bruxelles.

—— 1952b: *Atlas du Ruanda-Urundi.* Bruxelles.

Mungarulire, P., 1946: 'Déplacement d'un shebuja. Obligation de le suivre', *Bulletin de jurisprudence des tribunaux indigènes du Ruanda-Urundi.* Astrida. No. 1, pp. 49-50.

Murdock, G. P., 1949: *Social Structure.* New York.

APPENDIX THREE 191

Naigiziki, Saverio, 1950: *Escapade ruandaise*. Bruxelles.
—— 1955: *Mes transes à trente ans* (2 vols.). Astrida.
—— 1958: 'L'optimiste', *Jeune Afrique*. Elisabethville. No. 27, pp. 17-29; 28, pp. 27-35; 29, pp. 24-31.
—— 1959: 'Ruanda', *Women's Role in the Development of Tropical and Sub-Tropical Countries* (International Institute of Differing Civilizations, eds.). Brussels. pp. 151-7.
Neesen, Victor, 1953a: 'Le premier recensement par échantillonage au Ruanda-Urundi', *Zaïre*. Bruxelles. Vol. vii, 5, 469-88.
—— 1953b: 'Quelques données démographiques sur la population du Ruanda-Urundi', *Zaïre*. Bruxelles. Vol. vii, 10, pp. 1011-25.
Oberg, K., 1940: 'The Kingdom of Ankole in Uganda', *African Political Systems* (M. Fortes and E. E. Evans-Pritchard, eds.). London. pp. 121-62.
Opler, M. E., 1945: 'Themes as Dynamic Forces in Culture', *American Journal of Sociology*. Chicago. pp. 137-66.
Oppenheimer, F., 1922: *The State*. New York.
Pagès, A., 1925: 'Au Ruanda, sur les bords du Lac Kivu', *Anthropos*. Vienne. T. xx, pp. 860-80.
—— 1932: 'Cérémonie du mariage au Ruanda', *Congo*. Bruxelles. Vol. i, 5, pp. 645-63; ii, 1, pp. 42-68.
—— 1933: *Un royaume hamite au centre de l'Afrique*. Bruxelles.
—— 1934a: 'Cérémonies qui entourent la naissance d'un enfant et la réclusion de la mère', *Congo*. Bruxelles. Vol. iii, 2, pp. 203-20.
—— 1934b: 'La vie intellectuelle des Noirs du Ruanda', *Congo*. Bruxelles. Vol. iii, 3, pp. 357-89; 4, pp. 481-503; 5, pp. 657-71.
—— 1935a: 'Le mariage parmi les Banyarwanda', *Grands Lacs*. Namur. 51e année, 5-6, pp. 177-80.
—— 1935b: 'Kayi juka, le chef qui eut les yeux crevés', *Grands Lacs*. Namur. 51e année, 5-6, p. 231.
—— 1935c: 'Visions, oracles et prophéties', *Grands Lacs*. Namur. 51e année, 11-2, pp. 517-22.
—— 1937: 'Le mariage chez les Banyarwanda', *Bulletin des juridictions indigènes*. Elisabethville. 5e année, 4, pp. 114-15.
—— 1938: 'Note sur le régime des biens dans la province du Bugoye', *Congo*. Bruxelles. Vol. vii, 4, pp. 392-433.
—— 1947: 'Proverbes et sentences du Ruanda', *Aequatoria*. Coquilhatville. 10e année, 3, pp. 81-88; 4, pp. 144-50; 11e année, 2, pp. 53-59; 3, pp. 81-86.
—— 1949: 'Au Ruanda. Droits et pouvoirs des chefs sous la suzeraineté du roi hamite', *Zaïre*. Bruxelles. Vol. iii, 4, pp. 359-77.
—— 1950: 'Au Ruanda. A la cour du Mwami', *Zaïre*. Bruxelles. Vol. iv, 5, pp. 471-7.
Pauwels, M., 1946: 'La hutte au Rukiga de Byumba', *Grands Lacs*. Namur. 62e année, 3, pp. 173-9.
—— 1947a: 'Coutumes du Ruanda', *Grands Lacs*. Namur. 62e année, 7, pp. 25-30.

192 THE PREMISE OF INEQUALITY IN RUANDA

Pauwels, M., 1947b: 'Apothekerspraktijken in Ruanda', *Nieuw Afrika*. Anvers. 63e année, 10, pp. 403-6.

—— 1948: 'Au Ruanda. Quand et comment ils mangent', *Grand Lacs*. Namur. Nov. 15, pp. 51-54.

—— 1949a: 'Epousailles au Ruanda', *Grands Lacs*. Namur. Mars 15, pp. 47-50.

—— 1949b: 'La magie au Ruanda', *Grands Lacs*. Namur. Oct. 15, pp. 17-48.

—— 1949c: 'Kuraguza urugimbu', *The Uganda Journal*. Kampala. Vol. xiii, 1, pp. 27-30.

—— 1951a: 'Le culte de Nyabingi (Ruanda)', *Anthropos*. Fribourg. Vol. xxxxvi, pp. 337-57.

—— 1951b: 'Fiancée et jeune mariée au Ruanda', *Zaïre*. Bruxelles. Vol. v, 2, pp. 115-35.

—— 1952: 'Les couleurs et les dessins au Ruanda', *Anthropos*. Fribroug. Vol. xxxxvii, pp. 473-82.

—— 1953: 'L'habitation au Ruanda', *Kongo-Oversee*. Anvers. Vol. xiv, pp. 20-62.

—— 1958: *Imana et le culte des mânes au Rwanda*. Bruxelles.

Parsons, T., and Shils, E. A., eds., 1951: *Toward a General Theory of Action*. Cambridge, Mass.

Radcliffe-Brown, A. R., 1922: *The Andaman Islanders*. Cambridge England.

—— 1940: 'On Social Structure', *The Journal of the Royal Anthropological Institute*. London. Vol. 70, pp. 1-12.

—— 1952: *Structure and Function in Primitive Society*. London.

—— 1958: *Method in Social Anthropology* (M. N. Srininas, ed.). Chicago.

Risselin, T., 1949: 'La chanson savante chez les Watousis', *Jeune Afrique*. Elisabethville. No. 6, pp. 24-25.

Roscoe, J., 1924: *Immigrants and their Influence on the Lake Regions of Africa*. Cambridge, England.

Royal Anthropological Institute of Great Britain and Ireland, eds., 1951: *Notes and Queries on Anthropology*. London.

Rubinsztein, W., 1952: *Recherches sur l'imprégnation tuberculeuse et le virage après la vaccination par le B.C.G. des populations indigènes du Ruanda-Urundi*. Bruxelles.

Ruhara, Rwamasirabo, et Sendanyoye, 1948: 'Le buhake, une coutume essentiellement munyarwanda', *Bulletin des juridictions indigènes*. Elisabethville 16e année, 8, pp. 245-58; 9, pp. 261-5.

Russell, B., 1938: *Power*. London.

Saint Thibaut, Sœur, 1948: 'L'hygiène de la vie familiale indigène dans la région des Grands Lacs', *Grands Lacs*. Namur. Nov. 15, pp. 19-37.

Sandrart, G., 1930: *Cours de droit coutumier*. Astrida. (Mimeographed.)

Scaetta, H., 1932: *Les famines périodiques dans le Ruanda. Contribution à l'étude des aspects biologiques du phénomène*. Bruxelles.

APPENDIX THREE 193

Schumacher, P., 1910: 'Die Ehe in Ruanda', *Anthropos*. Wien. T. v, pp. 870-906.

—— 1927: 'Imana-Glaube in Ruanda', *Anthropos*. Wien T. xxii, pp. 617-18.

—— 1935: 'Sommaire historique des origines du sentiment religieux au Ruanda', *Grands Lacs*. Namur. 52e année, 11-12, pp. 554-60.

—— 1939: 'Die hamitische Wahrsagerei in Ruanda', *Anthropos*. Friburg, Vol. xxxiv, pp. 130-206.

—— 1942: 'Contribution au calendrier agricole indigène du Ruanda', *Bulletin agricole du Congo belge*. Bruxelles. Vol. xxxiii, pp. 500-9.

—— 1947: 'Psyché au centre africain', *Zaïre*. Bruxelles. Vol. i, 6, pp. 679-86.

—— 1948a: 'La fillette exposée dans la cîme de l'arbre', *Aequatoria*. Coquilhatville. 11e année, 4, pp. 143-6.

—— 1948b: 'Caractérologie au Ruanda', *Zaïre*. Bruxelles. Vol. ii, 6, pp. 591-624.

—— 1949: 'Au Ruanda: considérations sur le nature de l'homme', *Zaïre*. Bruxelles. Vol. iii, 3, pp. 257-78.

—— 1956: *Dictionnaire phonétique Français-Runyaruanda et Runyaruanda-Français*. Kabgayi.

Schwetz, J., 1948: *Recherches sur le paludisme endémique et le paludisme épidémique dans le Ruanda-Urundi*. Bruxelles.

Seligman, C. G., 1930: *Races of Africa*. London.

Sendanyoye, G., 1944: 'Le testament au Ruanda', *Servir*. Astrida. 5e année, 6, pp. 283-90.

—— 1945: 'La dévolution des biens par voie successorale', *Servir*. Astrida. 6e année, 4, pp. 200-2; 5, 249-54; 6, 302-6.

—— 1946: 'La tutelle en droit munyarwanda', *Bulletin de jurisprudence des tribunaux indigènes du Ruanda-Urundi*. Astrida. No. 1, pp. 12-25.

—— 1947a: 'Note sur les formes de testament dans le droit coutumier munyarwanda de la région d'Astrida', *Bulletin des juridictions indigènes*. Elisabethville. 15e année, 1, pp. 1-5.

—— 1947b: 'Conséquences du divorce quant à la dot et à la légitimation des enfants', *Bulletin de jurisprudence des tribunaux indigènes du Ruanda-Urundi*. Astrida. No. 4, pp. 201-7.

—— 1947c: 'Infractions et sanctions dans l'umurundo', *Bulletin de jurisprudence des tribunaux indigènes du Ruanda-Urundi*. Astrida. No. 6, pp. 305-38.

—— 1948a: 'De la légitimation des enfants naturels et illégitimes en droit munyarwanda', *Bulletin de jurisprudence des tribunaux indigènes du Ruanda-Urundi*. Astrida. No. 5, pp. 246-60.

—— 1948b: 'La dévolution des biens ab intestat', *Bulletin de jurisprudence des tribunaux indigènes du Ruandi-Urundi*. No. 6, pp. 305-38.

194 THE PREMISE OF INEQUALITY IN RUANDA

Sendanyoye, G., 1952: 'Le régime répressif coutumier en matière de viol au Ruanda', *Bulletin des juridictions indigènes*. Elisabethville. 20e année, 9, pp. 249-52.

—— 1957: 'Indagoranyo', *Bulletin des juridictions indigènes*. Elisabethville. 25e année, 3, pp. 74-81.

Seruvumba, N., 1948: 'A propos de la rupture du mariage', *Bulletin de jurisprudence des tribunaux indigènes du Ruanda-Urundi*. Astrida. No. 5, pp. 261-5.

Tenret, J., 1953: *Prospection anti-tuberculeuse au Ruanda-Urundi*. Bruxelles.

—— 1956: *Rapport sur l'activité de la section de prophylaxie de l'Organisation anti-tuberculeuse du Ruanda*. Bruxelles.

Tichelen, Henri E. van, 1957: 'Problèmes du développement économique du Ruanda-Urundi', *Zaïre*. Bruxelles. Vol. xi, 5, pp. 451-74.

United Nations Trusteeship Council, 1948: *Mission de visite dans le territoire sous tutelle du Ruanda-Urundi sous administration belge*. Lake Success, N.Y. (Mimeographed, ref.: T/217, Oct. 31.)

—— 1951: *Report of the United Nations Visiting Mission to Trust Territories in East Africa on Ruanda-Urundi*. New York. (Mimeographed, ref.: T/948, Dec. 27.)

Van Bulck, G., 1956: 'La conception coutumière d'enfant légitime, d'enfant nkuli et d'enfant umusambanano au Ruanda', *Zaïre*. Bruxelles. Vol. x, 7, pp. 729-37.

Van Hove, J., 1941: *Essai de droit coutumier du Ruanda*. Bruxelles.

Van Overschelde, G., 1947: *Bij de reuzen en de dwergen van Ruanda*. Anvers.

Vincent, Marc, 1955: *L'enfant au Ruanda-Urundi*. Bruxelles.

Wilde, Robert de, 1957: 'Les derniers nomades du Ruanda', *Jeune Afrique*. Elisabethville. No. 24, pp. 3-10.

Wittfogel, Karl A., 1957: *Oriental Despotism: A Comparative Study of Total Power*. New Haven, Conn.

Zangrie, Luc, 1951: 'Quelques traces ethnologique de l'origine égyptienne des Batutsi'. *Jeune Afrique*. Elisabethville. No. 15, pp. 9-15.

INDEX

Abanyiginya clan, 108, 116, 125
abatasi, 111
Abega clan, 108, 156
Abortion, 85
Administration, 100, 124, 128, 132, 142, 161, *ill.*; territorial, 101; description of structure, 101–3; analysis, 103–9
Adultery, 51, 74
Affinity, 1, 61–63, 64; system, 29–63; definition, 29; terminology, 52–53, 55–56; by marriage, 52–57
Agnatic relatives, *see* Patrilineal relatives
Agriculture (*see also* Cattle, names of implements, months), 14, 81, 89, 136, 145, 150, 153, 158; beginning, 11; Hutu, 15; implements, 15; crops, 15; yearly calendar, 15; dairy produce, 16, 18; cattle, 16–17; sheep and goats, 17; dues, 101, 102, 104, 108, 114, 139, 140, 176, 184
Ancestor, 36; name, 41; spirit, 46; worship, 47, 87
April, crops, 16; cattle, 17
Army, 109, 111, 145, 150, 156, 173–4, 177, 179; military service, 35; recruitment, 109–10, 155; warriors, 110–11, 112, 113, 116, 117, 118, 121–3, 145, 155, 174, 175, 178, 179, 180, 182; herdsmen, 110–14, 119, 121–3, 174, 178; encampment, 110, 115; tribute, 113–14; expedition, 111, 115, 116, 117, 125, 130, 175, 181; and lineage, 119–20; redistribution of wealth, 120
Army-chief, *see* Chief
August, 16
Aunt (*see also* Maternal and Paternal relatives), 53, 65

Banana, 15, 16, 18; -beer, 15, 18, 19, 91, 102; grove, 21
Bantu, 11, 12
Bark-cloth, 19–20, 24, 81
Basket work, 67, 81, 145
Bead work, 81
Bean, 15, 16, 18, 22, 23, 27, 36, 87, 102, 152
Beer (*see also* Banana-beer, Sorghum-beer), 18, 19, 38, 68, 87, 129, 130, 152; as marriage gift, 70; brewing, 81; as rent, 91

Beverages (*see also* Beer, Hydromel, Milk), 18; as bride-wealth, 69
Bill-hook, 15, 89
Birth, 79, 84
biru, 124–5, 126–7
Blood-feud, 36, 37, 38, 39, 45, 50, 130
Bride, 69
Bridegroom, 69, 71, 72
Bride-wealth (*see also* Cattle), 30, 38, 42, 43, 48, 49, 64, 66, 68, 69–71, 74, 75, 85, 92, 95, 130, 132
Brother, 44, 45, 71, 90, 92, 110, 130, 173, 177
Buffalo, 147
buhake, 5, 129–42, 148, 150, 153, 154, 155, 156, 158, 161
Bull, 87, 88, 174, 180
Burial customs, 38, 47, 88, 103, 176, 184
Butter, 16, 18; as cosmetic, 81

Cassava, 15, 16
Caste (*see also* Hutu and Tutsi), 16, 19, 66, 83, 85, 117–18, 120, 135, 136, 137, 148–53, 158, 164–71
Cattle, 13–14, 15, 36, 48, 111, 115, 116, 117, 120, 125, 130, 131, 135, 154, 161, 178; disease, 14, 127; rearing, 14, 17, 42, 81, 85–86, 89, 136; dairying, 16; magical beliefs, 17, 79; kraal, 20; as wealth, 33, 35, 37, 38, 39, 67, 78, 82, 120; as bride-wealth, 66, 69–70, 112, 129, 182; milking, 68; rights, 91–92, 93, 94, 95, 132, 134, 139, 173–5; dues, 101, 102, 103, 105, 108, 113, 113, 119, 123, 181; *nyambo*, 112, 175, 177, 182; *mabara*, 112; client, 111, 112, 121, 162; as power, 121, 141, 143, 148, 150, 164; cattle-lease, *see buhake*
Celibacy, 74
Chief, 33, 80, 82, 94, 95, 96, 98, 101, 106–7, 114, 116, 118, 124, 151, 155, 157, 168; hill-chief or sub-chief, 21, 102, 103, 105, 107, 142, 151, 153, 175, 176, 181, 183, 184, 185; of *inzu* or *umulyango*, 35, 110; power of, 35, 92, 119–20, 123, 132, 154; and council, 37, 128; land chief, 89, 90, 91, 92, 101, 102, 105, 108, 126, 151, 156, 163, 175, 176, 179, 181, 183, 185; cattle chief, 89, 90, 91, 100,

196 THE PREMISE OF INEQUALITY IN RUANDA

Chief—*cont.*
101, 102, 103, 105, 108, 126, 134, 151, 156, 163, 175, 176, 181, 183, 184, 185; army chief, 100, 106, 108, 109, 110, 111, 114, 115, 116, 119, 121, 122–4, 132, 134, 151, 153, 154, 156, 158, 173, 174, 175, 177, 178, 179, 181, 182, 183, 185
Child, 72, 82–85, 92, 93, 98, 117, 130, 162; of divorced parents, 74, 84; of nuclear and polygynous families, 75; adopted, 75
Child-wealth, 84
Clientage, 25, 46, 66, 82, 83, 100, 126, 129–42, 150, 151, 154, 162, 165, 173, 174, 178, 179; rights of client, 91, 129–30; obligations of, 22, 94, 130–1, 142; cattle client, 11, 112, 121; inheritance of client, 131; analysis of structure, 133–9; feudality, 133, 136–42, 148, 152, 155, 156, 157, 161, 164, 168, 170, *ill.*
Climate, 8–9, 23
Compound, 20–21, 83
Conception, 83
Concubine, 78; Hutu, 66, 76
Contraception, 85
Cooking, 23, 72, 81, 131
Cotton cloth, 20
Council, 37, 128
Court, 22, 66, 67, 78, 82, 86, 102, 104, 109, 117, 120, 130, 153, 174, 176, 179, 180, 184
Cousin, *see* Cross-line relatives and Parallel relatives
Cross-line relatives, 50–52, 64; definition, 29, 50; cousins, 30, 35, 84
Culture, 117, 143, 147, 160; influence of Western, 1, 8, 23, 158, 169; Arab, 1, 8; African, 24; Indian, 24; Tutsi, 170

Dancing, 19, 21, 42, 72, 109, 117, *ill.*
Daughter, 43, 45, 71, 75, 81, 84, 92, 93, 94, 95
Death, 27, 87, 98
Debt, 93, 115
December, crops, 15; cattle, 17
Descent, 29–47, 107
Diet (*see also* Beverages), 16–19, 22–25
Divination, 24, 26, 27, 87, 113, 174, 180, *ill.*
Divorce, 51, 73–74, 77, 84
Dress, 19–22, 95; Tutsi, 14; adornment, 20; inadequacy of, 24
Dwelling-place, 20, 24, 72, 75–76, 91; cleaning, 81

Dynasties, 29
Dysentery, 24

Economy, economic co-operation, 64, 67, 80–82; production, 89–95, 99, 125; of Ruanda, 145
Education, 85, 98, 99, 117, 171
Elephant, 147
Eleusine, 15
Erosion, 9
Exogamy, 34, 37, 46, 65

Family, 1, 2, 3, 92; familial pattern, 42–49, 99; marriage and, 64–88; polygynous and nuclear families, 75–76; economic co-operation, 80–82; head, 90, 95, 102, 104, 107
Father, 29, 42–43, 44, 48, 73, 74, 76, 84, 87, 92, 93, 106, 162, 163, 165, 166; terminology, 40, 52
February, crops, 15; cattle, 17
Fence, 20
Fertility, 67, 83, 145
Feudal organization, *see* Clientage
Ficus, 20; as bride-wealth, 70
Fiscal administration, 104–6
Fishing, 14
Food, 1, 14–19, 95, 98, 104, 174, 176, 180, 184; meat, 14, 18, 22, 120, 129, 130; fish, 14–15
Forestry, 9, 11

garagu, see buhake
Genitor, 69, 71, 84
Goat, 17, 36, 38, 42, 85, 88, 91; as bride-wealth, 69–70
Gourd, 15, 16
Government, 96, 99; central, 124–8, 145, 147, 148, 155, 156, 157
Granary, 16, 20, 48, 102
Grandchild, 44, 75; terminology, 41
Grandfather, 29, 44, 49, 53, 86, 148, 154; terminology, 40, 47, 52
Groundnut, 15

Health (*see also* Diet), 1, 22–28, 99; famine, 23; cleanliness, 23, 24; diseases (*see also* names of diseases), 23–24; clothing, 24; herbal medicine, 24; magical treatment of disease, 24; mental health, 25–26; effect of supernatural beliefs, 26–28
Herbs, 68, 71, 72
Hill, 21, 101, 147, 176, 184
Hoe, 15, 39, 85, 89, 114, 130; as bride-wealth, 69–70; as rent, 91
Homosexuality, 77, 78
Household equipment (*see also* Basket work, Implements, Pottery, &c.), 69–70

INDEX

Hunting, 14, 81, 114, 136; hunting areas, 91
Husband, 47, 73, 76, 86, 87; choice of, 64; duties, 67, 77, 81
Hutu, 2, 3, 4, 170–1, 173, 174; character and status, 10, 143, 145–7, 152–5, 164; arrival, 11; agriculture, 11, 15, 16, 17, 89; diet, 16, 18, 19, 22; clothing, 19; compound, 20; cleanliness, 24; fears, 25; kinship and affinity, 29–63; name of chief of *inzu*, 35; ritual, 36; feuds, 37; land rights, 39; treatment of children, 42–43, 75, 86; *umulyango* organization, 46; marriage, 65–66, 67, 72, 77, 81, 82, 120, 135; concubines, 66, 76; genitor and pater, 69; bride-wealth, 69; homosexuality, 77; homestead, 80; tribute, 102, 105, 114; chiefs, 105–6, 176, 184, 185; army, 109, 118–9, 120, 123, 180; *buhake*, 129, 130, 132, 138–42, 154; caste, 135, 136, 139, 143, 145, 149
Hydromel, 18, 36, 129; as bride-wealth, 70

Imana, 24, 26, 36, 84, 86, 116, 151, 156
Implements, 15, 23
Impotence, 73, 74
Incest, 37–38, 49, 51, 54, 57
Inequality, premise of, 26, 160, 172
Inheritance, 92–94
Initiation, 36, 42, 79, 149
Insanity, 74
Intestinal diseases, 23, 24
intore, 86, 109–10, 118, 123, 149, 173, 177, *ill.*
inzu, 73, 84, 87, 90, 92, 110, 116, 173–4, 177, 178; composition, 30, 35; organization and activities, 35–39; social and family roles within *inzu*, 39–45; chief, 35, 69, 88, 119; intermarriage, 65, 66, 67
Ivory, 14

January, crops, 15; cattle, 17
July, 36, 80; crops, 16; cattle, 17
June, crops, 16; cattle, 17
Jurisdiction, 122, 124, 130, 138

King, 5, 25, 29, 72, 82, 88, 89, 90, 91, 100, 105, 106–7, 109, 110, 111, 112, 113, 114, 115, 116, 118, 120, 121, 123, 124–6, 127, 130, 132, 147, 148, 151, 153, 155, 156, 175, 182, 183, *ill.*
Kinship, 1, 23, 3, 61–63, 107, 148, 151, 173, 177, *ill.*; system, 29–63,

97; definition, 29; terminology, 40–42, 58–61

Labour, 21, 94–95, 102, 103, 104, 120, 121, 139, 140, 153, 159, 175
Land rights, 89–91, 93, 94, 95, 108, 125; Hutu custom, 39; taxes, 105
Language, 12, 169, 171
Legislation, 124, 125
Leopard, 147
Leprosy, 74
Lineage, *see* Patrilineage

Magic, cattle, 17; Tutsi meals, 19, 23; in medicine, 24; fear of witchcraft, 25; king, 72, 125
Maize, 15, 16, 22
Malaria, 23
March, crops, 15; cattle, 17
Marriage, 1, 76; disputes, 35; role of *inzu*, 36, 67–68; proposals, 67–68; of son, 42; of daughter, 43; ceremonies, 47, 68, 69, 71–72; relatives by marriage, 52; marriage and the family, 64–88; prohibitions, 65; intercaste, 65–66; with aliens, 66; connections, 66, 67, 82
Maternal relatives, 62; definition, 29; uncle, 30, 48, 52, 85; aunt, 49, 52; cross-cousins, 48, 50; parallel cousins, 51; intermarriage, 64, 65
Matrilateral relatives, *see* Maternal relatives
Matrilineal relatives, definition, 29; terminology, 47–48
May, crops, 16; cattle, 17
Medicine, Herbal, 24
Menstruation, 17, 67, 77, 83
Mental Health, 25–28; effect of physical hardship, 25–26; effect of supernatural beliefs, 26–28
Methods of enquiry, 2
Migration, 11, 12
Military structure, 100, 101, 124, 132, 142, 153, 155, 161, *ill.*; description, 109–15; analysis, 115–24
Milk, 17, 19, 36, 68, 71, 72, 87, 88, 91, 102, 103, 113, 120, 129, 130, 174, 175, 180, 181, 184; cow, 16; sheep and goats, 17; curdled, 18; conservation, 23; as marriage gift, 70; churning, 81
Mother, 29, 43, 65, 74, 84, 85, 92, 165; descent group, 47–49
Murder, 35, 37, 38, 130
mwami, see King

Neighbourhood, 21, 102
Nephew, 43–44, 48, 53, 85, 173, 177–8
Niece, 44, 85, 173, 177–8

198 THE PREMISE OF INEQUALITY IN RUANDA

Nkole, 66
November, crops, 15; cattle, 17
Nyanza, 22, 125

Occupation of Ruanda, 10–14
October, crops, 15; cattle, 17
Orthography, 5

Parallel relatives, cousin, 45, 49, 50, 51, 54, 56, 57, 62, 63, 65, 71, 78, 84, 92, 130
Pastoralism, 11, 12
Pater, 69, 71, 84
Paternal relatives, 33, 62, 92; definition, 29; cross-cousins, 30, 45, 49, 50; uncle and aunt, 43–45, 49, 54, 67, 85, 110, 173, 178; intermarriage, 65
Patriclan, 34, 46, 149, 150, 151, 173
Patrilateral relatives, *see* Paternal relatives
Patrilineage, 32, 50, 61, 66, 68, 71, 78, 83, 91, 110, 113, 119–20, 121, 125, 127, 130, 148, 151, 159, 173; definition, 29; *inzu* and *umulyango*, 30, 34; head of patrilineage, 35, 73, 89, 92, 93, 102, 107, 134, 174, 177, 178, 180
Patrimony, 92
Patron, *see buhake*
Pea, 15, 22, 81, 87, 102
Pepper, red, 15
Physical environment, 1, 7–9, 143, 147
Physical Force, 96, 97, 137, 157
Planting, 81
Poetry, 109, 110, 111, 112, 116, 117
Poison, 26
Political organization, 1, 2, 3, 13, 96–128, 147, 152, 155, 156, 157–9, 161, 164, 168, 170, 173; cattle, 16–17; neighbourhoods, 21; power of king and chiefs, 25, 35, 119–20; organization and activities of *inzu*, 35–9; political authority in feuds, 37; organization and activities of *ubwoko* and *umulyango*, 45–47; land, 89–91
Polygyny, 68, 72–73; polygynous family, 74, 86, 93
Population, 10–14; density, 12–13
Pottery, 67, 114, 120, 136
Power (*see also biru*, Cattle, Chief, *inzu*, Political organization, King, *umulyango*), 99, 123, 158, 162; social, 135, 136, 137, 143, 147, 148, 153, 164, 165, 171; economic, 137, 171; political, 143, 147, 148, 155–7, 171
Pregnancy, 76, 86

Pumpkin, 15

Queen-mother, 124, 126, 156, *ill.*

Rainfall, 9, 15, 145
Recommendation, *see buhake*
Recreation, 21
Reproduction, 64, 99
Ritual, 87–88, 99, 103, 111, 124, 126, 149, 156, 175, 182; role of *inzu*, 36
Royal succession, 125, 156
Ruanda, physical geography, 7–9, 23; political boundaries, 7 (footnote); origin of political unit, 12; population, 12–13; food, 14; lakes, 14; local grouping of people, 22; philosophy, 26; supernatural beliefs, 26–28; realism, 27; initiation, 36; marriage connexions, 65; status of women, 80–81; king, 124–26; economy, 145
rugo, 20, 21, 75, 76, 93, 94, 95, 102, 130, 180
Ruler (*see also* Chief, King, etc.), 12, 98, 100, 161–3, 168
Rundi, 66
Ryangombe sect, 26, 36, 42, 149, 150

September, 16
Servant, 67, 95
Sexual intercourse, 63, 71, 99; prohibitions (*see also* Incest), 37, 38, 65, 76, 78; obligatory, 38–39, 71, 76, 78; between maternal cousins, 48, 49; privileged, 42–43, 45, 51, 54, 56–57, 62, 76, 78; between husband and wife, 76–80
Shallot, 15
shebuja, *see buhake*
Sheep, 17, 42, 79, 91, 114
Singing, 19
Sister, 44–45, 65, 68, 69, 110, 173
Skins, 14, 16, 81, 129, 130; goat- and sheep-skin, 17, 19; as clothing, 19–20, 24
Slavery, 8
Socialization, 85–87, 117–19, 149
Soil, 9, 94, 145, 158
Son, 42, 75, 76, 84, 86, 92, 93, 94, 106, 110, 125, 163, 173, 177; terminology, 41, 53
Sorcerer, 24, 26, 27
Sorghum, 15, 16, 18, 22, 36, 81, 102, 127, 152, 175; beer, 18; flour as marriage gift, 70
Sororal relatives, 69; nephews and nieces, 30, 51, 65; polygyny, 68
Sowing, 15, 16, 81, 90
Spirit of dead person, 24, 26, 27, 86, 87, 88, 104

INDEX

State, 98
Sterility, 68, 74, 76, 87
Subject, 98, 100, 161–3
Suicide, 79
Sweet potato, 15, 16

Tax (*see also* Tribute), 35, 102, 105, 108, 123, 154, 159, 175, 176, 177; taxpayers, 100, 105, 107, 145
Territory, 96, 97; administration, 101
Thrashing, 15
Tillage, 16
Tomato, 15
Trade, 21, 22
Tribute, (*see also* Tax), 22, 104, 108, 113–14, 120, 125, 142, 145, 147, 153, 155, 162, 175
Tuberculosis, 23, 27, 74
Tutsi, 2, 3, 4, 173, 174, 177, 179; character and social status, 10, 143, 145–7; arrival in Ruanda, 11, 86, 170; language, 12; hunting, 14; dress, 14, 20; diet, 16–19; agriculture, 17, 89; compound, 20, 21; cleanliness, 23–24; fears, 25; kinship and affinity, 29–63; size of *inzu*, 32; ritual, 36; land rights, 39, 91; education of sons, 42, 86, 117, 118; *umulyango* organization, 46; intermarriage with Hutu, 65–66, 120, 135; marriage, 67, 72, 77, 80, 81, 82; genitor and pater, 69; bride-wealth, 69; bachelors, 74; adoption of children, 75; homosexuality, 77, 78; power, 82, 124; chiefs, 105, 157, 176; army, 109, 114, 123, 174; descent groups, 127; *buhake*, 129, 130, 132, 138, 139–42; caste, 135, 136, 139, 141, 143, 145, 147, 149; domination, 143–59, 164
Twa, 2, 3, 173, 174; character and social status, 10, 145, 164; arrival in Ruanda, 11; hunting, 14; diet, 17, 19; clothing, 19; fears, 26; marriage, 67, 72, 81, 135; bride-wealth, 69; chiefs, 106, 176, 185; army, 109, 114, 118–19, 120, 123; caste, 135, 136, 149
Twins, 84
Typhoid fever, 23

ubwoko, 30, 176, 173; royal, 33; description, 33; organization and activities, 454–7
umulyango, 30, 92, 110, 173, 177; description, 33–35; chief, 35, 46; honour of ancestor, 45; organization and activities, 45–47; intermarriage, 64
Uncle (*see also* Maternal and Paternal relatives), 53, 65
Uterine relatives, *see* Matrilineal relatives

Venereal disease, 23
Virginity, 67, 71

Water supply, 9
Wealth (*see also* Cattle, Bride-wealth), 136, 137, 150; distribution, 120–2
Weapons, hunting, 14; teaching use of, 42, 190
Weeding, 15
Wife, 46–47, 48, 65, 66, 68, 69, 73, 76, 86, 87, 92, 94, 95, 130, 165; choice, 64, 66, 76; duties, 67, 77; number, 72; secondary wives, 75; economic position, 80–82, 93
Will, 94
Worship, 21

Yam, 15, 16
Yaws, 23, 27